Case Studies in
ORGANIZAT
BEHAVIOR and THEORY
for HEALTH CARE

D0932676

Edited by

Nancy Borkowski, DBA, CPA, FACHE, FHFMA
Clinical Associate Professor,
   Department of Decision Sciences & Information Systems
Executive Director, Health Management Programs
Chapman Graduate School of Business
Florida International University
Miami, FL

Gloria Deckard, PhD
Associate Dean,
   Landon Undergraduate School
Associate Professor,
   Department of Decision Sciences & Information Systems
College of Business
Florida International University
Miami, FL

JONES & BARTLETT
LEARNING

World Headquarters
Jones & Bartlett Learning
5 Wall Street
Burlington, MA 01803
978-443-5000
info@jblearning.com
www.jblearning.com

Jones & Bartlett Learning books and products are available through most bookstores and online book-sellers. To contact Jones & Bartlett Learning directly, call 800-832-0034, fax 978-443-8000, or visit our website, www.jblearning.com.

Production Credits

Publisher: Michael Brown
Managing Editor: Maro Gartside
Editorial Assistant: Chloe Falivene
Associate Production Editor: Rebekah Linga
Senior Marketing Manager: Sophie Fleck Teague
Manufacturing and Inventory Control
    Supervisor: Amy Bacus

Composition: Paw Print Media
Cover Design: Michael O'Donnell
Cover Image: © Jamesmmm/Dreamstime.com
Printing and Binding: Edwards Brothers Malloy
Cover Printing: Edwards Brothers Malloy

Library of Congress Cataloguing-in-Publication Data
Case studies in organizational behavior and theory for health care / [edited by] Nancy Borkowski and Gloria Deckard.
   p. ; cm.
Includes bibliographical references and index.
ISBN 978-1-4496-3428-5 (paper) -- ISBN 1-4496-3428-1 (paper)
I. Borkowski, Nancy. II. Deckard, Gloria J. (Gloria Jeanne), 1951-
[DNLM: 1. Health Services Administration. 2. Health Personnel--organization & administration. 3. Organizational Case Studies. 4. Organizational Culture. 5. Personnel Management. W 84.1]
  362.1068--dc23
       2012040060

6048

Printed in the United States of America
17 16 15 14 13 10 9 8 7 6 5 4 3 2 1

Contents

Preface

The goal of this book is to provide students, instructors, and practitioners with a compilation of case studies that allow the reader to "see" the theories and concepts of organizational behavior and theory being played out in stories. The case studies may be used in conjunction with my textbooks, *Organizational Behavior in Health Care, Second Edition*, and *Organizational Behavior, Theory, and Design in Health Care*. They may also be easily used without the referenced textbooks, as each case study can support the various learning objectives of leadership and management courses in nursing, health administration, or public health at both the graduate and undergraduate levels.

The cases included in this book were developed by a diverse group of individuals. Many of the contributing authors are practitioners who wanted to share their stories so others could learn from them. Other cases were developed by academicians with many years of classroom experience teaching organizational behavior and organization theory. As such, readers get the best of both worlds!

There are many individuals whose efforts contributed to this case book becoming a reality. First, many thanks to the contributing authors for sharing their knowledge and experiences through these case studies. Second, I wish to thank the many individuals at Jones & Bartlett Learning who collectively support the process that allows an author's idea to develop into a high-quality product. This book, as well as all of my other achievements, would not have been possible without the continuous support of my husband and children, who I am eternally thankful for having their presence in my life. Finally, I wish to acknowledge and thank the dedicated healthcare professionals who provide excellent care in a very complex, ever changing environment. It is my sincere wish that this book provides them with the knowledge and skills necessary to make their lives a little easier as they build a collaborative patient-centered care environment.

I look forward to receiving your feedback and suggestions for future editions. You may reach me at nborkows@fiu.edu.

With best regards,
Nancy Borkowski, DBA, CPA, FACHE, FHFMA

Introduction

The diversity of the 36 cases presented in this book is a reflection of the many situations that healthcare managers encounter on a daily basis. Each case provides the reader with a greater understanding of how and why individuals behave the way they do as they interact with others, groups, and their environments.

As you review the Table of Contents, you will notice that a few international cases have been included in this book. These international case studies demonstrate that although healthcare professionals may reside in different countries, human behavior is similar and managers must deal with issues of leadership, motivation, and conflict when confronted with situational and technological changes, poor communication, and misaligned resources.

You will find that some case studies are lengthy, which is necessary so a complex condition (i.e., change) with many characters and numerous interactions may be successfully played out for the reader. This is very realistic to the situations that healthcare managers encounter throughout their careers. Other cases are concise and directly on point to emphasize a particular theory or concept. All of the cases have extensive teaching materials that can be used to enhance the student's learning experience.

Contributors

Gülem Atabay, PhD
Izmir University of Economics
Faculty of Economic and
    Administrative Sciences
Department of Business
    Administration
Balcova, Izmir, Turkey

Frankline Augustin, DPPD, MSHA
Assistant Professor
Department of Health Sciences
California State University,
    Northridge
Northridge, CA

Michael Barrett, PhD
Professor
Judge Business School
University of Cambridge
Cambridge, England

Zulma M. Berrios, MD, MBA
Physician Practice Manager
Zulma M. Berrios, MD, LLC
Miami, FL

Becky Hayes Boober, PhD
Program Officer
Maine Health Access Foundation
Augusta, ME

Susanne Bruno-Ninassi, JD
Program Director/Associate Professor
Business Law, Paralegal Studies
    & Legal Administration
Marymount University
Arlington, VA

John Cantiello, PhD
Assistant Professor
George Mason University
Fairfax, VA

Eugenie Coakley, MA, MPH
Senior Biostatistician
JSI Research & Training Institute
Boston, MA

David Colton, PhD
Adjunct Professor
Mary Baldwin College
Staunton, VA

Lorri E. Cooper, PhD
Associate Professor and Director
MS in Management
School of Business Administration
Marymount University
Arlington, VA

Reeti Debnath
Assistant Professor
Department of Healthcare
    Management
NSHM College of Management
    and Technology
West Bengal, India

Jami DelliFraine, MHA, PhD
Assistant Professor
Division of Management, Policy
    & Community Health
University of Texas School of
    Public Health
Houston, TX

Karen McMillen Dielmann, DEd
Chair
BS in Healthcare Administration
Lancaster General College of Nursing
    & Health Sciences
Lancaster, PA

Diane Dodd-McCue, DBA
Associate Professor
Department of Patient Counseling
School of Allied Health Professions
Virginia Commonwealth University
Richmond, VA

Ebbin Dotson, PhD, MHSA
Assistant Professor
University of Texas School of
    Public Health
Houston, TX

Anat Drach-Zahavy, PhD
The Department of Nursing
The University of Haifa
Mount Carmel 31905
Haifa, Israel

Annelise Y. Driscoll, PhD
Director, The Executive Practice
    Management Certificate
    Program for Dentists
College of Dentistry
University of Florida
Gainesville, FL

Alyson Eisenhardt, DHS
Marymount University
Arlington, VA

Myron D. Fottler, PhD
Professor and Executive Director
Programs in Health Services
    Administration
University of Central Florida
Orlando, FL

Valerie A. George, PhD
Research Associate Professor
Florida International University
Miami, FL

**Debora Goetz Goldberg, PhD,
    MHA, MBA**
Assistant Research Professor
Center for Healthcare Quality
Department of Health Policy
The George Washington University
Washington, DC

Susan Grantham, PhD
JSI Research & Training Institute
Boston, MA

**Rev. Stephanie Hamilton,
   MDiv, BCC**
Chaplain/Instructor
Department of Patient Counseling
School of Allied Health Professions
Virginia Commonwealth University
Richmond, VA

Roger F. Hogu, MBA
South Broward Community
   Health Services
Hollywood, FL

Renee Brent Hotchkiss, PhD
Assistant Professor
Jiann-Ping Hsu College of
   Public Health
Georgia Southern University
Statesboro, GA

Eva Jarosová, PhD
Senior Lecturer
Department of Managerial
   Psychology and Sociology
University of Economics, Prague
Prague, Czech Republic

Susan J. Kowalewski, MBA, PhD
D'Youville College
Buffalo, NY

Carole Lalonde, PhD
University Laval
Department of Management
Quebec, Canada

Carolyn Massello, DBA
Associate Professor of Business
Milligan College
Milligan College, TN

Thomas Massello, MD
Surgeon
Quillen VA Medical Center
Mountain Home, TN

Alec McKinney, MBA
Senior Consultant
JSI Research & Training Institute
Boston, MA

Mary Helen McSweeney-Feld, PhD
Associate Professor
Office of Collaborative Programs
Towson University
Towson, MD

Carol Molinari, PhD, MBA, MPH
Associate Professor
University of Baltimore
Baltimore, MD

Eivor Oborn, PhD
Professor
School of Management
Royal Holloway University of London
London, England

Carole Paulson, EdD, MSN, RN
Assistant Professor
University of Wisconsin—
   Stevens Point
Stevens Point, WI

Şebnem Penbek
Izmir University of Economics
Faculty of Economic and
   Administrative Sciences
Department of Business
   Administration
Balcova, Izmir, Turkey

Clifford R. Perry, PhD
Distinguished Executive Professor
College of Business Administration
Florida International University
Miami, FL

Tracy H. Porter, PhD
College Associate Lecturer
Monte Ahuja College of Business
Cleveland State University
Cleveland, OH

Doris J. Ravotas, PhD
College of Health and
    Human Services
Western Michigan University
Kalamazoo, MI

Louis Rubino, PhD, FACHE
Professor and Health Administration
    Program Director
California State University,
    Northridge
Northridge, CA

Sarah J. Shoemaker,
    PharmD, PhD
Senior Associate
Abt Associates, Inc.
Boston, MA

Becky Staples
Research Assistant
Judge Business School
University of Cambridge
Cambridge, England

Richard J. Tarpey, MBA
Senior Vice President
HCA/Parallon
Nashville, TN

Natalie M. Truesdell, MPH, MBA
Consultant
JSI Research & Training Institute
Boston, MA

Robert Vazquez, MBA
Manager
Imaging Services
Miramar, FL

Melissa A. Walker, PhD, MPA
Associate Professor
Hugo Wall School of Urban
    and Politic Affairs
Wichita State University
Wichita, KS

Melina Ward, BA
Research Associate
JSI Research & Training Institute
Boston, MA

Melanie Wasserman, MPH, PhD
Senior Associate
Abt Associates, Inc.
Boston, MA

I Don't Want to Get Fired, But...

By Frankline Augustin and Louis Rubino

A small for-profit skilled nursing facility is located in a suburb of a major metropolitan area and is part of a local long-term care chain. The owner of the chain of facilities, Mr. Frank Dobbs, hired his long-time friend as the administrator approximately 2 years ago. It is obvious to the employees that the administrator, Mr. Bill Stevens, has a close personal relationship with the owner of the corporation. The nursing home has a good reputation, and its scores on various websites show historically being about on par with its local competitors. The nursing staff has generally been at the facility a long time and is considered stable in the current environment.

Olive Washington is a certified nurse assistant (CNA) who came on board approximately 6 months ago. She has been well received by the nurses and is happy to be working at the facility. Over the last couple of months, the administrator, Mr. Stevens, has decided to make executive rounds and as a result is becoming more known to the nursing staff. His remarks to the nurses as he makes his rounds seem inappropriate to Olive. She feels that the remarks are culturally insensitive, and some of the other nurses in her team have complained about his remarks to the director of nurses, Mrs. Alice Gonzalez. Olive has also heard from a new housekeeper she has befriended named Ramon Alvarez. He says that he, too, has been the recipient of inappropriate remarks by Mr. Stevens. Olive, having not been at the facility very long, did not want to complain and is waiting to see the outcome of the other nurses' discussions. None of the nurses are willing to approach the administrator themselves due to fear of losing their jobs. The director of nurses, Alice, listens to the various staff members' complaints regarding the comments made by Mr. Stevens during his rounds. Alice is somewhat hesitant to approach Mr. Stevens directly because he has a temper. She has seen him blow up over issues where he is criticized, and she is not sure if she wants to be subjected to his confrontational behavior. Alice is on good terms with the owner of the facility, Mr. Dobbs, and could go to him directly, but she is concerned that Mr. Stevens will be upset if she goes over his head. Alice considers taking a less interventional approach and attempts to coach Mr. Stevens on making more appropriate remarks to the staff when he makes rounds.

Alice is vacillating on which approach to take. While she agrees that the administrator's comments are unacceptable, she also does not want to ruin her chances of getting the raise that she's due for after her annual evaluation. Additionally, Mr. Stevens does have a history of letting people go when he is upset, and she is concerned about being able to find another job in the current environment. Yet Alice just heard through the grapevine that two new employees are also the targets of Mr. Steven's inappropriate remarks.

PART ONE

FIRST SET OF CASE STUDY DISCUSSION QUESTIONS

1. What are the various choices Alice has at this point to address the concerns raised?

2. What are the ramifications if Alice decides not to act at this time?

3. If you were Alice, what would you do and why?

PART TWO

Choose one of the following three options for Alice's next step:

    Option A: Alice talks to Mr. Stevens, the administrator, directly.

    Option B: Alice talks to Mr. Dobbs, the owner.

    Option C: Alice decides to talk to the new employees, Olive and Ramon.

After choosing your option, read only the corresponding option below and then answer the second set of questions that follows the dialogue.

The People

Administrator: Bill Stevens

Director of Nurses: Alice Gonzalez

Owner: Frank Dobbs

CNA: Olive Washington

Housekeeper: Ramon Alvarez

Option A: Alice talks to administrator (Mr. Stevens) directly

Alice: Bill, I need to talk to you in private.

Bill: What is it about?

Alice: I really like the way you are making executive rounds, but I want to talk to you about some of the comments that you make to my nurses as you're walking in their units.

Bill: Well, I'm always friendly with them. I think that's being a good administrator.

Alice: Friendly is good, but some of the remarks you say are not culturally sensitive.

Bill: You need to be more specific.

Alice: All right, let me tell you now since nobody is near us. One of my best CNAs, Olive, said that you told her that she has pretty dreadlocks but that you asked her "How do you keep your hair clean?"

Bill: I'm just concerned about infection control.

Alice: Olive took it as a racial attack. She's told me that she is very proud of her dreadlocks and how it represents her culture.

Bill: It was not meant to attack her background. I was just concerned about our patient safety.

Alice: Ramon also said to me that while he was mopping the floor, you walked by and said to him "Boy, you're doing a really good job. Did you learn how to mop like that at the car wash?"

Bill: I'm just being friendly. Do you want me to not acknowledge the staff at all when I'm making rounds?

Option B: Alice talks to the owner (Mr. Dobbs) directly

Alice: Mr. Dobbs, I'm sorry to bother you, but I have a big concern that I want to talk to you about.

Frank: Of course, Alice. You're such a loyal employee. How can I help you?

Alice: I have a concern about Mr. Stevens, and I'm hoping that you won't reveal to him that I was the one who told you this.

Frank: Well, I'll try. It depends on what you tell me.

Alice: Well, I'll tell you, but I'm concerned about retaliation because I want to keep my job.

Frank: Well, spit it out.

Alice: Mr. Stevens has been saying some inappropriate remarks to my minority staff, and they have been coming to me offended.

Frank: What did my old friend say?

Alice: Well, that's why I'm uncomfortable talking to you because I know he's your friend.

Frank: But this is business, and I want to protect my facility.

Alice: His remarks have referred to their cultural backgrounds in a disrespectful way, mentioning the hair of one of my workers and for another worker, he stereotyped him about prior work experience.

Frank: Oh, I know Bill. He didn't mean anything by that. He was probably just trying to be friendly.

Alice: Well he offended my workers, and it makes us vulnerable to potential discriminatory lawsuits.

Frank: Okay, okay, maybe I'll talk to him the next time we're playing golf.

Option C: Alice decides to talk to the new employees (Olive and Ramon) directly

Olive: Ramon and I are offended by Mr. Stevens's remarks.

Ramon: Yeah, he assumed I was a car-washer prior to working here.

Olive: And he implied that my dreadlocks were dirty.

Alice: We do need to address this. You need to document your concerns and send them up to Human Resources so that we can find out later if these were isolated incidents or part of a trend.

Olive: But what if he says something to me again? Am I supposed to ignore it?

Ramon: Maybe next time he'll slip on my floor.

Alice: We have to handle this per procedure. Any complaints must be documented and sent to HR.

Olive: I bet if you talked to the others, they'll tell you the same thing.

Ramon: We came to you thinking that you could help us, not send us to another department. Why can't you take care of this? I'm not good at writing things down.

Olive: Yeah, my friend got fired because she complained that while she was at the med-cart, he rubbed up against her as he walked by. Next day she was gone!

Alice: Oh, that had nothing to do with your friend's departure. But that's a confidential matter.

Olive: Well, I know the truth.

SECOND SET OF CASE STUDY DISCUSSION QUESTIONS

1. Based on the conversation that occurred, are you glad you chose the option that you did? Do you wish you would have chosen one of the other two options instead? Why?

2. Assess how you think your meeting went. Do you think you could have improved the outcome of the meeting?

3. Based on the conversation you did have, if you were Alice, what would you do next and why?

PART THREE

Now, Alice goes to her computer to try to keep up with her emails. She reads the following three messages received this morning:

Email #1

```
To:        All Employees
From:      Mr. Bill Stevens, Administrator
Subject:   Executive Rounds
```

I am pleased to announce that the executive rounds I started earlier this month are going well. I have already prevented certain family complaints escalating due to acting quickly on service recovery. I want to thank you for your cooperation as I make my daily rounds and your quick follow-through on any surfaced issues. This is important to resident and family satisfaction and also to improve our organizational culture. This is a good start, and I encourage all of you to be friendly to everyone you encounter as we work to further our goal of being the nursing home of first choice in our community.

Email #2

```
To:        Alice Gonzalez, Director of Nurses
From:      Mr. Bill Stevens, Administrator
Subject:   Friendliness
```

During my recent rounds, I have seen many unhappy faces in the hallways. I would expect that of our patients but not of our employees! Things need to lighten up around here, and I expect you to carry that ball and model that behavior to the staff. We will talk about this during your performance review.

Email #3

To: Bill Stevens, Administrator
From: Frank Dobbs, President
Subject: Resident Satisfaction Scores
cc: Alice Gonzalez, Director of Nurses

I just saw the latest resident satisfaction scores on the Internet. I am very satisfied with the upward trend I see. Bill, I am pleased you began the executive rounding that was recommended in the latest issue of the long-term care industry journal. Keep up the good work and maybe it will be my treat for drinks on the 19th hole next week. Alice, I hope you are supporting Bill on his rounds and going with him as your time permits.

THIRD SET OF CASE STUDY DISCUSSION QUESTIONS

1. Does having this new information change the way you would act if you were Alice? What would you do now?

2. Read the two options you did not select. Assuming these conversations also occurred, does this alter your next action steps? What would you do based on all the conversations that took place?

3. What about the cultural issues raised by the comments made by Mr. Stevens? Do these get handled in a different way than if the remarks made were not culturally related? How best are they addressed?

4. If you were Alice, what do you predict will be the outcome based on your final interventions selected? Do you think the issues raised in the case occur in real life?

Multidisciplinary Collaboration: Bridging Professional Differences for Service Improvement in Adolescent Mental Health Care

By Eivor Oborn, Michael Barrett, and Becky Staples

■ PART A: APRIL ■

INTRODUCTION

Paul Homilton, an esteemed academic psychiatrist in the Kesteven area of England, sat in his newly renovated office quite perplexed. He quizzically reflected on his early yet failed attempts to kick-start the new program of applied mental health research. He was initially excited at being a part of this winning consortium on knowledge translation. The launch of the Center had been attended by

This work was funded by the NIHR Collaboration for Leadership in Applied Health Research and Care for Cambridge & Peterborough (CLAHRC-CP) and the National Institute for Health Research (NIHR). The funders were not involved in the selection or analysis of data or in contributing to the content of the final manuscript.

high-ranking dignitaries from the Department of Health who celebrated what for many was a revolutionary collaborative approach to research.

It was hard for Paul to get his head around the almost paradigm shift for him following a successful career in conducting traditional research. Before, the design and development of the research had been his domain, and he would publish the results, sharing them when and with whomever he pleased once the research had been completed and validated. He was pensive and a bit tentative therefore in setting up the first research meeting to facilitate collaborative partnerships between healthcare and social care providers. What shift in mindset would be required of him and how might he successfully adapt to this new research approach? Further, how should he best facilitate communication and collaboration across health and social care in establishing the research effort?

Concerning the latter issue, these two services, *health* and *the social services*, together look after the child's welfare. For example, if a child experiences mental health problems that significantly impact upon their behavior and social interaction, then a doctor may look after the medication and talking therapy side of treatment, while social services might be involved in family counseling, providing home support, liaising with teachers or schools, and/or possibly working with the police. However, these two services have typically remained separate, in both aims and practice. In response to complaints about disjointed services and a lack of follow-through, the government administration recently emphasized multi-disciplinary collaboration between these parties as a vehicle for "joining up care" in welfare delivery. In addition, new applied health research streams have been developed that encourage knowledge exchange and translation between academic medical research and local practice communities.

A primary focus of the first set of meetings was to bring medical researchers together with these two provider groups and decide how funding provided by the government for research should be used; that is, what research should be conducted. The funding has been provided for research into adolescent care, but beyond this, decisions about what topics to consider are to be made by Paul and all of those he can persuade to commit to the meetings. Paul was aided by his research associate, Jessica Albright, whose task it was to carry through Paul's ideas and those brought out and defined in the meetings.

The first meeting had been a disaster, as well as something of a shock to Paul. Used to having Jessica arrange all his meetings by email, he had been surprised when he himself had to take a strong role in reorganizing, chasing, and cajoling, just to get the relevant individuals at social services to express a desire to participate, as they failed to reply to Jessica's emails and phone calls. And then, on the day of the meeting itself, no one had showed up from social services. It had not been a complete waste, as Paul and his research colleagues had used the opportunity to brainstorm their own ideas for the research with the one clinical psychiatrist who had attended (an individual with whom he had worked with on another research project), but he is anxious that the second meeting has more participation from social services.

BRIDGING THE PROFESSIONAL GAP

Paul and Jessica are convinced that a large part of the difficulty is in the strong history of differences between the two professions; indeed, until very recently the social services have resisted being defined as a profession at all. This resistance derives from a markedly different approach to care than that found in the medical profession.

Doctors, psychologists, and the majority of clinicians want to pass on the best possible health-related care to "patients" in a one-way exchange of knowledge in which cost is a largely secondary (though still important) consideration. They are used to relying on research to identify what this best health-related care is. By contrast, social services have so many potential "clients" that they must concentrate primarily on resource-constraints (thus are forced to leave many needs unmet), and the focus of their care is advocacy of their clients' needs in a broader social context, rather than any decontextualized "best practice" per se. It is this focus on advocacy that informs their resistance to professional status as they identify more with their clients than with other professions, seeking to work with them rather than for them.

Social care typically has a much weaker relationship with research, preferring to spend money on implementing its own ideas about what best practice might be, rather than determining precisely what it is through formal research. Recent government policy initiatives were key drivers in changing practice, rather than notable research. Due to their severe budgetary constraints, Paul is aware that most leaders in social care would prefer to spend the allocated money on human resources and the recruitment and training of more staff, than on research, which they had told him was generally "irrelevant, decontextualized and ivory tower like." This of course was a key reason why Paul was motivated to involve the social service workers in the research process—so that it would be more relevant and grounded in real context.

The difference in professional identity and perception is compounded by a distinct difference in status between the two professions. In the run up to the first meeting, Paul and Jessica spoke with social worker Jane Tome, who summed up the effects of this difference on their respective levels of power and influence:

> *The kind of resentment comes in because social workers feel you go to court and then the court listens to the doctor. The doctor who might see this person once comes along and says "Well this is how it is," and the court listens to that and the social worker might see the person 25 times, or have been working with them for a long period of time, but their opinion still isn't valued as much.*

Jane also discussed the fears held by many social workers, because of recent media scandals linked to severe cases of child abuse and deaths, that any interaction they have with other institutions (such as research organizations) will just leave them open for further scrutiny and judgment. It is this fear that Paul felt might have been responsible for the nonattendance at the first meeting. In his emails to arrange the second meeting, therefore, he was careful to stress his strong desire to solicit the opinions of the social services and to work in partnership with them.

OVERCOMING ONE-WAY KNOWLEDGE EXCHANGE

At first, Paul was hopeful that his reassurances to social services had worked as attendance at the second meeting was notably up. However, some of the key stakeholders were still absent, and even as the meeting was starting, emails of apology were pinging into his BlackBerry® smartphone inbox.

The meeting did not lessen the gaps in work status as Paul had hoped. Some of the problem was in the location and setting of the meeting: Jessica had booked a meeting room in Valerie House, down the road from where Paul's offices are based because this was the closest location where they were able to arrange meetings. While this was somewhat inevitable as Paul's office had set up the meeting, it did place the meeting physically on Health Service's property. This was compounded by the room's set up, with a large board room table dominating the middle of the room and giving a far more formal atmosphere than Paul had hoped to achieve (refer to Appendix B for diagrams of the room layout over time).

Such physical factors were compounded by the propensity of his medical and research colleagues to impart information, and far less so to receive it. The meeting got off to a troubled start when one of Paul's colleagues, John, noted the absence of the local head of social services, Helen. As the group began to discuss how they could get Helen's perspective, John answered, "We couldn't," before loudly adding that as per the reporting requirements specified in the grant he and his team would be recording who was turning up for meetings.

After this, the team from social services remained fairly quiet, while the health service clinicians and researchers shared the ideas they had formulated in the first meeting. Some social workers did pipe up with their thoughts, but as these tended to be less preconsidered or well-organized, they soon returned to listening in silence.

The unequal exchange of information was compounded by the differing definitions and interpretations held by the groups as the following exchange between Richard, a practicing psychiatrist, and Paul, the academic researcher, demonstrates:

> **Richard:** Children in Need [one of the categories of children within the English care system] are tricky to work with.
>
> **Paul:** Children in Need are *not* the tricky bit.
>
> **Richard:** We don't really know who these kids are. It is almost impossible to get information about these adolescents, and few of them have a social services file. This would make it problematic using them as cases for research. Children in Need has become a much vaguer term now, and it is difficult to understand how the category has been defined in the [health service].
>
> **Paul:** I disagree. I have written a paper about how they should be defined. I can tell you what the category should entail. I am sure that at least 360 of the children have some kind of [social services] record.
>
> **Richard:** Okay. In theory this should be the case. But I think all will become clearer when you go and track the records in person.

A lot of the meeting was thus spent clarifying the terms and perceptions of different individuals. This sparring was highly useful for professional equals such as Paul and Richard, and for the group, as it necessitated the consideration of different points of view (Richard's highly practical background contrasting with Paul's primarily academic career), but did create an environment of strong personalities, which may have negatively affected the confidence of the social services practitioners.

KEEPING A COLLABORATIVE FOCUS

In their discussion after the meeting, Jessica and Paul highlighted a number of problems with how it had progressed. A notable one of these had been the capacity of certain individuals to dominate the discussion and effectively shut down conversations from the wider group. One particular instance of this was with George, a psychologist who has experienced great professional success in running a residential care center for adolescents. He demonstrated a resistance to collaboration, stating:

> *I do my bit and I focus on doing my bit well. Rather than trying to do everybody's bit and doing nothing.*

George's reputation for strong performance affords him considerable respect among his colleagues and Paul was reluctant to stop anyone from having their say. However, George is employed on a far more isolated project than most clinicians in the field, and Paul worried that his strong opinions would have a negative impact on group motivation for the project and on collaboration between social and health services in general. Even within the healthcare community he was aware of the need to bridge between those focused on clinical practice and his own concerns for rigorous research.

A further difficulty was in staying on topic. The meeting was very long and in places circular in the material it covered. Although he feels this is inevitable in the first few meetings as people get to know each other and the concepts involved, Paul feels that it is vital that they learn to tread a path through this and to keep the meetings on track, if they are ever to make any decisions at all.

Though not quite as disastrous as the first meeting, there were still a lot of problems to be addressed. Paul and Jessica have arranged to discuss how to proceed and what Jessica should be doing to follow up the outcomes of the meeting, but Paul is unsure what to tell her. Where should they go from here to ensure engagement and input from practicing clinicians (e.g. psychologists and psychiatrists) as well as social workers into the research project?

CASE STUDY DISCUSSION QUESTIONS

Collaboration Theme Questions

1. What issues has Paul faced in attempting to create a collaborative working environment? Please consider broader organizational goals as well as professional differences between the groups.

2. How was the spatial arrangement of the room influencing the collaborative context?

   a. Reflecting on your own work environment, how does the arrangement of space and artifacts influence collaboration?

Knowledge Transfer Theme Questions

1. What types of knowledge boundaries are evident in the case and how might this influence collaboration?

2. Consider your own work practices. What knowledge boundaries have you and your colleagues faced, and how did you overcome them?

   a. Think about how Paul could use some of the examples from your work practices to facilitate sharing in his team.

Activity

In small groups, role-play a third meeting between the clinical and academic psychiatrists and the social services, attempting to avoid the issues of the second meeting.

- From the perspective of either the academic doctors or a member of the social services (depending on which part you are playing):

  - Write down your current position, stating your interests, your role, and your hopes and fears for the collaborative process.

  - Write down where you would like to progress to as a result of the collaboration.

  - From the perspective of your role, write down how you think the opposite group would have described where they are and where they want to be.

- Using what you have written, begin to role play, keeping in mind your own interests and the purpose of collaboration.

- Feel free to think about actions outside of simply what each group says might affect the process: for example, how are you going to sit?

■ PART B: SEPTEMBER ■

A POSITIVE ENVIRONMENT FOR COLLABORATION

One of the first meetings Jessica attended after her summer holiday was the September meeting between Paul, his clinical and academic colleagues, and the social services to determine the purpose and objective for the research funding. Though she knew that Paul had been working hard in her absence to improve the collaborative environment, Jessica was still pleasantly surprised by the far more positive attitude she experienced.

Key stakeholders were present at the meeting, even though it was still being held at Valerie House, on health service premises. The large table was no longer present, and people sat mixed together whereas before they had remained clumped together with those with whom they worked. The effect of this interaction was clear to see: at one point, while summarizing decisions that had been made, Paul was able to say, "This is the research question you [social services] really got excited about and wanted us to look at—this was never part of our initial research project." However, what surprised Jessica most was that, with a few moderations, the social workers seemed to have agreed on the importance of the research proposal initially suggested by Paul in their earlier meeting.

After the meeting Paul shared with Jessica that useful interaction was occurring in other, more informal areas, as well, spanning the traditional boundaries of how the two organizations interacted. Not only had Helen, the local head of social services, begun to attend the meetings, she had also begun an email exchange with Paul, seeking his advice on different issues and sharing news; something to which Paul had been pleased to respond in kind.

CREATING A TWO-WAY KNOWLEDGE EXCHANGE

In response to Jessica's queries as to how such an encouraging change in attitude could have been effected, Paul responded that the crucial factor had been in getting his clinical and academic colleagues to "shut up." As they had noted back in April, the greater confidence of the psychiatrists in sharing their views had led to an unequal information exchange: the psychiatrists knew the psychiatrists views, as did the social workers, but only the social workers knew the social workers' views as they were being denied the opportunity to express them.

So Paul had briefed and rebriefed his medical colleagues for the third meeting that they were not allowed to talk. The purpose of the third meeting had been to understand the thoughts and perspectives of the social work team. This had been a great success, allowing the social workers to establish confidence in their work and its relevance for the meetings and to actively be able to discuss the fears and reservations about being judged that Paul had attempted to address by email back in April. Just being given the opportunity to have their opinions listened to seemed to go some way to redressing the status gap perceived between the two professions.

There were two important outcomes of this session. First, word had clearly gotten back to Helen about the advances being made, and from this point, she began to attend and contribute to meetings. Second, it had emerged that, resource constraints aside, many of the views held by individuals in both groups were very similar; hence the agreement over the initial proposal for which adolescents should be researched.

AN OUTSIDE PERSPECTIVE

For Paul, a crucial factor in getting the teams to communicate more effectively, and to break down some of the conceptual boundaries between them, was his invitation to academics from the Engineering Department service design center of the nearby university to join the meetings. Paul had initially involved this group with the idea that they might serve as mediators, providing a neutral presence through which both social and healthcare professionals could present their ideas. However, these outsiders, with their interests in service design but with no understanding of the specific field under consideration, had proved to have a greater value than in mediation alone, and were helpful in asking the questions that others felt were too basic to ask. Their presence allowed everyone to get a clearer handle on the differences in perception that characterized the health and social services groups as they used the whiteboard to develop schemas and draw summary pictures.

The engineers' presence had two other major benefits in facilitating collaboration. Their outsider status ensured that they focused less on determining straight off what research the group should be funding and more on finding ways the different individuals could work together. Further, by considering ideas diagrammatically and encouraging lateral thinking, it was Paul's impression that they pushed everyone out of their "comfort zones" and created a sense of solidarity and wider meta group identity.

SCALING UP

Paul is greatly satisfied with how collaborative efforts in the meetings have advanced; however, he is aware that there is a great deal of work to be done. Although collaboration has been effective in determining the purpose of the research for which there is funding and ensuring that the research will be of interest to both healthcare and social services communities, it will have little long-term merit unless its impact can be sustained and widened out beyond the bounds of the meeting room.

The individuals from social services who have attended the meetings seem committed to the idea of joint endeavor, seeing it as a means to help combat their resourcing issues as well as gaining some insight into improving practice, and the numbers from this group attending the meetings are noticeably up. But Paul recognizes that there is a huge task ahead to convince the rest of social services, outside of the handful of committed individuals, that there is merit to be found in conducting and using research and in working with those from whom they have typically been quite separate. They would also need to address the sensitivity around issues such as external judgment and status perceptions to gain widespread support.

Another challenge will be in convincing psychiatrists and doctors to work outside the healthcare silos in which they have typically operated and to accept the validity of external viewpoints. This has the potential to be particularly problematic at times, such as in this case, where the healthcare professionals will need to take a distinct backseat in order to allow other ideas to be voiced and heard. Team collaboration is a difficult concept to scale up in order to influence and engage the broader community, but Paul is convinced that there is, in his case, evidence of the benefits that can be achieved through its achievement.

CASE STUDY DISCUSSION QUESTIONS

Collaboration Theme Questions

1. What was different about the third team meeting that better enabled collaboration?

2. Consider Appendix A, which stresses that it "is essential for patient outcomes that health and social care services are better integrated at all levels of the system."

    a. Is the document framed from a health or social services perspective? Why?

    b. What impact might this framing have?

    c. Consider an integration story in your local context. How might its framing affect the issues involved?

Knowledge Transfer Theme

1. Describe the features and boundary objects of the third meeting that facilitated greater knowledge sharing.

Looking Forward (Both Themes)

1. How can the positive improvements in the third meeting be scaled up beyond the initial participating team?

2. Using Appendix C as a template, think about the stakeholders who would need to be recruited and their likely attitudes and levels of influence.

RECOMMENDED READING

Gray, B. (2004). Strong opposition: Frame-based resistance to collaboration. *Journal of Community and Applied Social Psychology 14*, 166–176.

Newell, S., Robertson, M., Scarbrough, H., & Swan, J. (2009). *Managing knowledge work and innovation* (pp. 78–104). New York: Palgrave Macmillan.

Oborn, E. & Dawson, S. (2010). Learning across multiple communities of practice: An examination of multidisciplinary work. *British Journal of Management 21*(4), 843–858.

Appendix A

An excerpt from the July 2010 Whitepaper from the Coalition Government concerning its plans for the care structure in England.

EQUITY AND EXCELLENCE: LIBERATING THE NHS

Presented to Parliament
By the Secretary of State for Health
By Command of Her Majesty
July 2010

THE NHS OUTCOMES FRAMEWORK

3.5   The current performance regime will be replaced with separate frameworks for outcomes that set direction for the NHS, for public health, and social care, which provide for clear and unambiguous accountability, and enable better joint working. The Secretary of State, through the Public Health Service, will set local authorities national objectives for improving population health outcomes. It will be for local authorities to determine how best to secure those objectives, including by commissioning services from providers of NHS care.

3.6   A new NHS Outcomes Framework will provide direction for the NHS. It will include a focused set of national outcome goals determined by the Secretary of State, against which the NHS Commissioning Board will be held to account, alongside overall improvements in the NHS.

3.7   In turn, the NHS Outcomes Framework will be translated into a com-
       missioning outcomes framework for GP consortia, to create powerful
       incentives for effective commissioning.

3.8   The NHS Outcomes Framework will span the three domains of quality:

       ▪ the effectiveness of the treatment and care provided to patients—mea-
         sured by both clinical outcomes and patient-reported outcomes;
       ▪ the safety of the treatment and care provided to patients; and
       ▪ the broader experience patients have of the treatment and care they
         receive.

       For example, effectiveness goals might include how we compare interna-
       tionally on avoidable mortality and morbidity across a range of condi-
       tions. The criteria used will ensure that we do not exclude outcomes for
       key groups and services such as children, older people, and mental health.

3.9   The Department will launch a consultation on the development of the
       national outcome goals. We are committed to working with clinicians,
       patients, carers, and representative groups to create indicators that are
       based on the best available evidence. Later this year, in the light of the
       Spending Review, the Government will issue the first NHS Outcomes
       Framework. We intend it will be available to support NHS organisa-
       tions in delivering improved outcomes from April 2011, with full imple-
       mentation from April 2012.

3.10   The NHS Commissioning Board will work with clinicians, patients,
       and the public at every level of the system to develop the NHS Out-
       comes Framework into a more comprehensive set of indicators, reflect-
       ing the quality standards developed by NICE. The framework and its
       constituent indicators will enable international comparisons wherever
       possible, and reflect the Board's duties to promote equality and tackle
       inequalities in healthcare outcomes. It will ensure that clinical values
       direct managerial activity and that every part of the NHS is focusing
       on the right goals for patients. The main purpose of the programme of
       reform set out in this White Paper is to change the NHS environment
       so that it is easier to progress against those goals.

3.11   It is essential for patient outcomes that health and social care services are
       better integrated at all levels of the system. We will be consulting widely
       on options to ensure health and social care works seamlessly together to
       enable this.

Appendix B

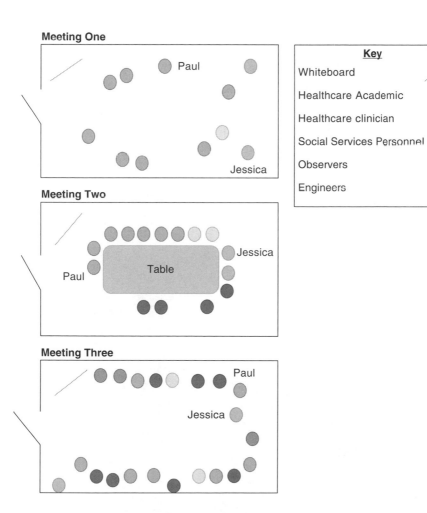

**Analysis of the Layout of the Meeting Room
Over the Course of the Collaboration Period**

Appendix C

READINESS FOR CHANGE:
Beckhard and Harris (1987)

Please describe a change effort that you would like to undertake.

Stakeholder	1	2	3	Readiness for Change	Resources for Change

Which stakeholders do you need to influence first? How might you do so? Which aspect of change is most critical for you, mobilizing resources or generating a sense of readiness for change?

What Just Happened?

By Zulma M. Berrios

It is the end of a busy Thursday at the office. Denise, the office manager, storms into Dr. Thomas's office, clearly upset. Denise relates to Dr. Thomas that she received a voice mail from Garnet, the billing and collections specialist, who has given an ultimatum: either remove her from handling Dr. Blandon's claims or she would resign. Denise retrieves Garnet's voice message for Dr. Thomas to hear. "I don't want to work for Dr. Blandon. Don't make me be in charge of his claims and collections! Nobody told me I had to work for him. He does not understand what I'm doing; this is too much. What is he expecting? I'm okay with Dr. Thomas and Dr. Williams's accounts, but you either outsource Dr. Blandon's accounts, or I'll resign."

The office is a single specialty practice managed by two physicians (Drs. Thomas and Williams). Most of the office staff, including Denise and Garnet, have been working together at the practice for over 10 years. Garnet is one of the most valuable employees. The practice enjoys an average of 30 days A/R cycle and a 90% collections rate, mainly because of Garnet's certification in medical coding, her experience in the field, and knowledge of the physician's clinical practice and claims experience. Garnet is dedicated, organized, and loyal to the practice. Her attention to detail and need for structure sometimes makes her a bit inflexible and resistant to the notion of change and the exploration of alternate ways of doing things.

In order to maximize the use of the expensive office space, Drs. Thomas and Williams have entered into an agreement with a third physician, Dr. Blandon, for the use of space, equipment, and personnel, and sharing of office expenses. Dr. Blandon has been working in the office for the last 4 weeks. His addition to the practice required rearranging the office space, hiring new personnel, and redistributing work assignments. Denise has been busy with all the arrangements required to bring Dr. Blandon on board. In addition to all her daily duties as manager, Denise was in charge of ordering new equipment; interviewing, hiring, and training new personnel; as well as bidding and contracting for the leasehold improvements. Although Denise has substantial freedom to carry out her duties, Drs. Thomas and Williams make the decisions regarding salaries, bonuses, promotions, and major operational changes. With Dr. Blandon's addition, Garnet is now responsible for the billing and collections for the three physicians.

Since Garnet has Fridays off and Dr. Williams is out of town, Dr. Thomas asked Denise to call Garnet and give her the opportunity to vent her frustration and to reassure her that the doctors will meet with her. Dr. Thomas doesn't want Garnet to be consumed with her dissatisfaction over the weekend. Denise calls Garnet from Dr. Thomas's office relating, "Garnet, I just heard your voicemail message. I'm sorry I could not answer your phone call. I was in the middle of a meeting with the contractors that will make the leasehold improvements. I want to talk with you and give you the opportunity to explain your concerns. You know you can always come to me with your concerns." Garnet, responding so loudly Dr. Thomas could hear her from across her desk, "That is one of the problems, you are so busy that there has been no time to talk. It has been 4 weeks since Dr. Blandon started working here, and no one has talked to me about what I need to do. I have this volume of work dropped on my lap that I was not expecting. On top of that, Dr. Blandon is constantly double-checking my work. Doesn't he know that I have more than 15 years of experience! Not only does he double-check my work, he also expects a high level of collections every week. Doesn't he understand the billing and collection cycle? I don't appreciate that he is looking over my shoulder all the time. I don't want to be in charge of his claims and collections. I'm not used to have work pile up. I don't want to be working overtime. You either outsource Dr. Blandon's collections, or I'll resign." Denise continued to listen to Garnet's complaints, trying to calm her down, and promised that Garnet would speak with Drs. Thomas and Williams first thing Monday morning. Although still upset, Garnet agreed to meet with the doctors on Monday.

Dr. Thomas asked, "What just happened?" Denise replied, "I'm as surprised as you are. I didn't know this was happening. I have been busy with the arrangements to bring Dr. Blandon on board. I didn't notice any changes that would alert me that something was bothering her. As you heard, she is expecting to meet with you and Dr. Williams on Monday. I'm confident we can reach a solution."

CASE STUDY DISCUSSION QUESTIONS

1. Describe the barriers to communication between Denise and Garnet and between Garnet and Dr. Blandon.

2. What should Denise have done?

3. What strategies would you recommend to improve communication in the office?

4. Describe the cognitive conflict illustrated in the case.

5. Describe how intrapersonal and interpersonal conflict is illustrated in the case.

6. Using the Thomas and Kilmann two-dimensional taxonomy of conflict handling modes, what conflict management mode did Denise use?

7. What conflict negotiation mode should be used in this case?

Readiness and Change Management During Electronic Medical Records Adoption

By Renee Brent Hotchkiss and John Cantiello

BACKGROUND

The Central Indiana Safety Net Clinics (CISNC) share the vision of establishing a community health information exchange for five partner healthcare clinics in a local urban area. Although the clinics partner in the region's safety-net planning council, each operate as independent organizations serving a disproportionately high number of the county's uninsured and underinsured (i.e., patient numbers ranging from 500 to over 10,000, annually). All of the clinics have been operational for at least 2 years.

Effectiveness of electronic medical record (EMR) systems and improvements in quality are well-documented benefits of adopting this technology. Member clinics of CISNC are interested in achieving the benefits of an EMR system's e-prescribing component. The clinics understand that this component will assist in reducing the number of handwriting errors, allow for immediate access to drug information and patient drug history, and provide FDA safety alerts regarding particular drugs. For the clinics' patients, e-prescribing would be a cost-effective, convenient process for reducing prescription filling time. However, some studies have shown that healthcare providers are hesitant to adopt EMR's e-prescribing due to high costs, slow integration, reduced efficiency, as well as decreased prescribing autonomy.

CURRENT SITUATION

Although CISNC recently received government funding to purchase an electronic medical record (EMR) and e-prescribing system, clinic leaders, Drs. Wyner and Alen, would like to perform clinic assessments before making such a big purchasing decision. They know that each clinic has unique needs, thus making the CISNC system selection complex. Drs. Wyner and Alen wonder, "Will there be one system that would be well suited for the entire group?"

To assist in the decision-making process, the first step for Drs. Wyner and Alen is to explore the "change readiness" of healthcare providers and patients in regards to their perceptions of EMR and e-prescribing. They decide to interview providers and patients in order to evaluate the attitudes, readiness, and acceptability to such innovative technology. Drs. Wyner and Alen hire a consultant to develop a survey to be administered over the next six months to the clinics' providers and patients (**Table 4-1** and **Table 4-2**).

PATIENT PERCEPTIONS

One hundred patients were interviewed over a 6-month period as they were waiting to be seen by the healthcare provider. Interestingly, staff reported that the majority of patients were familiar with e-prescribing and EMR. Other survey results found that patients identified a number of benefits for using the new technology. They liked the transportability of an electronic record and thought it would simplify the check-in process. They also thought it would allow the doctors to be more aware of the patient's history. Patients were hopeful that they would be able to access their own records online and gain a better understanding of their personal health.

Patient concerns focused primarily on access, security, and privacy of their records. They were concerned about identity theft, hackers, and system failures. They expressed concern about who would have access to their records and the possibility of it getting into the hands of people who were not their healthcare providers. They asked about password protection, encryption, HIPAA, and back-up files.

Table 4-1 Provider Readiness Assessment

Do you Agree/Disagree with the following statements:

If the resources are available, I will spend additional time to become familiar with electronic medical records technology.

It will be difficult to schedule time to complete electronic medical record and e-prescribing training.

It will be easy for me to learn to use this technology.

I feel that my needs will be accommodated in the electronic medical records and e-prescribing design process.

Most medical errors occur due to process failures in the current system.

The current practices are efficient; therefore, I do not see the need to implement the system.

Most medical errors occur due to process failures in the current system.

The current practices are efficient; therefore, I do not see the need to implement the system.

EMR and e-prescribing will lead to improved efficiency.

I feel that this technology will improve the effectiveness of the clinic.

The use of EMR and e-prescribing will reduce workloads and allow more time to interact with patients.

The new technologies are a good fit with provider workflow.

EMR and e-prescribing will lead to reductions in medical errors.

I feel that the use of the new system will improve our quality of care.

The new system will improve patient safety.

Our patient satisfaction will be enhanced through the adoption of EMR and e-prescribing.

Adopting these new technologies will enhance provider image.

Using EMR and e-prescribing will distract me and reduce my communication with patients and their families.

This technology will lead to communication issues between staff, colleagues, and coworkers.

EMR and e-prescribing create heavier workloads for providers and clinicians.

I feel that the use of these technologies will reduce provider autonomy.

Table 4-2 Interview Guide

Questions for Providers and Patients

Perceptions of EMR

Based on what you know or have heard about EMR and/or e-prescribing...

1. What are the *advantages* of using this technology?

2. What are the *disadvantages* of using this technology?

3. How do you think EMR will influence/impact your experience at the clinic?

Facilitators to Readiness

4. What are ways you think that an EMR and e-prescribing system will be beneficial for you?
   PROBE: What other benefits do you think there are?

Inhibitors to Readiness

5. What are ways you think that an EMR and e-prescribing system negatively affect you?
   PROBE: What other concerns do you have?

Additional Questions for Patients

1. Do you think your health will be affected by using this technology?
   PROBE: How do you think that such a system will affect your health?

2. How would this new technology negatively impact the amount of time your provider will spend with you?
   PROBE: What other concerns do you have?

Additional Questions for Providers

1. What are ways you think that an EMR and e-prescribing system will be beneficial to your patients?
   PROBE: What other benefits do you think there are?

2. What type of training/support would enable you to learn to use EMR and e-prescribing more easily/faster?

3. How would this new technology negatively impact patients?
   PROBE: What other concerns do you have?

4. Describe your overall willingness to implement EMR and e-prescribing?

5. Do you think that you have sufficient staff to handle day-to-day workloads?

6. Do you feel as though your facility is actively doing things to improve patient safety?

PROVIDER PERCEPTIONS

Healthcare providers were interviewed as well as completed the readiness assessment during their downtime at the clinic. The clinic leaders were disappointed with the low response rate.[1] However, Drs. Wyner and Alen knew that their relationship with the providers was somewhat fragile, and they didn't want to push too hard in fear that they would further strain the relations. They summarized the providers' perceptions based on the reports they received.

All were familiar with EMRs but some had not heard of e-prescribing. Based on the results of the readiness assessment, it was determined that providers were open to the idea of EMR and e-prescribing technology and would be willing to learn the new systems. Furthermore, their responses suggested that there was a need for change and that it would enhance their practice. The majority of responses indicated that the technology would be beneficial in that it would lead to improved efficiency and effectiveness, workload reductions, improved workflow, reductions in medical errors, improvements in quality of care and patient safety, enhanced patient satisfaction, and enhanced provider image. The interviews further identified a number of benefits to EMR and e-prescribing believed to be possible through the use of this technology. They felt that the transportability of EMRs would help to contain costs and reduce duplicative services. Also, it would result in shorter wait times, better coordination of care, and fewer errors. They hoped that the technology could be customized to meet the needs of the individual clinic.

Similar to the patients' perceptions, providers' concerns focused around security, access, and privacy. They also asked about system failures, password protections, user agreements, and back-up plans. Other concerns revolved around the possibility that the computers would be a distraction—taking the focus away from patients or that entering data and dealing with alerts would be a nuisance that would lead to inefficiency. Many providers discussed the high costs of implementing the systems and that it would need to be used to its fullest potential in order to deliver a return on the investment. The readiness assessment indicated that providers were concerned over the possible loss of autonomy; reductions in communication with patients and their families, as well as reductions in communication between staff, colleagues, and coworkers; and heavier workloads.

---

[1] Only 20 healthcare professionals were interviewed, and of those, only 12 completed a readiness assessment.

RESULTS

Drs. Wyner and Alen clearly have their hands full. The results of the interviews and surveys suggest that both providers and patients see a number of benefits to the implementation of EMR and e-prescribing. However, their concerns over security, access, and privacy are legitimate. They now must identify and evaluate alternative methods to address these concerns while striving to meet the needs of all parties.

Dr. Wyner suggests that the results of the interviews and surveys be shared with the clinics' managers at the next council meeting and solicit suggestions from the attendees. Dr. Wyner knows that each clinic will have unique needs that the managers will express at the meeting. He thinks that it is important to include the managers in the decision-making process so that they are more likely to embrace the upcoming changes. Dr. Wyner is concerned that a different approach might further stress provider relationships.

Alternately, Dr. Alen thinks it would be best to use a top down approach and simply make a decision and implement it. Dr. Alen would like to work with a consultant in order to make the best decision, believing that a consultant can provide expert knowledge on the available technology and the ways in which to implement it. Dr. Alen suggests that if they allow managers to make this decision, they will never be able to please everyone and will go over budget and over time.

While Drs. Wyner and Alen acknowledge each other's concerns, they are unable to come to an agreement about their next steps. They decide to share their dilemma with the board and have them vote on their alternative approaches. They prepare a memo and send it to the board members via email, asking for a reply with their vote within 3 days.

Board members are surprised by the memo and the current dilemma. They were not aware that the readiness assessments and interviews had been completed. They thought that the purpose of these interviews was to present alternative vendors to providers and patients and have them comment on their features. Board members feel that they are left with little time and limited information with which to make a decision. While they would have liked to have included managers in the decision and had hoped to do so through the interview process, over two-thirds of the Board members voted to use a consultant to select a system and implement it.

Based on the Board's decision, Dr. Alen hires a consultant and gives him the reports from each of CISNC's 5 clinics. He asks the consultant to do his best in meeting the needs of the clinics. Within a week, the consultant has selected a vendor and shares this news with Dr. Alen. Dr. Alen invites him to attend the next council meeting and present this news to the attendees.

CASE STUDY DISCUSSION QUESTIONS

1. Do you think the information gathering/problem identification process used in this case was successful? Why or why not?

2. Did the leadership of Drs. Myer and Alen help or hinder the change management process? What could they have done differently?

3. How do you think managers at the next council meeting will respond to Dr. Alen and the consultant?

4. List the human resource, management, budgetary, and IT challenges in this case. Which should have the highest priority and why?

5. What is the primary cause of the challenges?

6. What decision-making processes (pro/con lists, cost-benefit analysis, diffusion of innovation, etc.) would you have used and why?

7. How would you monitor the outcomes of your decision? How would you determine its success?

Choosing the Appropriate Electronic Medical Records System: A Clinic's Journey to Innovation

By John Cantiello and Renee Brent Hotchkiss

INTRODUCTION

Fairmont Clinic is a federally qualified health center (FQHC) located in the Midwest. Mr. Harold, the clinic administrator, is considering upgrading their current paper/file record system to an electronic medical records (EMR) system. He is currently researching different vendors to determine which direction the clinic should go in.

Harold knows that the government is providing financial incentives to FQHC's who adopt EMRs for meaningful use through the HI-TECH ACT (part of the American Recovery and Reinvestment Act). This sounds like a great opportunity to Harold, and he has heard a lot of positive things about EMRs. He knows that EMRs are known to improve care, reduce costs, and improve efficiency. He is also aware that in addition to the incentives provided by the federal government, there will be penalties for those practitioners and healthcare organizations who do not upgrade to an EMR system.

However, he also knows some practitioners and clinics that have not had such stellar experiences with their EMR systems. He has heard awful stories about clinics that could not get the IT support needed when problems arose and stories about how EMRs have slowed down practices. He also knows that there is a significant up-front cost in terms of capital and time.

Harold knows that he wants Fairmont Clinic to go "electronic," he just doesn't know how soon, what vendor to choose, and how extensive he wants Fairmont's EMR system to be.

CHALLENGES AND OPTIONS

Fairmont Clinic is a fairly busy clinic, but doesn't have a large staff. The clinic employs three full-time physicians, one physician assistant, two nurses, one receptionist, one biller, and two part-time medical assistants. On average, the clinicians treat 80–100 patients per day. The last thing Harold wants to do is slow down or create obstacles for the practitioners and staff regarding productivity. Therefore, he needs to ensure he implements a timeline for conversion that is fast enough so that the system can be in place without losing patient treatment days, and also so that it allows for the staff and clinicians to adjust to the system.

The most significant challenge faced by Harold is deciding which vendor to choose and how extensive he wants his clinic's EMR system to be. There are literally hundreds of vendors that Harold could choose from. After doing some extensive research on the Internet, talking to other practitioners in the area and at medical conferences, and reading professional trade journals, Harold was able to narrow down the list of vendors to the top 10.

Harold knows that the EMR system that he chooses must allow for the production of consult notes, the ability to store lab data, transfer of existing paper charts, and cross functionality with the local health system, Midwest Grace.

By examining the top 10 vendor list, Harold further narrowed down his choices to 3 that appeared to best suit the clinic's needs:

- E-Med-Clinic is the most affordable option. This vendor promises a quick installation process, additional support at an added cost, has fairly good reviews, and is not very complex. They meet the clinic's needs, but out of the three choices available to Harold, this seems like the most "bare bones" approach.
- IT Solutions meets all of the needs of the clinic, has excellent reviews, and includes extensive IT support; however, it is the most costly of the three choices.

- CareForward is a relatively new company. Their product meets the clinic's needs, they promise extensive IT support, and they are more affordable than IT Solutions. The biggest downside to this company is that they are not well known. Some early reviews indicated that this system is rather complex.

STAFF MEETING

Harold feels confident that he has narrowed down the list to three strong alternatives; however, he knows this is not a decision he can make on his own. Harold is an experienced administrator, and while he has never had to make a decision regarding upgrading an entire medical records system, he has had to make some very important decisions over his career. He has used a variety of different methods to make decisions and believes that a detailed pro/con analysis in consultation with those affected by the decision is the best approach for this situation.

Employees Present

He decides to hold a staff meeting where an open discussion can take place so he can learn the perceived pros and cons from the various stakeholders. Invited to the staff meeting are the following employees: Jennifer (receptionist and scheduler), Jim (billing coordinator), Dr. Haste, Dr. Pace, Dr. Kno, and Jenna Guichard (physician assistant), Linda and Sarah (nurses), and Jessica and Ron (medical assistants).

Employee Opinions

At the meeting, Harold updates the group on his research and selection of vendor. He knows that everyone in the room will be using the EMR system on a daily basis. He also knows that each of the clinic's employees has extensive experience in the medical field and, therefore, may know something about EMRs, or may have even used them in the past. For these reasons, he greatly values the opinions of those at the meeting.

Dr. Haste, Dr. Pace, and Dr. Kno all have varying opinions about "going electronic." Dr. Haste believes that the clinic should have already implemented an EMR system by now and was one of the people who pushed Harold into researching EMRs for the clinic. He wants Harold to invest in the most expensive option because he believes the clinic is already behind other healthcare providers in the local area. Dr. Pace can see value in updating the paper/file system but does not believe that the EMR system should be very extensive. He believes the clinic should go slow and start with the most affordable option and then upgrade later, if necessary. Dr. Kno is against an EMR system, stating that "he has worked his entire career without using an EMR and that the new system would only slow him down." Dr. Kno knows that one day all healthcare providers will be using EMRs and also about the government's incentives; however, he firmly believes that "you shouldn't fix something if it isn't broke."

Jennifer and Jim handle most of the administrative tasks in the office and both agree that updating the system is a good idea. Jim has never worked with an EMR system before, but he has heard great things about them and believes that an upgrade would make his job easier. Jennifer worked at a doctor's office previously that used an EMR system and she related to the group that "while it was difficult to get used to a new system that had flaws, it made things a lot easier." Neither Jennifer nor Jim had an opinion regarding which vendor the clinic should go with; however, they did state that "adequate IT support is crucial, so the cheapest option may not be the best choice."

Linda and Sarah both had experiences with EMRs. Linda related to Harold "my previous employer's EMR system was such a headache, which caused me to leave and accept the position at this clinic." Sarah stated that although her experience with EMRs was not the best, it did make some processes faster and easier. Sarah had previously worked for a hospital and noted that "even though the hospital went completely electronic, there was still a bin of papers in the medical records office that grew every day because no one knew how to combine them with the electronic versions of those patient's charts." Both agree that adequate IT support is necessary, but Linda concludes that "an EMR isn't needed in our clinic." Linda believes with everything going on in the clinic, the change would create unnecessary stress, and benefits from the change would not be realized in the long run.

Jenna had never used an EMR system before but she has many colleagues at other clinics who have, so she is excited about the possible change. She points out to Harold that "an EMR is very expensive and that you don't always get what you paid for because some vendors overcharge for subpar services." She promises to give Harold a list of contacts in the area and in other parts of the country that have experience with the vendors that he is considering for the clinic's conversion.

Jessica and Ron are the newest employees at the clinic and were trained on the use of EMRs in medical assisting school. They couldn't be happier that Harold is considering the upgrade and tell him that "no matter which system he chooses, they will be able to adjust quickly." Jessica and Ron are puzzled why some of the other employees are uneasy about the transition.

Harold thanked everyone for their comments. He reminds Jenna to send him the list of her contacts and adjourns the meeting.

HOW CAN THEORY BE USED TO MAKE A DECISION?

Harold is aware of Roger's diffusion of innovations theory which states that "*technological innovation is communicated through particular channels, over time, among the members of a social system*" and that individuals progress through five stages: knowledge, persuasion, decision, implementation, and confirmation. Harold believes that the clinic is past the "persuasion" stage and is now at the "decision" stage. He keeps in mind that the clinic's employees are only midway through the diffusion of innovations process and that now is a crucial time in order to ensure the best outcomes for the clinic.

Harold believes that he can use Roger's diffusion of innovation theory to guide the process of choosing the best EMR system, given the clinic's circumstances. He learned that with the diffusion of innovation theory that *important characteristics of innovation* are: 1) relative advantage, 2) compatibility, 3) complexity, 4) trialability, and 5) observability. Harold needs to ensure that the new system will 1) be better than the old one, 2) meet the clinic's needs, 3) not be too complex, 4) be experimented with on a small scale, and 5) the results of implementing a new system can be observed. Harold believes that he can reach the best decision by coupling his research with what he has learned from the clinic's employees with the characteristics of innovation.

CONCLUDING REMARKS

Harold knows he has a lot of thinking to do. The clinic is a public clinic, and while it will receive financial incentives from the government for implementing an EMR system and going electronic, Harold knows the budget is tight and does not have the funds to invest in an expensive upgrade. He also does not want to create any obstacles that may cause the clinic's productivity to decline—either in the short or long runs. He sits in his office and considers what to do next.

CASE STUDY DISCUSSION QUESTIONS

1. Outline the decision-making process you would use to decide which vendor to contract if you were in Harold's position.

2. How extensive should the system be? Does a FQHC need to have a very extensive EMR system?

3. Would the benefits of a more costly system outweigh the financial implications of going with such a system? How would you measure the financial implications in the short term and long term?

4. How important do you believe IT support to be?

5. How much say should the staff have in what type of system to go with? Should clinicians have more say then administrative staff? Should Harold have the staff vote or is this a decision for Harold to make alone?

6. How would you handle conflict if it arose from clinicians and staff who are against an EMR conversion?

7. Which vendor would you ultimately go with, and why? How would you evaluate whether or not the upgrade has improved care, reduced costs, and improved efficiency?

8. How specifically can Mr. Harold use the framework of diffusion of innovations theory (namely the important characteristics of innovation) to ensure that the clinic chooses the most appropriate system? Are some characteristics of innovation more important than others?

REFERENCES

Clarke, R. (1999). *A primer in diffusion of innovations theory*. Retrieved from http://www.rogerclarke.com/SOS/InnDiff.html

Rogers, E. M. (1962). *Diffusion of innovations*. New York: The Free Press of Glencoe.

Joint Patient Liaison Office: Building a Streamlined Unit

By Alyson Eisenhardt, Susanne Bruno-Ninassi, and Lorri E. Cooper

A s Colonel Green escorted Lieutenant (LT) Howard into the new office space where the newly created Joint Patient Liaison Office (JPLO) would be, she thought, "What exactly have I gotten myself into?" It is a joke in the military that the acronym NAVY translates to "Never Again Volunteer Yourself," and yet here she was volunteering to lead a new "joint" department as a Navy Officer working in an Army hospital.

Her Commanding Officer (CO), Captain Stans, briefed her on the recent complaints from the Pacific Commanders that the turnaround time for air medical evacuation (medevac) and specialty care services was a source of contention. Medevacs and specialty care services were often delayed, which caused a huge expense to patients and to their units while awaiting medical services. The proposed solution would combine all patient liaison services previously performed by each military service into one cohesive group.

This new office would require a leader. LT Howard thought, "I can fix this problem. There is an opportunity here. It would be a great challenge and great visibility." However, she now questioned if it was the visibility she really needed

---

to boost her career or if she would have been better off "flying under the radar." In any regard, there she was standing in a mess of boxes that would soon be her new office.

TAMC AND JPLO

Turner Army Medical Center (TAMC) serves the military population throughout the Western Pacific. TAMC is located on the island of Oahu, Hawaii (as seen in **Figure 6-1**) and houses a medevac office and service liaison offices. TAMC is the only inpatient military treatment facility (MTF) throughout the Hawaiian Islands. Out of 14 MTFs in the Pacific, it is the most diverse facility, offering over 30 specialties to service members, veterans, and their families in Hawaii and throughout the Pacific.

Each service liaison office is traditionally responsible for its own patients. Although these services are closely linked, each office operated independently of one another. In November 2005, the Joint Executive Committee, which consists of all leaders of the island military medical facilities, identified a service problem involving the Army medevac office and the patient liaison services.

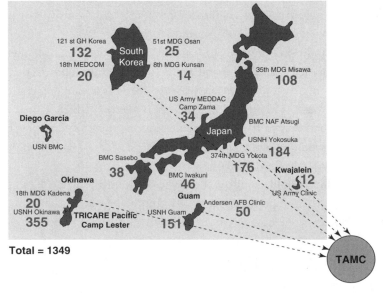

FIGURE 6-1 Patient Movement Throughout the Western Pacific

Numerous commanders from the Pacific complained about the specialty and inpatient turnaround time. Under the existing process, the commanders incurred extraneous costs to send their service members to Hawaii for treatment. The reasons for these costs were threefold.

1. While a service member received treatment, his/her position was vacant. In addition, if the injured service member held a lead position, without that member, operations were in jeopardy.
2. The cost of travel and outpatient stays in Hawaii was expensive. Many of the medevac flights were commercial and could cost as much as $1,500. Additionally, the per diem rate for the island, which includes meals, lodging, and incidentals, was $308 per day. To further add to this cost, many times service members, unable to travel alone, would be accompanied by a nonmedical attendant, who would also receive a paid flight and per diem expenses. As a result of these long unpredictable turnaround times, these expenses quickly depleted the command's travel budget.
3. The accountability of service members receiving treatment in Hawaii was difficult. Without a mandate to officially check-in to a unit, the service members were often getting into trouble. On the island, many service members engage in risk-taking behavior while awaiting medical services, thereby contributing to the cost and time away from duty. For example, a service member awaiting outpatient surgery was injured in a bar fight and broke his wrist. He had to wait for surgery, and due to recovery time, his return to service was delayed.

STREAMLINED COHESIVE DEPARTMENT

Colonel Green, the Patient Administration Division Leader responsible for medevac and utilization review services at TAMC, understood the importance of continuity of care for liaison services, and he recognized that the current organization of the patient liaison divisions had gaps. Ultimately, at the suggestion of Colonel Green, all patient liaison services were to be consolidated under one office with one manager. LT Howard, stationed at nearby Pearl Harbor, was awarded the job. LT Howard had a stellar service record and was the patient administration service leader for the Navy. She had strong connections with the Air Force, understood medevac well, and had proven herself to be a team player. She showed promise, and Colonel Green had faith that she could make the department a team. Her first order of business was to develop and create a streamlined functioning department.

Historically, the service liaisons and the medevac offices had provided assistance to patients traveling to and from TAMC for medical care since the 1980s. As a Navy Officer, LT Howard would now take charge of a staff, which included Army, Navy, Air Force, Marine, and civilian personnel. Previously, each service provided similar patient liaison services independent of each other. With the consolidation of the services, the staff members, who never worked as a team before, would now perform streamline functions as one "cohesive group."

This consolidation took approximately 1 year to complete (see **Figure 6-2**). There were considerable efforts and resources devoted to training that focused on providing each service member the capability to perform as a team. During this year, there was a massive cross-training. Upon completion of this training, all service members were able to perform each other's functions. However, each group remained responsible for a specific function as follows:

- Army personnel coordinated medevac movement, served as the main point of contact for the air force flight deck, ensured patients met all requirements for travel clearance, handled all ambulance movement, and entered all patient movement data. In addition to the medevac coordination, the Army handled their patient liaison services.

The Army service members were:

- Sergeant First Class (SFC) Alan—Sergeant Alan; the second most senior Army enlisted member in the office and was the supervisor below the LT. He was stern and a bit macho. He was a hard-driver and took his job and his service seriously. He was definitely what the military would call a "lifer."

- Corporal (CPL) Odom—Corporal Odom was young and energetic. She was a bit stubborn in her ways and had a hard time adjusting to new situations. She had an opinion at all times and was not shy to share it.

- Specialist (SPC) Stevens—Specialist Stevens was ambitious and eager to gain and share knowledge. She was a team player and wanted to do well.

- Navy, Marines, and Air Force service liaisons obtained data and assisted with patient needs. All liaisons assisted with travel and accommodations for service members, checked-in with service members, and were the liaison for the MTF and command needs, coordinated continuity of care issues, and served as the main point of contact for the parent commands.

There were three Navy liaisons:

- HM1 Jones had 15 years in the military. He was the most senior Navy service member in the office. Coming from a ship to an MTF, he was accustomed to division. He had trouble integrating into a team approach. He was concerned more with the responsibilities of other parties and less with his own.

- HM2 Arber was a motivated sailor, who took on any task. She was interested in becoming an officer and was good at offering suggestions and recommendations to senior shipmates. She had a knack for teamwork and would be a good leader someday.

- HM2 Janner was quiet and friendly. She was a hard worker and committed sailor. However, she often needed direction in her tasks.

There was one Marine liaison:

- Sergeant Cooper was a solid worker and committed Marine. He was devoted to his fellow Marines and lived by its commitment to brotherhood. He worked well with teams and had an enormous respect for authority, as do all Marines.

There was one Air Force Liaison:

- Master Sergeant (MSgt) Miller was the oldest and most senior enlisted service member in the office. Despite her seniority, she was not assigned to be the leading enlisted member of the office (as is traditionally the case). This was a role that MSgt Miller's commander, LT Howard, agreed would be better served by Sergeant Alan. Miller was one year shy of retirement from the Air Force and not interested in taking on any additional work.

- The Utilization Review Coordinator coordinated with specialty care clinics and other Case Managers from the home clinics.

- The Utilization Review Coordinator (and BSN) was Ms. Kingley. Ms. Kingley was a "take charge" kind of person. There was nothing she would not do for her patients. She often went above and beyond for patients and for her fellow staff members. She was more than devoted to her job.

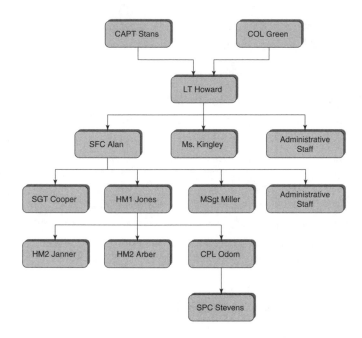

FIGURE 6–2 Organizational Chart

BENEFITS AND CHALLENGES

The consolidation produced many benefits, such as internal processes gained efficiencies, redundancy was eliminated, and wait and turnaround times were cut down. As a result, service members sent to TAMC were spending less time on the island awaiting services and more time back at work. The commanders were beginning to recognize the benefit of the consolidation and the JPLO.

During the year of consolidation, in addition to the JPLO accomplishing its mission, there were many challenges that had to be overcome. Teamwork is not always innate, and it took time to build a functioning and effective team environment. Furthermore, this effective teamwork was often challenged by reality. Some of these challenges are illustrated in the following scenarios.

MIXING EXISTING CULTURES

LT Howard had been in the military for 5 years. Hawaii was only her second duty station, but having worked as part of several tri-service disaster response teams, she knew enough of the military to understand that the different branches of military service had different core values, different mission, and different cultures. She was now charged with blending those cultures into one effective team.

"But, what do they do?" Hospital Corpsman 1st Class (HM1) Jones asked. LT Howard bit her lip and responded, "HM1 Jones, the Army handles the patient input data. We need to supply them with the correct information to do that efficiently. This department has had too many medical evacuation discrepancies in the past. We cannot afford to make errors." LT Howard knew the cost of one discrepancy meant wasted fuel, wasted money, and possibly a wasted airplane.

HM1 Jones replied, "I just feel like we are learning their job, and they are not helping us out at all. We have more sailors coming through here than they have soldiers, marines, or airmen combined. It should be our process."

"It is *our* process, Hospital Corpsman 1st Class Jones. We are a joint office now, and we need to work as one process," LT Howard responded as she turned to address her entire team. "I need everyone to understand that we are all on the same team now. If you have any issues or objections, we need to discuss them now. If not, I assume we will be working together from this point on."

MISSION IMPOSSIBLE

LT Howard was staring at the dry erase board above her computer until the words blurred when Ms. Kingley entered her office.

"Lieutenant, are you okay?" Ms. Kingley asked. She had been a nurse at TAMC for over 10 years and in her current position as case manager/utilization review specialist for over a year. She did her job well and went above and beyond for the patients and the rest of the staff.

"Ms. Kingley, will you read aloud for me please?" LT Howard gestured to the words on the dry erase board entitled "JPLO mission," Ms. Kingley read:

"The Joint Patient Liaison Office seeks to provide superior and streamlined medical liaison services to all patients served by TAMC via proper and efficient communication and coordination with the patients, the commands, other facilities, and community resources. The office aims to excel in both internal and external customer satisfaction. We are the link to quality care in the Western Pacific Region. No need will be unmet!"

When she was through, she looked back at the LT.

"What does that mean to you?" the LT asked.

"Honestly?"

"Yes, honestly," LT Howard replied.

"Well, not a whole heck of a lot, Lieutenant," Ms. Kingley went on, "I wasn't there when they wrote it."

LT Howard laughed to herself, although the situation was really not all that funny. Ms. Kingley was correct. She was an integral part of the success of the JPLO, yet she and the other staff members were not part of the key decisions made regarding the consolidation of the services.

"How do I get people to accept and commit to a mission that they did not create themselves?" The LT wondered how this was going to work. She knew she would have to answer this question before moving on with other department goals.

A TEAM THAT RUNS TOGETHER, WORKS TOGETHER

There was much about the culture of the military that was difficult for LT Howard to take at times. But one thing she enjoyed and was inspired by was the culture of fitness that thrived in this environment. Being a "fit force" is mandatory of all services. There are quarterly fitness tests to ensure that all service members are "within fitness standards." LT Howard's devotion to fitness went beyond what was mandated by the Navy. Fitness was important to her, and she liked the fact that she could make it part of her team building.

One morning, she decided physical training (PT) should be a priority in this department. When she returned to the office that morning she announced a fitness plan to the team at the weekly department meeting. PT sessions would begin at 6:30 a.m. Monday through Friday. Participation was not mandatory, but recommended.

Instantly, MSgt Miller let out what seemed to be an adult-like whine. LT Howard was not a big fan of spontaneous displays of emotion like this. Miller grumbled as the meeting adjourned, "I have to give report at the Air Force Base at 7:30 a.m. I'm not running in the mornings." LT Howard replied it would be great if everyone participated, and if Miller could join the group for a bit prior to her report that would be appreciated. Miller stated that if the PT sessions were not mandatory then she was not going to rush around in the morning prior to report.

LT Howard recognized that Miller had some underlying resentment toward her and the rest of the staff. MSgt Miller was the highest-ranking enlisted in the office; as such, it was expected that Miller would be second in charge of the office. However, this was not the case. LT Howard believed that Miller, who was close to retirement, had what is known in the military as "short-timers disease." She was not interested in performing at her best because at this point in her career she felt her performance did not matter. LT Howard knew that this was not something that would be able to be overcome. LT Howard and MSgt Miller discussed the structure of the office, and it was mutually agreed that because Miller was due to retire in less than 6 months, the job of senior enlisted would go to someone who needed the responsibility and growth for their career. Sergeant Alan was chosen as the next in charge.

MSgt Miller was known for her "independence." It seemed to the team that she preferred to rely on the Air Force and not her new joint office mates whenever she could. Her team members noticed this and often made comments to the LT. This was a difficult situation for LT Howard; since MSgt Miller was a senior enlisted, LT Howard had really expected more from her.

MOTIVATING WITH PURPOSE

As she looked back on the past 6 months, LT Howard knew that her staff had come a long way together. They were finally working together as an integrated team. Prior to the office cross-training efforts, annually, there had been 30 medevac discrepancies that caused delays or cancellations of medevac flights. After the cross-training, discrepancies decreased to zero and as a result there were no cancellations or delays in flights. Patient safety became key to the office as illustrated in the following:

1. Wait times for ambulances were eliminated and backup services established.
2. Reporting from civilian hospitals was immediately received as opposed to 24–48 hour reporting.
3. Services consolidating return times were down from 3 to 4 days to 1 to 2 days after the patient was medically cleared. Estimated cost savings of $300,000 per year.

It was obvious that the team had good momentum, and LT Howard wanted to keep it going. She knew one of the best ways to motivate her staff was through service awards or ribbons. Service ribbons/awards are military decorations, which acknowledge service and personal accomplishments while a member of the

United States armed forces. Such awards are a means of displaying the highlights of a service member's career and are to be worn in order of precedence. Service members wear these awards proudly. The number and types of ribbons worn speaks volumes for the service member. In the military, this is a matter of status and a step toward promotion.

LT Howard thought how great it would be to award her staff with service awards generally not awarded to members outside a particular service. "I am going to put the Army personnel in for Navy service awards," she announced to Sergeant Alan. "I'll need your help with the paperwork," she told him.

"The paperwork is not problem, ma'am, but I think you are wasting your time. The Army is old school. This ain't the Navy. They won't go for it," he told her.

"I'm not willing to hear that, Sergeant. Just help me out with the administrative stuff, will you?" She asked rhetorically.

"Yes, ma'am," was his answer.

Two weeks later, Sergeant Alan placed the request for the award on the Lieutenant's desk. "Sorry Lieutenant," he said, sliding the papers toward her.

LT Howard looked over at the ever-growing pile of paperwork. "Sergeant this is the third time the Army has denied this award. No offense, but what the heck is their problem?"

LT Howard was referring to the Army Awards Office. This was the third time she had attempted to give an Army soldier a Navy award. She had meticulously combed over the award. It was well written and concise. Every time the award was returned, she would add to it, tweak it, and send it back. Apparently, it was not her grammar the Army did not like, but rather that she was a Navy lieutenant trying to give a soldier a formal Navy award. This was not within Army protocol.

PUTTING PRACTICE IN ACTION

LT Howard was pulling into the hospital parking lot when she received a call from Colonel Green. The Colonel wanted her in his office as soon as she walked in the door. There was an emergency that required her team's full attention.

"This isn't a drill, Lieutenant," Colonel Green spoke with a tense voice as he explained the situation. There had been a boiler explosion aboard a submarine off the coast of Guam early that morning. Five sailors were seriously burned; one was killed on-site. The others were being medevaced to TAMC and then off to the Army's burn center in Texas.

The JPLO was becoming visible now, ready or not, and the team needed to be a team now! LT Howard received her orders from the Colonel. The hospital's chief of staff was holding a meeting to plan the receipt and stabilization of the patients. LT Howard needed to be there, and her crew needed to be ready to move these patients whenever they arrived on the flight deck. Time was a moving target. Uncertainty existed regarding when patients would be stable enough to leave Guam and then stabilized at TAMC to continue their travel to the burn center. The JPLO needed to be ready.

LT Howard returned to her office and called the team together for a quick briefing before she moved to join the hospital coordination meeting. She alerted the team to the urgency of the incoming situation and left orders to begin coordination with the flight deck and with the ambulance.

The urgency and the seriousness of what was about to transpire gave her pause. Lives were at stake. The team needed to respond efficiently and without error. Already on CNN, the world was watching and waiting for the injured sailors to be received at Burns Medical Center, stabilized, and then transported safely to the burn center in Texas. The injured, while in critical condition, would make a 7,000+ mile medevac, requiring speed and seamless coordination. This would be the first real test of the new unit.

LT Howard had come to know her team members well. She knew they had devoted themselves to developing the necessary actions to respond at the highest performance level to this type of event. She had confidence in them. Still she was nervous. She knew they would be looking to her to guide and support their efforts and more important, she knew her superior officers would judge her leadership capability based on the success of this mission along with the success of her team.

As she walked down the hall toward the hospital organization meeting, she wondered, "are we ready for this now?"

LT Howard briefed her staff as soon as she returned to her office. She told them that she was on her way to the coordination meeting and that she would return to report on further action. She left orders to begin coordination with the flight deck and with the ambulance. As she gathered her notepad, she thought this was the moment the department had prepared for over the past year.

CASE STUDY DISCUSSION QUESTIONS

1. At the end of the case, LT Howard is wondering about the outcome of her team's urgent and serious "test." What do you predict will happen?

2. In terms of leadership, what did LT Howard "give" to "get" an engaged, effective team? What did team members have to "give" to "get" the same?

3. If you were Colonel Green, the person who originally formed the new unit, how might you determine the success of the new Joint Patient Liaison Office? How would judge LT Howard's leadership of the office?

4. What qualities and characteristics do you look for in a person you are willing to follow? What do you expect from a leader you "want" to follow? Is it different from a leader you are required to follow because of their position or status?

5. Individuals, the public, the media—all are demanding "transparency" for both leaders and organizations today. Why? What is it that we want when we ask for or even demand transparency? Just exactly what is the "promise" of transparency?

6. How valued is transparency in your organization? Is it safe to bring bad news to your boss? Is it safe to bring bad news to those at the top of your organization?

7. Based on the profiles contained in the case, project an assessment of the two dimensions for each team member.

8. Consider groups or teams you have worked with—was there a balance along the dimensions or were there some outliers? What effect did this have on the group? What effect did this have on the leader of the group?

9. For your ideal group, what is the best mix of followers? Does it change based on different expected outcomes of the group's purpose?

10. When LT Howard's attempt at creating awards for team members was unsuccessful, what other means of motivation and rewards might she have established?

11. One of the strongest elements of motivation involves the integration of "purpose" among team members. What evidence in the case highlights the sense of purpose among team members? What other ways might LT Howard have chosen to imbue this "purpose" among team members?

Working in a Critical Care Unit: Experiences of a Nurse

By Reeti Debnath (India)

Tanima Bose is a married 38-year-old nurse, who has worked in Medinova Multispecialty Hospital (India) for the past 6 years. The hospital is a 230-bed facility and is considered one of the best in the city.

When Tanima first joined Medinova Multispecialty Hospital, she was assigned as a staff nurse to the cardiology unit on the third floor. Her supervisor and colleagues were very helpful and the work environment in the unit was quite motivating. Tanima was a hard worker and within 5 years was recognized for her efforts with a promotion and reassignment to the hospital's fifth floor intensive care unit (ICU). The ICU not only had a greater bed capacity than the cardiology unit but sicker patients to manage, but Tanima was up for the challenge.

Tanima's schedule was the 8 a.m. to 2 p.m. shift, but she very rarely left the hospital without incurring overtime. At times, her colleagues would call in sick, and due to staff shortage, her supervisor would ask her to stay and assist the other nurses with patient care. On many occasions, she had to miss out on participating in important social events at home. Tanima also felt that she was not properly trained to carry out some of her assigned duties since there was no formal training by the hospital when she was transferred to the ICU.

Tanima is starting to feel that her job is negatively impacting both her professional and personal lives. Recently, she has been encountering nonworking monitors in the ICU as well as malfunctioning ventilators and blood pressure equipment. Last week, one of Tanima's patients expired during her shift and she felt helpless. Tanima thought to herself, "If all the equipment worked in the ICU all the time, we can save half of our patients because they are so sick. If the equipment doesn't work, we can only save a few. I don't know how much longer I can put up with this situation. I am losing my enthusiasm for nursing."

CASE STUDY DISCUSSION QUESTIONS

1. What sources of stress can be identified in this case study?

2. If you were in Tanima's situation, how would you handle it?

3. In your opinion, what measures can be adopted by the healthcare institution to manage the stress of the nursing staff?

The Tardy Drama Queen

By Karen McMillen Dielmann

Eastside General (Eastside) is part of the Sun Valley Healthcare System. Eastside is one of Sun Valley's smaller, community-based hospitals located in a rural area of the Midwest. Sally Moreno, the Admissions Department supervisor, has worked for Eastside for 10 years, with her job as registrar in the small, but busy emergency department (ED). She appreciates the importance of her staff's roles in contributing to the financial health of the hospital. In addition, Sally's manager frequently reminds her that she needs to keep productivity high in the department in order to avoid layoffs in this poor economy. Sally feels a strong sense of responsibility to Eastside and the surrounding community. Eastside is the largest employer in the area and Sally grew up in this community. Many of her family members work for the hospital.

Since the Admissions Department is a 24/7 operation, all staff need to work together as a team to ensure that there is adequate coverage in all areas of the department. One Admissions Department staff member, Rosetta Samuels, transferred in 18 months ago from the Dietary Department where she had worked for

2 years. About 9 months ago, Sally noticed that Rosetta began to have a tardiness problem. It was becoming worse, causing grumbling among her coworkers, who were tired of having to either stay late (from the night shift) to cover for her or having to deal with angry patients who are waiting to be admitted for services (from the day shift) when Rosetta was late for her 7 a.m. shift.

Rosetta breezes into work 15–30 minutes late several times per month, complaining loudly and dramatizing the situation that led to her being late. Some of the reasons for her tardiness have been:

• Losing track of time when tidying up her apartment before leaving for work
• Taking too much time to pack her lunch, get dressed, or take a shower in the morning; she just can't seem to get out of the door on time
• Running out of gas on the way to work or having car problems, such as the car not starting in the rain
• Having trouble deciding what to wear to work

Sally has been keeping daily documentation on the time Rosetta arrives for her shift as well as a list of complaints from her coworkers. Rosetta has been verbally counseled about the problem. Today, Sally was giving Rosetta a written warning and called her into the office:

Sally: Rosetta, you know that we have talked about you needing to be on time.

Rosetta: Yes, and I have really tried to be on time. I just can't help it sometimes. I get a late start in the mornings, or my kids won't get out of bed…You know that yesterday my youngest, Georgie, he's my biggest problem, well he wouldn't get out of bed. I kept pestering him, 'Georgie, I'm going to be late for work,' but he wouldn't listen. I don't know what to do about him anymore…

Sally: [interrupting] I know you have problems at home and you've told me about your issues causing you to be late, but, Rosetta, you must be here on time. It creates problems for the department and the other employees when you're late.

Rosetta: I know. I will try, I really will…Who has been complaining about me? I bet it's that old biddy, Jane. She never liked me…

> Just last week she told the other ladies in the break room that I
> don't do my share of the work. I do work hard; I just have a little
> trouble getting to work on time. It's not my fault…I don't know
> why she dislikes me, I never did nothing to her….

Sally: [interrupting again] This isn't about Jane or anyone else; it's
about you needing to be on time. I have to write you up and if
you don't start showing up on time very day, you will get fired.

Rosetta: [crying out loudly] Please don't fire me! I need this job. My
husband lost his job and I am the only one working. My kids
need to eat. Please don't fire me. I promise to be on time.

Sally: I know Rosetta. Please try to be on time. I have to write you
up; it is the company's policy and my manager will be asking
to see this report. Please, Rosetta, be on time.

Rosetta: I will, Sally. I promise. Maybe I should transfer to another
department where it's not so important that I be at work right
at 7 a.m. everyday…

Sally: Rosetta, it is important to be on time in every job here at Eastside General.

Rosetta: Okay. I will try from now on.

Since that conversation two weeks ago, Rosetta had been on time…most days.
She was a few minutes late here and there, but most of the time, she had arrived
very close to the start of her shift…that is, until today.

Today, Rosetta was 20 minutes late, complaining in a loud voice when she
arrived about the "traffic jam." Sally is dreading the thought of having to deal
with her again about her tardiness.

Interestingly, yesterday Sally received a transfer form from the Human Resources Department regarding Rosetta's request to transfer to another job within
the hospital. The form requires Sally, as Rosetta's direct supervisor, to complete
information about her performance and attendance. Sally is torn about this; if
she completes the form honestly, Rosetta will most likely not be considered for
the transfer (Sally and the Admissions Department will be stuck with her). However, if Sally "overlooks" Rosetta's tardiness issues, she may get transferred to the
other area—perhaps with a more amenable schedule? After all, Rosetta is a good
employee when she's at work.

CASE STUDY DISCUSSION QUESTIONS

1. Does Maslow's Hierarchy of Needs apply to this situation? If yes, how? If no, why not?

2. What are some of the motivational factors affecting Sally's and Rosetta's behaviors? In what ways, do each person's behaviors impact the other employees?

3. What is your assessment of Sally's conflict management style? What are your suggestions for Sally for dealing with this situation?

4. How would you describe Sally's leadership in terms of being a transactional or transformational leader? What are your suggestions for Sally in terms of her leadership style or approach in this situation?

5. How should Sally approach the situation with Rosetta's tardiness today? Should the request for transfer play a role in her decision? What should she do about that?

CASE **9**

It's Just Not Fair!

By Karen McMillen Dielmann

JoAnne Martin is the manager of the environmental services department for Lake Simon Healthcare System's Central Rock facility, which is located in a mid-size community. Lake Simon is considered one of the largest systems in the Midwest, owning and operating numerous but small inpatient and outpatient facilities in several states. JoAnne started with Lake Simon 25 years ago as a per diem housekeeper working her way up the system to her current manager position. She is a "hands on" manager, working as hard as or harder than her staff. JoAnne's staff respect and admire her because she "gets her hands dirty" and is compassionate toward their work, health, and family needs.

Martha and Lydia are long-term employees in the environmental services department at Lake Simon's Central Rock facility. Both employees have serious health issues (this should be confidential, but things get around) and have been approved under the Family and Medical Leave Act (FMLA) for occasional work restrictions due to their health issues.

Martha has worked for Lake Simon for 30 years and is viewed as a dedicated and knowledgeable employee. New employees gravitate to Martha because she assists everyone in learning the intricacies of their job duties; in fact, she is known as "mom" in the department. Martha has a serious disease that may require an eventual liver transplant.

Lydia has worked for the health system for 8 years and has been battling breast cancer for the past 3 years. Lydia is fun loving and a jokester. She is the social planner in the department, organizing the many retirement parties, baby showers, birthdays, and so forth. Although ill, Lydia has a positive attitude and she is always encouraging and supportive of others. Employees seek her out when they need a hug or some encouraging words and she is the first person to volunteer to help out by covering another employee's shift, if she is able to do so.

Martha and Lydia rarely miss work and do as much as they can within their health restrictions. In fact, both usually step over the line working beyond their restrictions to help out when staffing is short or the patient census is high and rooms need to be turned over quickly for readmissions. When they need time off for surgery or other medical treatments, other employees are willing to cover for them or donate vacation time to help them financially through their medical leave.

Betty also works in the environmental services department at Central Rock and is an occasional relief supervisor. Betty has had a variety of medical treatments over the 10 years she has worked for the system, mostly due to her suffering from fibromyalgia and a blood clotting disorder. She is often approved under the Family and Medical Leave Act (FMLA) for work restrictions due to her health issues. Although Betty is a good worker, she is not sought out as frequently as Martha and Lydia. Betty has a tendency to move slowly, complain about her health and family issues, and not extend herself beyond her required job duties.

Wanda works at Central Rock as well. She is avoided by others most of the time because of her negative attitude, constant complains regarding management, her assigned workload, and others "not pulling their share of the work." Wanda has numerous family issues that she freely discusses in the workplace and that have caused employees to complain to JoAnne that Wanda needs to spend more time working and less time "sharing."

Entering the monthly staff meeting, JoAnne senses an underlying tension among the departmental staff. However, her concern is preparing for a relicensing visit from the Department of Health. JoAnne starts the meeting reminding everyone about the upcoming visit.

JoAnne:	The Department of Health will be arriving on Monday and we need to make sure all hallways and stairways are clean, especially the baseboards and in the corners.
Martha:	I am working this weekend and will make sure that the north wing's hallways and stairways are all up to snuff. Sally and Joe are here too; they'll help.
JoAnne:	Great.
Betty:	I can't do more than I already do. It's all I can do to get my own work done by the end of the shift and my doctor won't let me do too much.
	[After Betty's comment, some of the other employees rolled their eyes and started snickering.]
Lydia:	We can do this folks. We've done it before. Remember the last time the Health Department was here, we received excellent comments about the cleanliness of our hospital…
JoAnne:	That's right. Let's pull together and make this place sparkle!
Wanda:	But some of us work harder than others and we resent having to cover extra days and do extra work all of the time.
	[Some of the other employees gasped at Wanda's statement; some nodded their heads in agreement and others rolled their eyes.]
Betty:	I do what I can and at least I don't whine and complain all the time like some people…
JoAnne:	We need to focus on the upcoming inspection. Let's pull together and get this done.
Lydia:	And then we'll have a celebration party!

All went well during the inspection and the administration again received great comments about the cleanliness of the hospital, but the tension continued in the environmental services department.

Wanda is a member of Betty's church and relates to all that she "always" sees Betty helping out at the monthly church supper. Wanda feels the need to mention this fact at every opportunity when employees gather in the break room as well as the coincidence that Betty is usually not at work the day after the church supper because she taking her "FMLA time off." Wanda has been counseled in the past about her negative attitude toward others, in addition to not completing her work in a timely manner. Just last month, JoAnne spoke to Wanda about this.

JoAnne: Yesterday, you were seen in the break room well past your 30 minute lunch. I was told that you were complaining about administration. I've told you that we are all on the same team here and that you need to have a more positive attitude.

Wanda: Why do you care what I say? It's a free country. I can say what I want as long as I do my work.

JoAnne: Well, that's part of the problem. You are not getting your work done by the end of your shift and the next shift has to pick up and finish your work, or I have to do it before I leave for the day.

Wanda: That's not fair. What about the others in the department who call in sick when they're not really sick and we have to cover for them!

JoAnne: Wanda, I am not going to discuss other employees. You need to complete your own job duties by the end of the shift and I don't want to hear any more issues about your negativity.

Betty called in sick today asking to use FMLA time; according to the rumor mill, she worked the church supper last night. Although Wanda has been counseled in the past about her negative attitude, again today the other employees in the department are tense and gossiping (JoAnne can hear them whispering) because of Wanda's comments to them. JoAnne knows that Wanda will be coming to her sometime during the shift to complain once again, that this situation with Betty is not fair. She mumbles to herself, "What am I going to say to her this time? I just want this nonsense to stop."

CASE STUDY DISCUSSION QUESTIONS

1. What do you think are some of the motivating factors behind the behaviors of the manager and these four employees?

2. How do individuals' perceptions relate in this situation?

3. How should JoAnne deal with Wanda? Does anything need to be done relating to Betty?

4. Would you recommend making changes to the way JoAnne is managing this department? If yes, what recommendations and why? If no, why?

Broken Ribs

By Diane Dodd-McCue and Stephanie Hamilton

D r. Roberts, a young medical doctor, was entering his third week as a resident in a busy university hospital's emergency department (ED) and was again pulling night duty on a late summer weekend. Ever since his first ED experience, as a tree-climbing 7 year old with a broken arm, Dr. Roberts had wanted to be in trauma care. He had directed his energies toward academic perfection, foregoing the rollicking spring break and summer antics of his less focused school friends. He had excelled in medical school, and his reward was this plum assignment in one of the most innovative trauma centers in the country. Dr. Roberts knew others thought of him as bright, eager, and intense, and that was fine with him. He didn't want to do a good job—he wanted to do an excellent job—and he tried to be attentive to any guidance provided by his superiors.

It was early in his duty shift but Dr. Roberts had already interviewed a number of patients to assure charted information was thorough and accurate. One was a disheveled middle-aged man dramatically holding his side and moaning.

"Hi. I'm Dr. Roberts. And you are?"

The patient repeated his name, nodded, and let out a loud sigh. Dr. Roberts continued. "I see you are visiting us with some broken ribs. So I can better understand how we can help you, can you tell me how this happened?"

Dr. Roberts sat down and began focusing on putting information into the medical chart.

"Well, doc, it just shouldn't have happened if they'd just let me do my job. See, I'm an accountant and not an action hero. Work for a bail bondsmen. Things pretty busy these days. My boss and his brother usually do the meet and greet, apprehend these guys. I stay with the numbers. But this week I had to help apprehend them because it's his brother's vacation time. That's how I come to get hurt. Oh! This hurts. It hurts real bad!"

Dr. Roberts nodded sympathetically but didn't look up from the chart. He was intent on recording patient information.

The patient groaned loudly and then continued. "These ribs, wow they hurt. I am in pain, bad pain. Need something real quick. Can you get me…" At this point, the patient reels off the name of a specific pain medication as well as a specific dosage.

Dr. Roberts continued to dutifully record this information and then moves on, assuring the patient his case was being reviewed. A few minutes later Dr. Able, the attending physician, comes by and asks Dr. Roberts for a review of this patient. Dr. Roberts repeats the patient's account in a straightforward manner. Dr. Able asks Dr. Roberts what he thinks he should do. Dr. Roberts replies that the patient was in pain and probably needs pain relief.

Consider the following three possible scenarios.

SCENARIO 1

Dr. Able: [Pulling up a chair and sitting next to Dr. Roberts at the nurse's station] So, tell me some more about your impressions of the patient. It sounds like an unusual situation.

Dr. Roberts: Yes. I guess not everybody comes in because they were helping a bail bondsman. I know we see a lot of weird things here. But rib fractures can be so painful. It seems clear cut that he is in extreme pain and needs these meds.

Dr. Able: It sounds like he knows the specific medicine he needs. [pause]

Dr. Roberts: Yes. Hmm. You know, now that I think about it, it was unusual that he told me an exact dosage and medicine. I actually would not have chosen that medicine for him. He must have taken a lot of pain medicines before. At first he was really moaning and then became matter of fact in telling me about needing meds. I think I should ask him some more; like, if he has had other injuries before and why he knows pain meds so well; is he allergic to other pain meds and therefore knows to ask for that one. If he has done other risky things like this before, he may have a lot of experience with injuries and meds.

Dr. Able: That is a good idea to ask him some more questions and clarify about the meds and previous injuries.

Dr. Roberts: Yes, and it is an unusual story. I am definitely going to dig deeper to clarify 1) previous injuries and 2) previous meds taken for pain.

[Dr. Roberts comes back to Dr. Able in a short while.]

Dr. Roberts: Hey, got a minute? [They pull up two seats at the station.] Can you believe this? When I went in to talk with him again I overheard him on his cell phone laughing and talking before I pulled the curtain to go in and he realized I was there. He did not look to be in pain to me. When I asked about previous injuries or pain meds he reiterated his story about tonight's happenings, but the details were slightly different about what had happened as he compared it to another time he was injured before. That man is lying. So calm and cool about it too. I am going to check the system to see if he had any previous ER visits, complaints. I am thinking that he knows dosages etc. because he abuses pain meds.

Dr. Able: [Pats Dr. Roberts on the shoulder] Excellent plan. Good work in assessing to go back and talk with him and dig a little deeper. We always need to be comprehensive, don't we?

SCENARIO 2

Dr. Able: [Standing over the resident who is sitting at the nurses' station] Needs pain relief? You've got to be kidding. That man needs a kick in the ass. You're a physician, you idiot! Can't you see the man is lying and simply abusing narcotic drugs? [Dr. Able's voice is raised and a nurse and care partner look over.

Dr. Roberts is clearly embarrassed.] Open your eyes and ears man. Get in there and tell that *%@ patient not to come to this ER again seeking drugs but to get himself into drug therapy! Let this be a lesson to you to be aware most of our patients are abusing the system and us too!

Dr. Roberts: [With his eyes down] I should have seen that sir. Yes, sir!

SCENARIO 3

Dr. Able: [Sitting down next to Dr. Roberts; fatherly tone] Now, Dr. Roberts, I realize you may not be street smart but let me tell you a couple of things. Listen up because this has served me well over the years. Not everyone who comes in here is really sick, injured, or "emergent." This "accountant" is really addicted to those narcotics that he so readily gives you details about. Note how he knows the exact dosage? Here, let me show you on the computer here. Watch me. [Dr. Roberts meekly watches as Dr. Able pulls up previous visits of the patient to this ED.] And not only this ED. Note the cross-reference here in a previous visit that he was seen at three other hospitals for supposed "injuries and in extreme pain."

CASE STUDY DISCUSSION QUESTIONS

1. How does the attending physician respond to the new resident?
2. How might this response be received by the resident?
3. What is the possible long-term impact on the resident as he continues his work in this unit?

When Increased Diversity Improves Team Performance

By Ebbin Dotson and Jami DelliFraine

Bridgestone Health System (BHS) is a nationally renowned health system, operating an integrated delivery model in every region of the country. It is in a growth mode, where despite healthcare reform issues, has been able to grow in four of its five regional markets. This growth can be attributed to the high performing Corporate Leadership Team (CLT). As part of the last strategic planning process, the System CEO, Ralph Stuart, made sure to take the CLT through the stages of group development until he was sure they were performing well. One of the highlights of the past 3 years of sustained growth has been the chief diversity officer's aggressive marketing campaign targeted at minority populations, highlighting BHS's culturally relevant services and programs. Upon review of the data, Ralph concluded that it has been the major part of their growth success.

In meetings, Ralph often points to the innovative thinking and skills of Roosevelt Ford, the chief diversity officer (CDO), and his ability to identify opportunities to turn problem areas into viable institutional practices that both clinicians and administrators can implement with success. Roosevelt has made an impact in his 20 years in the organization, most notably helping the organization respond to the legal problem it faced when the courts ruled in favor of minority patients that were discriminated against early in the 1990s, and was forced to respond with institutionalized diversity practices. Recently, based on Roosevelt's 30 years of human resources experience, his track record in the organization, and the value that Ralph wants to place on culturally competent care, he promoted Roosevelt to senior vice president from his role as vice president and CDO.

This promotion was not made lightly, but strategically in Ralph's eyes. The Corporate Diversity Department (CDD) that Roosevelt directs is seen in the organization as merely a compliance stamp. Ralph's CLT is not that diverse, and many are uneasy with the cultural diversity attention that has come to Roosevelt and his very racially and gender diverse Corporate Diversity Department. He knows that getting the CLT to buy into integrating diversity in each department is going to be an uphill battle but has made it part of his vision.

In particular, the other senior vice presidents and vice presidents are not happy that Roosevelt has picked Mikayla Johnson as his successor. In public, questions around her age and experience are mentioned. She is 36 years old and has been in the department for the past 7 years. In private, the CEO has been told she is too ethnic and might not be the right choice, even though the current CDO, Roosevelt, is an African American man in his 60s.

Roosevelt has already notified Ralph that he will likely retire in the next 12 months and would like to put in place a departmental succession plan for the same time. He is asking Ralph to support his plan, and seriously consider Mikayla Johnson as the new CDO. Ralph is trying to figure out how to make a good strategic decision but is well aware of the team dynamics and atmosphere. He cannot afford to jeopardize their growth strategy, nor his CLT performance.

THE QUIET PLATITUDE OF THE CLT

The Corporate Leadership Team (CLT) is Ralph Stuart's executive team. In his 7-year tenure, he has been able to lead a major growth strategy in an environment that has been tough for many of BHS's competitors. Before the diversity marketing campaign, the growth rate had been less than 3% in the previous 3 years. It was a major point of contention between the Board and the previous CEO. The Board expected 5–7% growth for the next 3-year strategic plan but did not have the confidence in the previous CEO. Ralph Stuart was brought in after a yearlong national search. He came with over 20 years of experience in the healthcare industry and most recently had been a partner in The Howser Group, one of the most prestigious management consulting firms known for stabilizing and turning around large organizations. It was said that his reason for going back into the C-suite was, in part, because both he and his wife's parents lived in the state and they wanted to be closer to them and other family.

It was a great decision on the part of the Board, as Ralph was able to produce a 5% growth rate in his first 3 years. With the second 3-year strategic plan, he was able to reach a 7% growth rate, in large part because of Roosevelt Ford's aggressive diversity plan. The Board was elated with the CLT performance, and is hoping that the success can continue for the next strategic plan that is currently underway. The major selling point of the current strategic plan, Ralph's third to get approval from the Board, is its diversity impact initiative.

BHS comprises a myriad of integrated services, departments, and facilities. It is a nonprofit health system that operates in every region of the country. It has 34 hospitals, with one in almost every major metro area. There are over 100,000 total workers at BHS. **Figure 11-1** provides a breakdown of diversity by profession. In addition, the Board of Directors is one of most diverse of all its competitors. It has nine members: five men, three African Americans, one Latino, and one Asian. One of their key reasons for hiring Ralph was his commitment to diversity.

To make good on his diversity pledge to the Board, Ralph wanted every department to implement aspects of their corporate diversity plan. At the year-end retreat, he described the organization's past 3-year growth success as stemming from the diversity plan's ability to draw in new customers through their increased visibility in certain markets and by retooling their service offerings in a way that Roosevelt often described as the "business imperative of diversity and our need show customers we are culturally competent." He wanted to implement a more robust version that customers would be able to understand as a "brand of

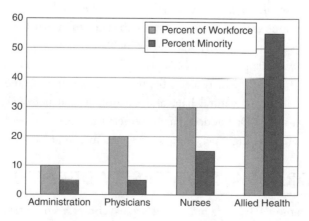

FIGURE 11-1 BHS Workforce Diversity

service." Roosevelt provided the details for the initiative and cautioned the team that each of them would be challenged to increase diversity efforts in ways that might make them uncomfortable but that would be necessary for success.

On one occasion, in a meeting with two of his senior executives, Ralph brought up the cost for the new diversity strategy that Roosevelt and his department proposed in the previous monthly CLT meeting. Dan Fausty has been with BHS since he interned with the organization 20 years ago. He has worked his way up the ranks and has held all of the senior positions in the finance department. He has been the SVP of Finance for the past 5 years and has been vocal in his opinion that investments in diversity are not a good itemized expense because they cannot be easily associated to outcomes for any one department. Reba Hollaway is the VP of Marketing and Relations and has been with the organization for 5 years. Ralph was her mentor at a previous healthcare organization, and was able to bring her onboard when the previous VP left shortly after Ralph's arrival. She has been very aware of the lack of gender and racial diversity in the CLT, and has expressed to Ralph that gender balance is more important than racial balance. He considers the two of them straight shooters and often asks their opinions in sociopolitical issues that arise between senior executives.

Ralph thought the discussion would go like many had before with two of his most trusted advisors when he asked if they believed the proposed $1 million investment Roosevelt was asking for over the next 3 years would be returned in growth and new business. The two of them cautioned Ralph that the CDD might be using the diversity plan to increase management diversity and are not truly focused on growth. They then bantered on a bit with small talk about forecasting and segmented markets, but then Dan stopped and said his biggest worry was that the investment would be lost if Roosevelt left and they had to count on Mikayla Johnson to continue as the diversity person. Reba chimed in that she is the one that works most closely with the Corporate Diversity Department and, although admittedly said she was a supporter of Mikayla's efforts, felt the CDD might become too "diverse righteous" if Mikayla gets the helm. Her specific comments were that Mikayla's style of dress, natural hair, and confrontational personality make her intimidating at times. Dan added that Roosevelt has a presence with his size but did not come off as an angry person in the same manner that Mikayla has at times.

THE CORPORATE DIVERSITY DEPARTMENT

The CDD is a model department, and its success comes from understanding how to address the diverse needs of patients with cultural and linguistic differences. It includes: Alice Yen, an Asian American woman directing Linguistic Services;

Jorge Gonzalez, a Mexican American man directing Workforce Diversity; Richard Witlock, a mixed race man directing Cultural Competency; and Mikayla Johnson, an African American female as the head of Diversity Strategy and Marketing. Staffed with only six other employees, it is able to carry out a remarkable amount of programming, consulting, and material for the organization.

Alice, Jorge, and Richard were all seasoned BHS employees, each with multidepartmental experience and vast networks that have been key to the CDD's success. Mikayla was a student intern before being hired in the department, and was nearing the completion of a PhD program in organizational psychology when she started. Since starting in the CDD, she has been trained by each of the other Directors, and has earned their respect and loyalty. Roosevelt and his Directors created the position of Diversity Strategy and Marketing, in part because they wanted to keep Mikayla, but also because it was the perfect diversity position that they felt could make the most impact in the organization after Roosevelt retired.

In the last performance evaluation meeting, Mikayla mentioned her desire for a more visible role in the organization. She was aware of Roosevelt's desire to retire and asked if he felt she was ready to compete for his position if he chose to retire. She also mentioned being courted for a CDO position from a competing organization but was not ready to leave BHS and her current life in the city. Roosevelt talked with her about her skills and supported her development and readiness for a senior position. He said that he would be happy to provide more senior level responsibility to help with her executive leadership development, knowing fully that she was their best chance at his replacement in the organization.

THE RETIREMENT CONVERSATION

In preparation for the retreat presentation, Ralph and Roosevelt met to discuss some of the components of the expanded diversity plan. Toward the end of their conversation, Roosevelt mentioned his desire to retire within the year and felt it would be good to do so right after the new strategic plan was put into place. Ralph was surprised, but was calmed by Roosevelt's subsequent outlining of a succession plan that included Mikayla. He informed Ralph that she was more than ready and was twice as good as he was at her age when it came to the skill set that made him a successful CDO. He wanted Ralph's support to begin preparing his exit and Mikayla's entrance as CDO.

Ralph was vocal about the pushback he would receive from the Board and the CLT. His main concerns were her age, her extroverted personality, and the undertone of becoming too diverse too fast that might be conveyed with a new

CDO and diversity plan. He asked Roosevelt to provide a formal evaluation of Mikayla that spoke to her skills and qualifications. He wanted information on her track record, especially measures of success for growth and strategy. Roosevelt complied and, before leaving Ralph's office, reminded him that Mikayla was instrumental in drafting and implementing the previous diversity plan, having performed all of the legwork. He stated that she knew the plan better than anyone in the organization. His sentiment was that it would be a detriment to the organization if they were not able to keep her in the department or organization. Ralph responded that he agreed, but it was going to be hard to move from a "Roosevelt" to a "Mikayla," apologizing for the racial tone, but being sincere that it would be a real issue to address.

CASE STUDY DISCUSSION QUESTIONS

1. What diversity issues are present in the case?
2. How would you define diversity? What makes an organization diverse?
3. How should Ralph open up the diversity conversation to the Corporate Leadership Team (CLT) as a whole?
4. What conflict management tools should Ralph use to address the perceived cultural bias issues with the Corporate Leadership Team (CLT)?
5. What effect did promoting Roosevelt to Senior Vice President (SVP) have on the organization? Why?
6. Why did Ralph promote Roosevelt to Senior Vice President (SVP)? What did that signal to the organization and CLT?
7. Which team is more important to have as high performers, the Corporate Leadership Team (CLT) or the Corporate Diversity Department (CDD)? Why?
8. What impact will increasing diversity have on team performance? Why?
9. What leadership traits will be important for Mikayla to develop for the Chief Diversity Officer (CDO) position?
10. Is the current workforce diverse? In all professions?
11. How much does the composition of the Board of Directors contribute to Ralph's decision-making?

Whose Patient Is It?

By Anat Drach-Zahavy (Israel)

Sara is 45 years old with a BA degree in nursing and has worked in a large urban hospital (Israel) for the past 20 years. Sara has been assigned to the ophthalmology/eye surgery inpatient unit for most of her time with the hospital. Until recently, she has enjoyed her job although stressful at times with a high patient-to-nurse ratio of complex cases. The hospital specializes in the extensive use of the newest technologies in the ophthalmology field and has developed a reputation of successfully treating complex ophthalmological conditions. The hospital's ophthalmology/eye surgery unit has 19 inpatient beds and employs a team of 5 physicians and 12 nurses. However, efficiency considerations by the hospital have led the administration to use a strategy referred to as "satellite patients." Satellite patients refer to patients that are placed in units' beds that have available space and not in the specialized unit. As an example, a cardiology patient may be placed in a bed in the orthopedic unit if no space is available in the cardiology unit at the time of patient's admission. Although this is considered an efficient use of resources (i.e., hospital bed) there have been major concerns raised by the clinicians regarding the quality of care being received by the patient in a "satellite" bed.

And this is where our story begins, with Sara retelling her experience from the previous night's shift…

On occasion in the unit I work (ophthalmology/eye surgery), a few patients from different units will be placed due to a lack of available beds in their units. These patients are referred to "satellite patients," and they place a great burden on nurses who find themselves accountable for providing nursing care for patients outside their area of specialization. Nurses are uncomfortable caring for patients with problems outside their specialization area due to lack of experience and training in these fields. In addition, they have to continue providing care for all the other patients in their frequently overloaded unit. Often these patients' treatment plans are complex due to the type of surgery performed and the patients' care needs.

Last night, an orthopedic patient was transferred to the ophthalmology/eye surgery unit after undergoing a complex thigh surgery due to a motor vehicle accident. A few minutes after I started my shift, the patient began to moan, complaining about a strong pain at his surgical site. I followed the physician's orders as noted in the patient's medical file and administered a dosage of pain medication to the patient. The patient continued to experience a high level of pain that also caused him to become sick. I needed assistance with this patient's treatment plan and paged the orthopedic physician who was on duty. After a brief description of the patient's condition, the orthopedic physician promised he would come and see the patient.

An hour passed and the physician did not arrive. When I tried calling his cell phone, it went directly to voice mail. I contacted the physician's colleagues, supervisors, as well as the hospital administrators, trying to reach him so he could advise me how to take care of the orthopedic patient. I was panicking, "What am I going to do now?" I have no knowledge regarding how to treat this patient, nor do I have time to learn more about his condition. I have 10 other ophthalmology patients that need me! How can I manage everything? What was this physician thinking? Why is he not answering my calls?

The patient continued to complain about strong pains at his surgical site, pushing the distress button, and begging for my assistance: "Please help me!" I ran from one side of the unit to the other in an attempt to provide care for all my patients, and support him as much as I could. I felt helpless…not being able to provide the proper care for him while attempting to provide care for my other 10 patients, some of them in complex situations after their surgeries.

After 3.5 hours of continuous calling and paging, another orthopedic physician arrived on my unit. Imagine my surprise when I found out there were two orthopedic physicians on duty last night that could have been involved in the patient's care, and neither one came until 3.5 hours after my first call for assistance.

The physician checked the patient and provided new pain medication orders. The patient achieved immediate relief and fell asleep quickly thereafter.

In the morning, I reported the case to my head nurse. She supported my decisions and promised to raise the case in front of the hospital's management. I am sure she did so, but unfortunately, this is neither the first nor the last case where a patient did not receive the appropriate care. I fear there could be serious adverse consequences for a patient's health if the hospital's management does not take the necessary actions to correct the situation.

CASE STUDY DISCUSSION QUESTIONS

1. Define the main sources of conflicts described in the case.
2. Discuss barriers for effective patient care by referring to the following issues
   a. Hospital's organizational structure and task structuring
   b. Interprofessional teamwork and team composition
   c. Organizational and professional/job commitment
   d. Individual coping with stress situations: the perception of challenge versus threat
3. Imagine that you are appointed as a consultant in this organization.
   a. Suggest organizational structures to prevent such conflicts
   b. Prepare a program for the head nurse of team-building activities to address the above barriers
   c. How would you recommend Sara cope with the stressful situation?

The Impact of Profitability on Leadership and Accountability in a Public University Dental Clinic

By Annelise Y. Driscoll and Myron D. Fottler

INTRODUCTION

The Southern University dental clinic was built with student monies from a capital improvement fund. It took 1 year to design and build, using state-of-the-art technology and the latest in equipment and services. It was opened for students, but faculty and staff were welcome to use the facility on campus as well. This was particularly attractive to all, as the fees for the services were set at the lowest percentile for the region. Therefore, it was in high demand from the opening day until the last day of the first year of operations.

At first, faculty and staff were skeptical, but word-of-mouth marketing on the high quality of care, high levels of comfort and service toward patients, and low fees soon spread around campus, and the schedule was full almost immediately. All aspects of the design and build-out of the dental clinic came from the Dental Consultant who was hired to handle the project from inception to opening day, including establishing systems, hiring staff, designing protocols, setting fee schedules, and choosing equipment/technology/décor.

The Dental Consultant had 30 years of experience plus the operational aspect of managing newly built dental clinics. She was responsible, well respected, and given full authority for the project with very little oversight from the Leadership Team from the first discussion to the opening day. She also provided monthly progress reports that were acknowledged with praise. Since no one in the Leadership Team had any background or experience in dental offices, systems, design, or operations, they relied heavily and totally on the experience and reputation of the Dental Consultant. The project went off flawlessly, with the clinic built in less than the allotted time and under the $550,000.00 earmarked budget. The consultant then became the Founding Director of the Dental Clinic.

The clinic was built with no debt load, paid for with student money, and had the responsibility of being financially self-sustaining within the first 18 months and thereafter. No subsidies were to be provided for its operational costs, which the consultant knew and took into consideration when creating the operational systems that would lead to financial viability with high demand. All of the key concepts were included in the operational systems: 1) Access to care in a convenient location on campus, 2) high-quality care by experienced and nurturing staff using the latest technology, and 3) low-cost services able to be provided to students, faculty, and staff due to the fact that no debt load was incurred. Coupled with a strong marketing and promotional plan, and a myriad of financing options for all patients, the dental clinic was destined to succeed.

During the building phase, the Dental Consultant worked with the Human Resources department to contract with the employee dental insurance companies as well as the student dental insurance program. In addition, the consultant promoted and marketed the opening across campus to colleges, departments, student groups, faculty, and key leaders. The Dental Consultant incorporated private practice profitability and operational strategies while working within the parameters of a state university public setting. This was a unique concept, and admittedly a risky one, but one that succeeded financially almost immediately.

DENTAL CLINIC SETTING AND ENVIRONMENT

The Dental Clinic was housed within the Student Health Center in the middle of campus. It included 2,000 square feet of space with the reception room, administrative offices, and clinical areas. It utilized state-of-the-art technology and advanced digital imaging systems as well as paperless electronic health records and a fully integrated software system that encompassed both the clinical aspects and business aspects of a patient's chart. The reception room contained a flat-screen TV with dental educational software viewable by patients waiting.

Each patient's electronic chart contained an electronic patient information and check-in system, digital images of referral letters, patient identification and insurance cards, HIPAA/FERPA, and all consent forms within the patient's electronic record, and digital signatures from each patient. All papers and documents were stored in each patient's electronic "document center" within their accounts that were built into the dental software. Insurance claims were filed electronically, payments were processed electronically, and patients' appointment confirmations were completed electronically, as well as all aspects of their financial accounts. This created a streamlined approach to viewing all aspects of a patient's chart at a finger-touch from any computer within the administrative or clinical area.

The clinical area consisted of state-of-the-art technology used in every aspect of the clinical experience for patients. Advanced technology used in the clinical area included a digital X-ray system, intra-oral camera for a virtual tour of the mouth, voice-activated periodontal charting, wireless headphones to watch TV while undergoing procedures, flat-screen TV monitors overhead to view patient X-rays, photos, educational programs on dental procedures, computerized work stations in each clinical room ("operatory"), wireless handpieces and equipment, an oil-less and maintenance-free mechanical room, automated lights, motion-sensitive electricity, and a high-tech sterilization center.

The dental chairs looked like black leather lounge chairs with no trays/or dental equipment looming over a patient's chest while in the chair and all drills/suction/equipment placed behind the patient's head so not to view it or feel claustrophobic while undergoing treatment. Each clinical room, or operatory, used an open-bay design, again, to decrease apprehension and invite relaxation. The soothing aesthetics, coupled with the aromatherapy, was a natural extension to the warm reception room. Patients were put at ease upon entering the clinical area, which quieted nervous patients and created a positive dental experience.

Photos were taken on each patient of the inside of their mouths during their virtual tour and were added to insurance claims to substantiate claims. At the same time, patients were confident of explained dental issues when able to view them directly overhead in close view and receive a copy of their photo, if desired. Photos of dental issues confirmed the need for treatment, which increased case acceptance of recommended treatment. This contributed to the significant success of the dental clinic within its first year of operations. Visual proof of the need for dental treatment, the soothing environment, and the low fee schedules for treatment insured the growth of demand very early on.

The décor of the dental clinic was very soothing, and cozy, with little reminders to patients of their presence in a dental clinic. Warm colors, soothing art and décor, blankets, aromatherapy, and natural lighting were used to reduce patient apprehensiveness. Unlike the rest of the health center, which had a more "sterile" and "colder clinical" feel to it with minimal décor or warmth, the dental clinic was designed to soothe and welcome patients as an integral strategy of patient comfort first. It worked wonders, as patients felt at home and comfortable in the dental clinic.

The décor and atmosphere was unique and other departments requested similar décor and aesthetics within the health center. Visitors immediately complimented the warm décor and feel of the dental clinic. It became nicknamed the "Taj Mahal" of the health center. No expense was spared in the design, build-out, and decoration of the dental clinic, yet the entire project was completed in less time than originally estimated, with no issues or problems, and cost less than the proposed budget for the job.

As a result of the "private dental practice feel" and the streamlined processes, along with the reduced fees (for students as well as faculty and staff), and emphasis on customer comfort and service, over 3,500 patients were seen within the first 12 months, with a total revenue of over $625,000 in dental services provided. Of those services provided, more than 93% of services were paid for and collected. This went beyond the usual collection ratio of 40% ($0.40 collected out of each $1.00 billed out) that the other departments of the health center collected for the services they provided and billed out. The profitability of the future of the dental clinic was extremely attractive to the Health Center Director as a future source of revenue to subsidize other nonprofitable departments and services. Within a month of opening, the dental clinic was touted as the "rising star" of the health center.

DENTAL CLINIC STAFF

Dental Clinic Director: After an outstanding job creating and building the dental clinic, the dental consultant was hired as the founding Director. A PhD, with an MBA and 30 years of a successful track record, references, and experience building and operating profitable dental clinics in both private and corporate settings, the Director had the responsibility of establishing financial sustainability and viability of the dental clinic almost immediately. Pressure was applied early on from the Health Center Director to establish policies and procedures based on established best-practices while complying with all regulations.

The Dental Director reported directly to the Health Center Director and was on a lateral placement on the organizational chart with the Business Director. The founding Director had worked on campus for 7 years prior in health administration research and teaching and was well known and well liked at the university. She worked well with the construction and design teams as well as other departments within the university during that time. No conflicts arose with any parties during the building of the facility.

Dentist: The Dentist brought 15 years of private practice ownership experience with him plus an additional 3 years of working as a dentist for a busy corporation serving mostly an HMO population. After 15 years of owning his own practice, and declining revenue from an impending recession, he sold his practice and worked for a corporate practice. Not wanting to continue working in a corporate dental facility with long hours and significant pressure to "sell" dentistry, the position as the first university dentist at Southern University was an attractive offer; although the university dental salary was two-thirds lower than his corporate salary.

The dentist had experience in providing high-volume dental services and understanding the importance of his role in working with and for the Dental Director in creating financial sustainability of the fledgling program. The Dentist reported to the Dental Director for operational matters and the Medical Director for clinical issues not addressed in the existing clinical policies manuals. The Dentist agreed to provide a very comprehensive set of dental services to patients to avoid the need to refer them out to specialists.

Financial Counselor: The Financial Counselor brought 15 years of corporate and dental practice administration experience with her. A perfectionist with an outstanding work ethic, she maintained all patient accounts, payment, and insurance billing functions. All patients met with the Financial Counselor at their check-out process to pay for their services or set up payment plans and sign promissory notes for them. Extremely professional and efficient, she was an overachiever with high expectations of herself and others. The Financial Counselor was aggressive in nature with very high career goals.

Office Assistant: The Office Assistant brought 5 years of front desk experience working part time in a dental specialist's office. While she had front desk and dental software experience, this was her first job with all of the front desk responsibilities on a full time basis. As English was not the Office Assistant's first language, her propensity for spelling and grammar errors quickly became apparent.

Dental Hygienist: The Dental Hygienist had 6 years of experience working in a fast-paced, high-end private dental practice where there was significant pressure to produce significant revenue. She was experienced, with a warm and likable personality and brought with her an extensive background working with state-of-the-art dental technology. Ambitious and taking on a natural role as technical trainer/expert, she became an informal clinical leader.

Dental Assistants: Two Dental Assistants, both of whom worked for the Dentist at his prior corporate dental practice, came to work at the Southern University Dental Clinic, per the request of the hired Dentist. Both Dental Assistants had 3 years experience as Dental Assistants, working with the Dentist at his prior corporate dental practice. They had limited experience in a fast-paced environment, worked well together, and were extremely loyal to the Dentist. Both Dental Assistants were able to "sell" dental services and were accustomed to receiving monthly bonuses in their prior jobs as an incentive to get treatment acceptance from patients.

EXECUTIVE LEADERSHIP TEAM

This group of healthcare executives included the Health Center Director, Medical Director, Nursing Director, IT Director, Pharmacy Director, Administrative Assistant, Dental Director, and Business/Financial Director. Meetings were held every 2 weeks, and all major decisions were voted on and approved through the Leadership Team. In addition, individual meetings were held between the Health Center Director and each member of the Leadership Team every 2 weeks to discuss departmental issues and performances. The Leadership Team, with the Health Center Director at the helm, discussed and resolved through voting, all major decisions regarding all aspects of the operations of the Health Center. All meetings were documented by the Administrative Assistant, and all meeting minutes were sent out to the Leadership Team within 24 hours of each meeting.

These protocols and procedures were approved and documented by the University Vice Presidents, and were an integral aspect of the fulfillment of the accreditation standards for performance improvement plans. The function of the Executive Leadership Team served to have checks and balances in place, as well as an overall consensus of all key leaders to be made aware of all major issues, situations, and successes, and strategize cohesively on solutions and planning. In addition, all policies, protocols, and procedures were approved unanimously by the Executive Leadership Team.

BACKGROUND AND CHRONOLOGY

The Dental Clinic was built with no issues, no problems, with the entire project taking less time than initially estimated (12 months instead of 18), coming under budget than originally proposed ($535,000 instead of $612,000), and opened 9 days before Christmas as a "soft opening." One hundred fifty-five patients were seen in 9 days as the staff dealt with new demands for services, urgent care appointments, and performed root canals and crown preparations right up until the close of business on Christmas Eve. The staff expressed concerns about the busy schedule and not wanting to work on Christmas Eve.

January was busier than anyone expected as the Director had spent the 9 months prior to opening day on marketing and promoting the Dental Clinic all over the Southern University campus and in various media advertising. As a result, the demand was immediate and higher than originally estimated. Also, the poor condition of the majority of patients' dental condition and oral health surprised all staff and required the Dentist to provide the extensive array of services to treat patients "in house" as much as possible almost immediately. Affordability being a key marketing factor, the wider array of services provided "in house" by the Dentist (as agreed to in his job interviews) became needed from the very first week. By mid-January, the Dentist began referring patients out for procedures to be completed at specialists' offices, which were part of his job description to perform himself. The Director discussed this with the Dentist, who stated it was in the patient's best interest to refer them out.

INTER-/INTRAPERSONAL RELATIONSHIPS AND COMMUNICATION

Dialogue from the Dental Director included conversations such as: "Can you tell me why we are referring this patient out instead of having you perform the services?" to which the Dentist would reply, "I'm not comfortable doing this so we are referring them out for their own best interest." To which the Dental Director queried, "But this was the agreed upon scope of your capabilities which you indicated you were willing and able to perform at your job interview with us. This is becoming a habit, soon to be protocol, that patients are being referred out for services that we are advertising that we are able to perform here. Our financial viability depends on the service mix we have marketed to patients. We can't afford to not perform these advertised services. How are we to be financially self-sustaining if we cannot perform the services we advertised that you agreed to perform?" To which the Dentist would reply, "I'm not doing them. The specialists are going to do them. I'm not comfortable, and I don't care about your bottom line. I didn't sign up to work this hard for so little money. You're not a clinician, therefore, you shouldn't even be questioning what I will and will not perform and that's that."

This was usually followed by the Dentist meeting with the Medical Director and Health Center Director indicating he was unhappy answering to a nonclinician and performing services that were not in the patient's best interest. The Health Center Director would then call the Dental Director upstairs and state the Dentist's concern for not being clinically questioned. It became apparent to the Dental Director that the Dentist was undermining the chain of command and requested the Health Center Director send the Dentist back down to resolve the issues at hand with the Dental Director, according to the organizational chart and protocols, to which the Health Center Director stated there was always an "open door policy" for staff to share concerns.

February brought the "Grand Opening," including a ribbon-breaking ceremony from the President of the University. Media articles and photos were distributed on campus and in the surrounding community. The demand for services by patients grew even faster. Revenues (and their successful collections) from dental services provided became apparent immediately and were extremely attractive to the Health Center Director. The financial success of the Dental Clinic, while a great reflection of the experience of the Dental Clinic Director, became an even bigger reflection of success of the leadership of the Health Center Director. The immediate profitability of the Dental Clinic, unheard of in public university settings, became coveted by the Leadership Team as a shining new model of a private practice business model in a public bureaucratic university. The Dental Director received significant accolades for the success of the Dental Clinic from all attendees including the Health Center Director and President.

TEAM DYNAMICS AND STRESS IN THE WORKPLACE

While the operational aspects of the Dental Clinic were streamlined, efficient, and profitable, the underlying personality clashes and unwillingness to adhere to job descriptions and job responsibilities were exacerbated by the increasing demand and became very unmanageable. The Dental Assistants, Dentist, and Dental Hygienist complained of working much harder than they were hired to do. Their expectation was to work less in a public setting for less money but to enjoy a higher quality of life due to reduced stress and work hours. The immediate and continually growing demand for services negated that.

Typical responses from clinical staff members to seeing urgent care patients who walked in without appointments, swollen or in pain, consisted of "Another patient? I took a cut in pay to come work here, not to work harder for less money. That's the third extra patient put on the schedule today plus our regular full schedule. I really don't want to work this hard or this fast paced for such little pay." To which the Dental Director would reply, "That's true, you do make less salary, but your 6 weeks of paid time off and fully funded retirement plan combined equal what you made in the private sector, and you do get to leave every day at 5 p.m.—that's a plus, right?! Besides, lots of demand from patients equals job security, which is rare in this economy." Clinical staff members then rolled their eyes, stated "whatever," and walked away while the Dental Director thanked them for seeing another patient not originally scheduled.

The Financial Counselor required more information for billing and patient accounts than the clinical staff was willing to provide, causing tension between both groups. The Office Assistant, not used to working a busy front desk on her own, made daily, consistent errors that caused extra work for the Financial Assistant and Director to resolve. In addition, as the errors were numerous and daily, the Office Assistant would frequently lie to avoid being blamed. The Financial Counselor did not receive needed clinical information and had to correct administrative errors in addition to her growing job responsibilities. She became increasingly frustrated and expressed that to all staff members early on in an abrasive fashion. "I shouldn't have to fix your mistakes everyday and I'm tired of doing your work on top of mine," was frequently stated to the Office Assistant by the Financial Counselor. Daily conversations included "Where is the insurance information for this patient and why hasn't it been verified yet?" to which the reply was "I'm very busy, the phones are ringing off the wall and I didn't get to it yet. I'm not perfect, you know." This abrasive communication added to the staff division and conflict. The Director played a dual role of managing the successful operations of the facility while resolving staff conflict, coaxing the clinical staff to adhere to their hired responsibilities, coaching the Office Assistant on job performance and skill improvement, and discussing more successful communication strategies for the Financial Counselor to use to build stronger relationships with the rest of the staff.

ORGANIZATIONAL LEADERSHIP

Biweekly leadership meetings with the Dental Director and Health Center Director included status updates on the Dentist's inability to work toward a resolution and goals with the Health Center Director vacillating back and forth between "Don't let him walk all over you. Enforce your goals and motivate him to change," and "I told you not to question him or make him feel uncomfortable so why is this still an issue?" Attempts by the Dental Director to involve Human Resources' conflict resolution services were denied by the Health Center Director.

By March, with the schedule consistently full, the Dentist stopped communicating with the Director and referred out all patients needing more than fillings and crowns, to specialists. When confronted, the Dentist advised the Director that he was working much harder than anticipated for less money than desired, regardless of job descriptions. The Director reminded the Dentist of his terms of hiring and job description that was a needed component of financial sustainability and viability. As the Dental Clinic Director tried numerous approaches to reopen communications, the Dentist refused and submitted a letter of resignation to the Health Center Director stating his inability to "work with that woman" (the Dental Clinic Director).

The Health Center Director was simultaneously being congratulated on the successes of the new Dental Clinic and confronted with the aforementioned issues. He then made a decision and informed the Dentist only that he would split the lines of leadership in the Dental Clinic. More specifically, he unilaterally changed the organizational chart so that the Dentist and the clinical staff reported directly to the Medical Director while circumnavigating the Dental Director. In addition, to keep the Dentist from resigning, the Health Center Director promoted the Dentist to Clinical Leadership of the clinical staff. This removed the clinical staff from the locus of authority of the Dental Clinic Director. None of the changes to the organization chart or the job descriptions for the Dentist or Dental Clinic Director were submitted to the Human Resources Department. The Health Center Director advised all staff that they were welcome to come to his office to resolve issues but no one was to discuss anything with the HR department on campus.

WORKPLACE COMMUNICATION

The Dental Director was informed of the policy change and organizational chart change after the Dentist agreed to the terms and rescinded his letter of resignation. She protested the change internally and behind closed doors to no avail. In addition, the Executive Leadership Team was not informed of the changes nor were they discussed during Executive Leadership Meetings, nor documented in minutes. No documentation was submitted to the Human Resources Department. Changes to the job descriptions were hand written by the Health Center Director and initialed. Neither the Dentist nor the Dental Director was required to sign any new job descriptions.

While the Dental Clinic Director objected to this new policy change, warning of a greater division within the Dental Clinic with the potential for greater staff conflict and divisiveness, the Health Center Director advised her to improve her leadership skills and team building skills to avoid having a "program in jeopardy." He then signed her up for leadership classes through the Human Resources Department with a warning to learn much and say little.

LEADERSHIP STYLES AND ORGANIZATIONAL POLITICS

The division in leadership, along with the different leadership styles of both the Dentist and Dental Director, continued to create conflict among the staff. The Dentist avoided confrontation with the clinical staff, did not address any issues with them, and fostered a low key, "less is more" work ethic. Speaking only to the Director when necessary, the Dentist informed all clinical staff they were no longer supervised by the Director. The Health Center Director allowed the Dentist and clinical staff to have an "open door policy" which circumnavigated chains of command on the organizational chart.

The Financial Counselor and the clinical staff continued to have conflicts as the level of attention to detail diminished with regard to clinical standards and documentation needed by the Financial Counselor to handle patient finances, present treatment options, and submit insurance claims with clinical narratives. After complaining to the Dental Clinic Director about the lack of details from the Office Assistant and the clinical staff, the Financial Counselor grew increasingly frustrated by the Director's inability to resolve the issues. The clinical staff as well as the Office Assistant aligned themselves with the Dentist as his casual leadership style was preferred. The Dentist, as clinical leadership, did not resolve issues and continued to avoid confrontation. He became friends and "colleagues" with those aligned with him. As a team, the clinical staff routinely advised the Office Assistant to reschedule patients to loosen up the schedule.

CHANGE MANAGEMENT

Increasingly frustrated, the Dental Clinic Director requested weekly management meetings with the Dentist in an attempt to unify the newly split leadership team, which the Dentist refused to attend. The Director then implemented team building workshops, which the clinical staff did not want to participate in. The

Director then completed a 3-month leadership excellence series of workshops to improve on leadership skills. The Health Center Director advised the Dental Director to apologize to all dental staff members in an effort to "throw out the olive branch," which she did under protest to the Health Center Director.

Throughout June, July, and August, the Health Center Director scheduled a series of meetings with the entire Dental Clinic staff and excluded the Dental Clinic Director from the meetings. In an effort to establish where the problems existed, the four meetings were attended by all full time Dental Clinic employees except the Director. In many of the meetings, volatility and hostility ensued as the Financial Counselor expressed dissatisfaction with the lack of leadership, lack of accountability, lack of team morale, and lack of help from all staff members.

As a result of one particularly heated discussion, the Financial Counselor received a written reprimand, by the Health Center Director, which she appealed but lost. The Health Center Director advised all dental staff that if they could not begin to work harmoniously, they would all be terminated, the Dental Clinic closed, and only certain personnel would be "invited to reapply" for positions after a complete structural reorganization.

ORGANIZATIONAL CHANGE AND RESTRUCTURING

By November, the Dentist recommended a reorganization of the Dental Clinic to allow more profitability to generate while utilizing clinical staff members in different capacities. The Health Center Director accepted the recommendation, informed the Dental Director of the procedural changes. The Dental Director informed the Health Center Director the new procedural changes violated the state's legal statutes for "delegatable duties" that Dentists must perform themselves and warned against adverse actions from the Board of Dentistry. Proceeding against the Dental Director's warning, the Dental Clinic was reorganized for additional and enhanced profit maximization.

THE FIRST YEAR: GROWTH, PROFITABILITY, AND OUTCOMES

From the outside, financially and operationally, the first year of operations at the Southern University Dental Clinic was highly successful. The size of the staff doubled to accommodate the demand for services. Over 3,500 patients were seen, with revenue of over $625,000 earned. The collections ratio was over 93%. The patient satisfactory surveys reported over 93% satisfaction rate for services performed, oral health education provided, and overall quality of customer service given. The schedule was consistently booked 3 weeks out and cancellations were rare. The revenues generated and fees collected surpassed the initial estimates by over 200%. In short, the Dental Clinic illustrated the successful blending of private practice business systems in a public university could indeed exist and be profitable and efficient.

From the inside, however, the unresolved staff conflict, division of the administrative and clinical departments, different leadership styles of the Director and Dentist, and lack of trust in all levels of leadership, had a significant impact on the staffing of the Dental Clinic. At the end of the first year, the original Dentist resigned, the founding Director's position was eliminated along with the founding Director, both the Financial Counselor and one Dental Assistant went out on medical leave and never returned to their positions. Other part-time staff positions were eliminated. Three months later, employee satisfaction surveys from the Health Center employees reported an overall lack of trust in the Health Center Director, who then lost authority over three additional departments. However, he continued to exercise authority over the Dental Clinic even though he knew little about dentistry and was never on site.

No leadership was hired to oversee the Dental Clinic, dissention continued, while efficiency dropped dramatically along with the capability to keep up with demand for services. The positions that were vacant were not approved to be filled, as revenue collected from patients at the Dental Clinic dropped dramatically with insurance billing 90 days behind schedule. Without a Financial Counselor, revenue collection was not addressed, leaving the Dental Clinic chronically understaffed and overworked. This negatively impacted patient satisfaction levels as the business model, without leadership, failed to operate efficiently or profitably. Six months into the second year of operations, the Health Center Director suddenly and hurriedly resigned. By the time the announcement of his resignation was made public (2 days later), his office was cleaned out, and he was gone.

No documentation was sent to the Human Resources Department throughout the first year except the recommendation to eliminate the position of the Dental Director and save cost of the salary and benefits. The Executive Leadership Team was not informed of the decision to eliminate the Dental Director's position until the day after the Director was eliminated. No performance evaluations were completed nor were allowed to be completed on any dental staff member by the Dental Director, per the Health Center Director's decision.

The revised organization chart and meeting minutes were documented and kept internally with the Health Center Director. They were never made available to either Human Resources or to the Executive Leadership Team.

CASE STUDY DISCUSSION QUESTIONS

1. How did the different leadership and management styles of the key leaders (Dentist, Dental Director, and Health Center Director) impact the team dynamics in the Dental Clinic?

2. What actions could have been taken, regarding the attitudes and behaviors of staff, which negatively influenced staff's perceptions of their accountability for their job performances?

3. If you were the Dental Director, how would you have handled the Dentist's resignation attempt 3 months after the clinic opening and the subsequent empowerment of the Dentist as clinical leadership? What steps would you have taken to minimize the organizational decline of the Dental Clinic?

4. How did the organizational culture created by the Health Center Director impact both interpersonal and intrapersonal relationships and conflict management issues in the first year of operations?

5. What were the pivotal turning points or decisions leading to the Dental Clinic's performance decline at the end of the first year and beginning of the second year?

6. How do you think the significant profitability of this program impacted the leaderships' decisions and the eventual organizational restructuring? Evaluate the resistance to change management in the three key leaders: Dentist, Dental Director, and Health Center Director.

A Multicultural Healthcare Team and Patient Care

By Valerie A. George

THE SITUATION

Recently, Linda, Director of the Hearts Open Home (HOH), a 150-resident assisted-living facility established in 1990 in Southern California, received a phone call from Phyllis, the niece of Ethel Backer. Ethel is 88 years old and has been a resident of HOH for the past 8 years. During the call, Phyllis expressed concern that Ethel's needs were not being met. Phyllis related to Linda that she was very upset about the care her aunt was receiving and was considering contacting a lawyer. Linda suggested that Phyllis attend the next case management meeting for Ethel, which would be held in 1 week. Phyllis agreed to attend the meeting even though she lives in Salt Lake City, Utah.

THE PEOPLE

Linda: Director for the past 10 years of HOH. She is Caucasian, 52 years of age, born and raised in the Midwest. She moved to southern California with her husband and family approximately 15 years ago.

Suzanne: Nurse, African American, age 38, native of Los Angeles, new to the HOH staff, previous position was Nursing Supervisor at a large urban hospital's very busy emergency department.

Juan: Physical Therapist, age 36, originally from Colombia but completed his studies in the United States.

Stephanie: Psychologist, Chinese, age 42, from the Bay Area near San Francisco, married to a man of Spanish descent. She speaks Chinese, English, and Spanish.

Maria: Nursing Assistant, age 28, originally from Columbia. Maria speaks with a strong Hispanic accent, immigrating to the United States only 3 years ago.

Dianne: Dietitian, age 42, from Venezuela. She has been employed at HOH for 5 years.

Phyllis: Niece of Ethel Backer, 68 years of age, a Mormon, retired school teacher living with her husband in Salt Lake City, Utah.

THE CASE MANAGEMENT MEETING

Linda begins the meeting introducing Phyllis to the HOH care team members. However, before Linda can complete her statement, Phyllis begins addressing the group.

Phyllis:	I try to come and visit my aunt as often as I can, but I live in Utah and I can't afford to travel to California that often. We pay HOH good money to take care of my aunt, and we expect you to be more responsible and attentive to her needs.
Linda:	Phyllis, can you explain your exact concerns regarding your aunt to the group?
Phyllis:	Well, 2 weeks ago when I came to visit Ethel, she appeared very lethargic and would not consider going for a walk with me using her walker. Also, her hair looked terrible, like it had not been washed in a week, and she looked like she lost weight. I also saw there was a plate of horrible looking food in her room—rice and beans or something similar. She needs meat and potatoes, not that Spanish food! But, what really is upsetting upset me is that I noticed this morning that she has a

nasty sore on the back of her shoulder. When I went to look for someone to help her, I saw lots of staff, but they were just standing around, joking, and speaking Spanish. I don't think they were really caring for the residents. What is going on here, why aren't you looking after my aunt?

Suzanne: I am new here but according to the notes in her chart, Ethel has had a number of colds this year as well as problems with her feet. She has been provided with medication prescribed by her physician and the podiatrist has been treating her feet. Phyllis, you must remember that your aunt is 88 years old. As for the sore, I was not aware of this problem. I will stop in after the meeting and see what is going on. Marie, did you advise the nursing staff of Ethel's sore?

Maria: There are so many residents at HOH with so many needs that I am overwhelmed at times. I can only do what I can do! I have tried to encourage Ethel to use her walker, but she just sits there in her wheelchair and will not move. She tells me to go away and let her be. It is the same thing for everything I try to do for her. When I try to help her take a shower so her hair can be washed, it is a major drama making it almost impossible. Suzanne, I said you need to visit each resident daily, and Dianne, I told you that Ethel did not like the food! (Maria begins to cry.)

Dianne: According to my records, it was requested that Ethel be served her meals in her room. There are no specific dietary restrictions or requirements on her chart so she is served the regular daily menu. Here at HOH, we strictly follow USFDA dietary guidelines, but if the resident does not like what is being served, there is not much I can do. Most of the residents at HOH are Hispanic so we design the food menu to be sure that they get foods they are familiar with and that they enjoy. With 150 residents, I don't have time to visit each patient individually to see what they like and don't like to eat. I need to stick to my budget. Perhaps the family can get more involved and bring Ethel some of her favorite meals or take her out to eat when they visit.

Juan: The last time I saw Ethel was about 2 months ago. According to my records, I have seen her 6 times this year. We have a care plan that includes her walking with a walker daily so she is just not sitting in her wheelchair. As you know, 2 years ago she fell and had a hip replacement, and sometimes it is very difficult for older patients to recover and become active after that type of operation. They need to be motivated, and I believe that seeing family members more regularly is important. Phyllis, maybe you and your family should consider moving to Southern California so you can be closer to your aunt."

Stephanie: Yes, regular visits from the family are very important for the well-being of an older person like Ethel. Phyllis, your family needs to be more involved. Seeing the family will provide stimulus for Ethel and then perhaps she will be more alert overall. Family always comes first.

Phyllis: It sounds to me, that although each of you are a member of my aunt's care team, you are not working together and communicating. As a result, my aunt is not getting the attention and care that she needs. What are you planning to do to ensure that she is getting adequate care? I don't live in this city and I can't be flying in every week to check up on her care. Perhaps this Hispanic community is not really interested in caring for someone who is not Latino.

Linda: Phyllis, we hear and appreciate your concerns. We will do whatever it takes to ensure that your aunt is getting the care she needs. Although we are located in a primarily Hispanic area of the city and many of our residents are Latino, we try to be sensitive to the cultural backgrounds of all. We embrace the differences that we have and keep this in mind in the foods that we serve as well as our approach to our residents. I would like to think about this situation and meet with my team later this week to see how we can improve the situation.

CASE STUDY DISCUSSION QUESTIONS

1. Identify any shared values (cultural or professional) in the group.

2. What is the primary means of communication among the team members? Is there a formal or informal network of communication? What factors are involved? How can communication be improved among this culturally diverse team?

3. Identify where you think the individuals in this case are in reference to stages in the Model of Intercultural Sensitivity? Are they in the Ethnocentric stages (denial, defense, minimization) or in the Ethnorelative stages (acceptance, adaptation, integration)? Explain why you have selected the stage.

15

Renovation of the Pediatrics Department

By Valerie A. George

THE SITUATION

The administration at a large urban hospital has decided that changes need to be made regarding the physical organization of the Pediatrics Department's outpatient clinic. The Director of Operations has called a meeting to be held in the pediatric clinic after hours to discuss the necessary renovations with the individuals that he believes are key to the success of the project.

THE PEOPLE

Jorge, age 40, Director of Operations for the Hospital

Jorge relocated with his family from Mexico 6 years ago to Southern California. He received his MBA from the University of California. He is very happy with his position and wants to continue his professional career at this hospital, hoping to eventually become the CEO.

Kyoto, age 36, Architect

Kyoto, born in Osaka (Japan), is a junior staff member within the hospital's architect department. She is new to the health industry with limited experience with outpatient settings, but she is very dedicated to her work and wants to find a successful solution so her abilities are recognized by the department's director. She is the only female architect in the department. She is concerned about the functionality, aesthetics, and spatial balance for the clinic area. She has a 2-year-old daughter with health problems so she has visited the clinic on numerous occasions and found the environment to be very dysfunctional.

Marsha, age 60, Director of Pediatric Nursing

Marsha, originally from Philadelphia, has been working with the team of nurses and doctors employed in the Pediatrics Department's clinic for the past 15 years. She believes that although there is some congestion at times, they have established routines that make the system work. She believes making changes in the current space would be very disruptive to the patients, families, and staff, and not helpful unless there was actually an increase in the clinic's space allocation.

Raj, age 40, Director of Physical Management

Raj, originally from Pakistan, immigrated to the United States 10 years ago to join his family. After completing his mechanical engineering in Pakistan, he worked in the Middle East construction industry gaining valuable experience. For this project, Raj and his team would need to engage a general contractor but with much of the work being done by his team. Raj is very much vested in this project because he wants his team to have additional work as recently there have been some lay-offs within his department.

THE MEETING

Jorge calls the meeting to order and asks everyone to introduce themselves to the group. He then explains that the Pediatrics Department's clinic has been losing money. He believes this is being caused by the inefficient operations of the clinic due to the spatial arrangements. He notes that the waiting room is too small, which limits the number of patients that can be seen each hour since every patient has at least one or more family members accompanying the child. In addition, the examining rooms are located at the opposite end of the corridor from the waiting room so time is wasted moving the patient from the registration/waiting room to the exam room and back to the check-out area. This leads to the problem of continual traffic/congestion in the hallways.

Jorge relates that although the hospital's administration is concerned about the renovation cost, status quo is unacceptable except for the fact that there would not be any additional space allocation. He indicates to the group that administration wants a fiscally acceptable solution fast! As such, Jorge tells the group that he is directing Kyoto to design a plan incorporating everyone's feedback regarding the issues after they conclude tonight's meeting. Jorge thinks to himself, "I hope she can do it. I have never worked with a Japanese female architect before!"

DIALOGUE

Jorge: Thank you all for coming to this meeting. As noted, I would like to get some feedback from you as to how you think the clinic space could be arranged for servicing more patients."

Kyoto: I think not just the rearranging of space needs to be considered but how the space is used in reference to feng shui.

Marsha: Feng-what?

Kyoto: Feng shui considers the balance of the energy to assure that the space provides the best health for the patients. It is important to provide the opportunity for the patients to experience a spiritually balanced environment, especially if they have health concerns. It is also important for the staff.

Marsha: The staff works very hard at their jobs. All they want is to paint the walls a different color.

Raj: Jorge, what is the timeline for this project? Do you have a budget? I would like to start organizing my team as soon as possible.

Jorge: Yes, we do have a budget and we can start as soon as we have the architectural plans. Marsha, perhaps you could explain to us the "traffic" pattern when a patient arrives at the clinic for his/her appointment.

Marsha: Patients (or a family member) register by signing-in at the window over there and their insurance forms are processed behind the counter. They are asked to take a seat either in the front waiting room or the small area around the corner. They are then called from the waiting room when the doctor is ready to see the patient and walked down the corridor to one of the examining rooms. When the visit is completed, they again walk down the corridor to the front area's check-out window/counter so a new appointment can be scheduled. The system works just fine.

Jorge: Marsha, administration has received numerous complaints about lack of space in the waiting areas from both staff and patients/families. I personally have seen patients/families sitting on the floor, waiting outside the clinic's front door for their scheduled appointments. The noise level permeates into other departments and is quite disruptive. One thought I had was removing the waiting room chairs and replacing them with benches to provide for more seating.

Kyoto: I see there are many files behind the sign-in window, perhaps these could be relocated. Also, I am sure you are going digital soon so you will not need all those files in the future. If the files were relocated, that area could be opened up and some of the space could be used for additional seating or possibly a children's play area. The entrance to the clinic should be changed as well as the bathroom locations. With these changes we can redesign some of the corridors, allowing for more seating. This would also increase the light into the space and create a more harmonious environment.

Marsha: The staff is happy with the current design of the sign-in and check-out areas. I have made sure that these work spaces meet the needs of the staff.

Raj: Jorge, if we have to change the bathrooms and create a new entrance it will be very costly. But my team is ready and willing to do the job, just tell us when to start.

CASE STUDY DISCUSSION QUESTIONS

1. How did the diverse nature of the group impact communication and what were the lines of communication?

2. Are there different levels of motivation for making changes among the individuals in the meeting and if so what are these differences?

3. Describe any apparent conflict or support (culturally, professionally, or personally) in this group for this project.

4. What is the best approach for Jorge in making his final decision, what variables should he consider in terms of group feedback (i.e., cost benefit analysis, employee or client satisfaction)?

Practice Transformation: The Case of a Small, Independent Primary Care Practice

By Debora Goetz Goldberg

CURRENT SITUATION IN PRIMARY CARE

Primary care is a critical component of the healthcare system in delivering acute, chronic, and preventive care services. The Institute of Medicine declared that primary care services should be integrated across health system components, accessible, delivered in the context of family and community and through an ongoing partnership between the clinician and patient (IOM, 1994). Current challenges in primary care include: patients' lack of access to services, inconsistencies in providing standards of care and evidence-based medicine, difficulty coordinating care across health system components, and complexity involved in caring for individuals with chronic illnesses.

There are many external pressures on primary care practices to improve healthcare services. Primary care practices face increasing demands from regulatory sources, an increasing rate of change in technologies and care delivery processes, and increasing patient and community expectations. Practices are expected to be more transparent and accountable through performance measurement, to provide evidence-based medicine and patient-centered care, and to make strategic alliances in the move toward integrated care models. These pressures come in the form of pay-for-performance compensation methods, public reporting of performance, government requirements for adoption of electronic health records (EHRs), and medical specialty board recertification.

Over the last several years, there have been many efforts in primary care to respond to the challenges presented by the external environment. The majority of these efforts focus on redesigning healthcare services and improving business functionality at the practice level. These innovations include incorporating a patient-centered team approach to providing care, increasing use of advanced technologies, improving functional office space, and emphasizing quality and outcomes. Small and independent practices (those not owned and operated by a larger group or healthcare system) find it difficult to transform because they lack financial knowledge and material resources. Small practices are struggling to develop efficient and effective models of care that best suit their needs.

TRANSFORMING A SMALL INDEPENDENT PRIMARY CARE PRACTICE

Valerie Brennan[1] graduated from medical school in midlife, fulfilling her lifelong dream of becoming a family medicine physician. She was a single parent with one daughter and was thrilled to begin a new career in medicine. To offset the costs of medical school she participated in the Loan Repayment Program with the National Health Service Corps, Health Resources and Services Administration (HRSA) (National Health Service Corps, 2012). After completing a requirement for the program by serving as a primary care physician in a medically underserved rural area, she started a solo family medicine practice in a small town in southwest Virginia in 2005. Her goal was to have an independently run physician practice that provides high quality care to individuals and families in the community.

Dr. Brennan is currently instituting major changes to expand capacity and improve office operations, cash flow, services to patients, and physician and staff satisfaction. Her goal is to transform the current practice model to one that is team-based, supported by effective office systems and technology, and a focus on quality and improvement. While her medical education provided her with the clinical skills necessary to take care of patients, Dr. Brennan had little experience

---

[1] Names of individuals have been changed to maintain confidentiality.

or knowledge in starting and managing a medical practice and engaging in quality improvement activities. She is faced with many challenges including complying with a multitude of requirements for financial reimbursement, government regulations, and practice certification; ensuring financial stability of the practice; responding to patient and community needs; and managing personnel during major transformations in practice operations.

Physician Practice Setting and Community

Dr. Brennan's practice is located in a semirural area on the southwest border of Virginia. The practice provides acute and chronic illness care and disease prevention services to patients that live in town as well as individuals from neighboring rural areas. The practice currently schedules patients between 9 a.m. and 5 p.m. Monday through Friday. Dr. Brennan plans to change the office hours to better meet patient needs and at the same time retain reasonable hours for clinicians and staff.

While the practice is located in an independent city, it is combined with Washington County for government statistical purposes. Washington County ranks 82 out of 132 counties in the Commonwealth of Virginia in Health Outcomes, according to the County Health Rankings (2012), which is calculated by the number of premature deaths, low birth weight, individual reported health status, physical health days taken, and mental health days taken. The county ranks 79 out of 132 in Health Factors, which include health behaviors, clinical care, socioeconomic factors, and the physical environment. The county has a high number of adults who report poor health and smoking on a regular basis.

The county population of 17,526 consists of 54.1% females and 45.9% males. The racial diversity is 90.7% Caucasian, 6.4% African American, and 2.9 % Native American. The average household size is 2.12 and average household income is $31,797. The homeownership rate in 2009 was 65.6% with the median value of the home being $89,600. The majority, 78.6%, of residents graduated from high school and 18.9% went on to finish a bachelor's degree. The main industries in this area are manufacturing and service-related businesses. The recent economic downturn has severely influenced the population with dramatic increases in unemployment and individuals losing their health insurance coverage.

There are over 200 physicians in the surrounding area. The closest hospital is 20 miles away from the practice. This hospital is a 300-bed, 700,000 square-foot facility that opened in 1994. There are also several small community hospitals in the area as well as mental health and drug rehabilitation centers and laboratory and diagnostic services.

Practice Staff

Over the past few years Dr. Brennan has slowly added staff to the practice to expand the practice's ability to meet the needs of the community. There are currently seven employees including Dr. Brennan, a nurse manager, one licensed practical nurse (LPN), two medical assistants, a front office assistant, and an office manager. Dr. Brennan hopes to add a part-time nurse practitioner (NP) and other physicians to build capacity to see more patients and their families. Practice employees are not offered employee benefits such as health insurance or merit increases due to the high cost of practice operations and low reimbursement rates for clinical services. The practice has had a high turnover rate of staff during recent transformation efforts as some employees found it difficult to follow new protocols and procedures, did not understand the purpose and rationale for changes, or were unwilling or not prepared to learn new skills such as those required by use EHR functions.

Health Information Technology

Dr. Brennan opened the practice in 2005 with an EHR and practice management system to assist with the practice's financial, administrative, and clinical activities. The EHR is a longitudinal electronic record of patient health information generated by one or more encounters in a care delivery setting (HIMSS, 2012). Clinical staff use the system for ambulatory care progress notes, patient problem lists, allergies, medications, and potential drug interactions, and have electronic access to clinical information external to the practice such as lab results, radiology results, and record of prescriptions. The EHR is also used to e-transmit prescriptions to pharmacies. Patients cannot access their records online; however, Dr. Brennan would like to add a patient portal to the EHR that allows patients to enter their medical history and medical complaints before they arrive at the practice and to possibly view limited portions of their chart. The practice has also installed various electronic software packages to assist with organizing calendars and tracking human resources management issues such as tracking applicants and professional licenses.

The practice has updated the EHR software multiple times. Occasionally the EHR system crashes and causes major disruption to office operations and patient care since there is no access to the patient medical records during this time. Dr. Brennan's goal is to incorporate as much health information technology into the practice as possible to record and track patient medical records, measure and improve quality of care, and assist with office operations. The practice is currently awaiting a major upgrade to the EHR system to meet CMS meaningful use criteria that would add the following capabilities: clinician decision support such as prompts for care and treatment, connections to other health providers such as hospitals and medical laboratories, and quality outcomes measurement and improvement tracking. Dr. Brennan and her staff do not know how to utilize these functions and are unsure whether and how practice processes and procedures will need to change in order to fully utilize these new EHR functions.

Facilities

Dr. Brennan's practice resides in a colonial style red brick building that is shared with several other medical offices. The practice is near shopping centers, restaurants, and the access to a major highway that runs through southwest Virginia and into Tennessee. Her office has three examination rooms, one physician office, several rooms for storage of supplies and computer equipment, a screening area for nurses to take vital signs, and a front office for the office manager and administrative staff that also serves as the check-in area for patients. The waiting room seats five to six individuals and has health education materials spread out for patients to view while waiting to see the doctor. Dr. Brennan realizes that the current space and practice layout will not meet the future needs of the practice. She would like to expand the facility to improve flow and allow for more providers, which would include additional exam rooms and waiting room space. She would also like to add space that would accommodate several computer stations with privacy screens for patients to enter their medical history and reason for visit.

Finances

The majority of reimbursement for healthcare services provided by the practice is based on fee-for-service arrangements. The percent of annual revenues for patient care comes from each of the following major sources of insurance coverage: commercial health insurance, 60%; Medicare, 30%; Medicaid, 3%; and other insurance such as workers' compensation, 2%, and self-pay, 5%. Several recent initiatives in pay-for-performance (P4P) are now a part of commercial insurance plans and Medicare payments whereby part of reimbursement for services is provided to providers that meet or exceed evidence-based performance targets such as the percentage of female patients in a specific age group that have had a mammography in the past year. Dr. Brennan is considering participating in the voluntary Medicare program; however, does not fully understand how or why she should participate. The practice has experienced cash flow problems in the past; the office manager suggested that to improve the financial situation of the practice they may need outside assistance in evaluating the practice's patient insurance mix and process for coding.

Organizational Relationships

The practice has informal relationships with other specialists, diagnostic services, and treatment centers for patient referrals. The practice has a formal relationship with an independent practice association (IPA) that assists with negotiating contract rates with insurance companies, and measuring and tracking clinical performance for reporting to insurers. Dr. Brennan attempts to attend the annual conference organized by the state primary care association; besides this she has little interaction with other primary care practices and health providers in the community. Dr. Brennan and her staff primarily utilize websites such as the American Academy of Family Physicians (AAFP) and the Center for Medicare and Medicaid Services (CMS) to obtain information on practice improvements and changes in Medicare and Medicaid reimbursement policies.

Practice Transformation Efforts

Dr. Brennan's goal is to transform the practice in order to provide quality care and patient access to needed services. As noted in the following statement, she believes transformation efforts should coincide with financial stability of the practice and employee and provider satisfaction.

"Financially, last year was slim, as I cut my personal income by over 30% to invest in my improvement project, and I haven't changed that rate, as we are still investing and developing. We embarked on a process last year to revolutionize the practice of medicine and provide a business environment that is good for physicians, employees, patients, and insurance companies. I am certain that if doctors are able to transform their practice in a financially sound manner, both patients and insurances will benefit, and though not the only ingredient, I feel this is one of the key ingredients in improving the quality of care.

My budget is probably going to force us to expand slowly, locally. My tentative plan is to bring on a nurse practitioner and have her seeing patients on Tuesday, Thursday, and maybe even Saturday afternoon. With that and some help with office hours on other days, that should free me to train new doctors coming into our practice. I will help them to be successful right from the start and ensure that their clinic enjoys top notch quality and that they are able to strike a good work-life balance while obtaining maximum reimbursement and maintaining control of their career."

CASE STUDY DISCUSSION QUESTIONS

1. Describe the current issues in delivering primary health care.

2. What are the external pressures on practices to make improvements? Where do these pressures originate from?

3. What challenges do practices face with instituting major changes to their practice?

4. What steps could the physician take to improve the practice?

5. How could the physician gain trust and engage employees in these major change initiatives?

6. Identify health policies that affect primary care practices and discuss potential implications on practices.

REFERENCES

County Health Rankings & Roadmaps. Retrieved from http://www.countyhealthrankings.org/#app/

HIMSS. Electronic health record. Retrieved from from http://www.himss.org/ASP/topics_ehr.asp

IOM. Defining Primary Care: An Interim Report. Retrieved from http://www.nap.edu/openbook.php?record_id=9153&page=1

National Health Service Corps, Health Resources and Services Administration (HRSA). Retrieved from http://nhsc.bhpr.hrsa.gov/

Working Toward Collaborative Care

By Susan Grantham, Becky Hayes Boober, Alec McKinney, Natalie M. Truesdell, Eugenie Coakley, and Melina Ward

I continue to be optimistic about the benefits of integrating behavioral health and physical health. I think, ultimately, it provides higher quality of care for our patients. We all now recognize 'health' as having a physical and mental component. Gone are the days of just focusing on a disease or presenting symptoms; especially in primary care, where our intent is to treat the whole person. But 9 months after having brought in two behavioral health specialists to the practice, it's not working as well as I hoped. We are colocated, but not necessarily 'integrated.' I feel like what I've done is colocate a specialty behavioral health practice in the primary care setting. They operate fairly independently. I'm unsure as to the next steps. How do we go from a colocated practice to a truly collaborative approach to care?

—CEO, Maine Primary Practice

INTRODUCTION

"This is the third time this month that Mr. Smith has come in, complaining about neck pain and feeling lethargic," Dr. Appleton explained in the early morning "huddle" with her six colleagues. "Results are back from his scans and the lab, and I'm just not finding anything. I doubt he's drug seeking because he hasn't filled the script I gave him at his first appointment. Mark, will you have time to see him this morning when he comes back in? I'd like to have you assess him and maybe see if there's a behavioral health issue that is impacting his health. I thought about what you said yesterday and agree that we might need to rule out depression." Dr. Appleton and Mark, the Behavioral Health Care Provider, discussed how they would coordinate the "warm hand off."

Finally after 2 years, Maine Primary Practice's (MPP) efforts to implement integrated behavioral health and primary medical care were paying off. The data showed a substantial drop in emergency department usage by their patients. Patients with depression had improved health scores, as measured by a screening tool (PHQ-9), and were adhering to the lifestyle changes necessary to improve their health as outlined in their individual care plans. The behavioral health providers (BHPs) and primary care providers (PCPs) were working with patients to overcome a range of barriers that were interfering with patients' abilities to get to appointments, such as transportation, and as a result, no-show rates were dropping. As a clinic, they were also learning how to better track various data so that they could more regularly review and improve their clinical operations and meet patients' needs. Just last week, Dr. Baker, another physician, commented to Dr. Appleton how nice it was to have an on-site behavioral health provider. More than ever, they could now focus on the areas of primary care that they were most equipped to handle and work with others to truly improve the lives of patients. The integrated care approach was, as Mr. Savard, MPP's CEO, had always expected, making a meaningful difference both for the clinic's staff and, more importantly, the clinic's patients.

After 2 years, the providers and staff really do feel they are integrated. They can hardly imagine how they functioned prior to the integration initiative without the behavioral health providers. Getting to this point, however, had been a rocky road. It had required a range of iterative changes that all together had a major impact on the way they provided care, as well as in the clinic's financial and billing operations. It is a tribute to everyone on staff that they persisted in pursuing their vision of integrated care, driven by their commitment to providing the highest quality, patient-centered, care possible to their patients. This case details some of the discussions that they had along the road they followed.

BACKGROUND

Better integration of mental health and primary care offers the opportunity to improve access to mental health care, improve patient well-being through treatment of mental health issues, and to decrease medical costs associated with mental and addictive disorders. The majority of care for mental and addictive disorders is provided in the primary care setting, the "de facto" treatment setting as characterized by Regier et al. (1993). Less than a third of those with mental or addictive disorders receive treatment in any one year (Regier et al. 1993). Of the nearly half who have a mental disorder but receive no treatment, 80% report at least one visit to their primary care provider during the year (Higgins, 1994). Persons with mental or addictive disorders also incur increased medical utilization and costs compared to those without behavioral health disorders (Strosahl, 1998; Simon, Von Korff, & Barlow 1995).

Clearly the primary care setting is important to the discussion of mental health services provision both for the care currently provided as well as the opportunity to reach those not being treated. Despite its importance, studies show that mental and addictive disorders often go unrecognized and untreated by primary care providers (Bolestrian, Williams, & Wilkinson, 1988). Some of the reasons that contribute to this under-recognition are lack of training by the primary care provider, lack of confidence on behalf of the provider to address mental health issues, and lack of time and/or competing medical priorities. Additionally, patients may be reluctant to disclose mental or addictive disorders and providers may feel uncomfortable addressing these issues due to stigma. The prevalence of mental health disorders, their under-recognition and under-treatment, and the increased costs to the healthcare system of those who suffer, indicate the importance of addressing the nexus between behavioral health disorders and primary care.

Collaborative treatment approaches, particularly those where mental health providers are colocated in the primary care setting, have been shown to be effective, particularly when these approached have served patients with depression and anxiety, two of the most prevalent primary care conditions (Katon et al., 1995; Schulberg et al., 1996). However, there is not one "model" or definition of collaborative care, and approaches in the research have varied. Colocation is a relatively easy step. Essential to successful integration is moving from colocation to collaboration, with the coordination between the primary care providers and mental health providers at the core of collaboration.

SETTING AND CONTEXT

Rockybay is a small, coastal town in Maine with a population of just over 10,000. The healthcare and social service providers in the town are at the heart of the region's safety net and also serve the large, rural county surrounding Rockybay. These providers do a very good job, but despite their efforts, care is relatively fragmented and resources are tight. The demographic and socioeconomic characteristics of Rocky-bay and the county for the most part mirror the state. There is limited racial and ethnic diversity, larger than usual proportions of middle-aged and older adults, and a great deal of poverty, particularly the farther you get away from Rockybay and the coast. Over the past 5 years, Rockybay has become a favored destination for two small but high need refugee populations, which have become an increasing burden on the health, social service, and public education systems. There are a couple of more densely populated communities in and around the town, but overall the county is very rural and the population is widely dispersed. As a result, transportation is a major problem for many people in the region.

The economic downturn has hit the area hard. The town's biggest employer, Coastal Plastics, was forced to cut its staff a year ago from three shifts to two and as a result laid off about 30% of its employees. Due to these lay-offs, the low-income population has been increasing and there are more uninsured and Medicaid insured individuals and families in the area than usual. The lay-offs at Coastal Plastics were a real blow to the town's morale, and MPP's providers have seen their patients getting sicker and more stressed as the hard times continue. Most of these patients have had nowhere else to turn except to MPP, and the practice has never been busier.

The Rockybay clinic is MPP's largest and serves approximately 4,200 patients who logged roughly 11,000 patient visits in the last full year. The other 4 sites are much smaller and 2 of them are only open 3 days per week. The Rocky-bay site employs 2 full-time family practice physicians, and 1 full-time nurse practitioner along with a case manager, a team of nurses, medical assistants, and front-desk staff. Prior to implementing their integrated approach at Rockybay, they provided mental health services much like the rest of the state by referring patients presenting with acute mental health or substance abuse issues to outside providers. For the small number of patients who were insured privately or had the means to pay cash, referrals were made to a small handful of private providers. For the remaining low-income patients with no behavioral health coverage or with Medicaid insurance, referrals were made to the county mental health clinic in Rockybay. In either case, capacity was very limited and typically only those with serious or particularly acute issues were provided care.

Dr. Appleton, now MPP's medical director, had been one of the first doctors at MPP to recognize the high prevalence of behavioral health issues and, more importantly, appreciate the impact that these issues were having on the physical health of her patients. People in the rural town of Rockybay were simply uncomfortable with the idea of mental health services and were reluctant to follow up on referrals with mental health therapists. Even when they were willing to engage in behavioral health care, there were often barriers, such as transportation issues or long delays before getting an appointment, which prevented them from getting the care they needed. Given the growing body of evidence to support the integration of behavioral health and primary care, it seemed to make especially good sense in rural communities like Rockybay. It did not take much to get the other primary care providers and staff to make the same connections, and they all agreed that something different needed to happen so their patients could receive comprehensive, coordinated care. Luckily, a local foundation also agreed and awarded MPP a 3-year, $300,000 grant to explore how to best implement an integrated care approach.

THE PEOPLE

CEO: Mr. Savard

Office Manager: Kate Allowitz

Quality Improvement Manager: Maria Torres

Nurse: Desmond Jackson

Patient 1: Susan M.

Patient 2: Jim R.

Patient 3: Roberta T.

Behavioral Health Provider 1: Mark

Behavioral Health Provider 2: Terry

PCP/Medical Director: Dr. Jennifer Appleton

Primary Care Provider: Dr. Jim Baker

PCP/ NP: Lily Kowalski

ADMINISTRATIVE PERSPECTIVE

Over lunch in the break room, some of the practice staff met to talk about integrated care at MPP. "It is hard to believe a year has gone by since we started this integration program," Kate Allowitz, the Office Manager, said. Desmond Jackson, RN, agreed, "I still remember when Mr. Savard, our CEO, announced that new funding was available to hire two licensed clinical social workers to provide behavioral health services. It was clear he really expected us to integrate them into the practice—even if it wasn't very clear what they'd be doing." Maria Torres, the Quality Improvement Manager, chimed in, "It was inspiring—it's what makes MPP such a great place to work. We're always willing to innovate and make changes in order to serve our patients better. But I knew it would be a ton of work—over the 7 years I've worked as the quality improvement manager, and I've definitely learned that organizational change is never an easy process."

Kate agreed. "It has been a bit of trial-and-error. Do you remember the discussions we had with Mark and Terry when they first started at MPP? Something seemingly simple, like adopting a screening tool, turned out to be a huge undertaking for us. Mark and Terry advocated for employing a comprehensive psychosocial screening and assessment questionnaire they had both used previously in their mental health organizations. Our doctors were really opposed. They thought it was just way too long. They also thought that some of the issues the questionnaire raised were very sensitive and that they might alienate patients; especially new patients with whom we had not yet had the opportunity to develop trust and rapport. The doctors were also afraid of how much time it would take to review the questionnaire and uncertain as to what to do with all the information it yielded. To tell you the truth, even though I didn't say so at the time, I thought it would have been incredibly difficult to incorporate the screening into our practice. Who was going to administer it? When was it going to be administered? How were we going to incorporate it into our electronic medical record (EMR)?"

"Yes, I remember those discussions well," said Maria. "We finally settled on the PHQ-9 depression screener (Kroenke & Spitzer, 2002) (see **Appendix 17-A**). It was definitely a compromise. We all agreed that some screening tool was necessary. Our doctors liked the fact that the PHQ-9 was relatively short, depression focused, easily interpreted, and they knew what to do with the results."

"As with all compromises, there were some trade-offs, and I'm not sure that the PHQ-9 was the best choice," interjected Desmond. "I worry sometimes that the PHQ-9 is potentially missing some important things going on with the patient, like stress, alcohol misuse, or PTSD (post-traumatic stress disorder), given the number of veterans we serve. It's these types of issues where I see the social workers being able to contribute. Fortunately, some patients do disclose these issues or concerns to me or to the other nurses. Sometimes they will talk about this with their doctor, too. Some patients, though, wish they had more time with their doctors. They feel rushed. I think the doctors are in the same bind. They'd like to spend more time with the patients, but they know they are on a schedule and need to stay within the usual 15-minute visit when possible. Especially with patients who have a chronic disease or complex medical condition; even though the doctors would like to take the time to talk about other issues, they really have to use their time with the patient to focus on these medical conditions."

Kate sighed. She had heard all the complaints about the 15-minute appointment before. She hated being the one who constantly had to be pushing the doctors to adhere to this standard. However, given how insurance plans reimburse for care, she had no choice if the practice was to continue to be financially sound. "It's actually one of the benefits that I had envisioned the social workers providing. I was hoping that the doctors could refer the patients who seemed to need more time to talk about their mental health to the social workers, which could make things more efficient around here. I know there's not a clear line between mental health and medical care, but the idea was that the social workers and doctors would work as a team to serve the patient.

Now, it's not only the doctors that I have to keep haranguing about the 15-minute appointments, it's the social workers, too! Mark and Terry had very little understanding of the pressure we're under financially. The incentives and reimbursement they were used to from their previous employment are completely different in our primary care setting. They were used to having counseling sessions with patients that lasted up to 50 minutes. For the first few months they were here, I couldn't understand why they were seeing so few patients. When we sat down together, they explained it to me. The doctors were only referring cases to them when the PHQ-9 score was 10 or higher, indicating a risk for depression. Mark and Terry would then work with the patient and the patient's doctor to develop a treatment plan, which might include an antidepressant and therapy or just therapy. Mark and Terry would then help monitor the patient on the meds as well as provide the therapy, which generally consisted of these 50-minute appointments, often with no limitations on the number of appointments. I'm not so sure that is the model of care that Mr. Savard was envisioning when we went down the path of integration. I think this is what he is referring to when he says we've "colocated" a specialty mental health practice in a primary care setting. We haven't quite figured out yet what it means to provide mental health in a primary care setting—clinically, operationally, or financially!"

"Actually the new screening process raised awareness of mental/behavioral health issues, but then the question was what to do about it," Desmond countered. "In the past, it would be my role to check in with a patient over the phone who seemed down or withdrawn—especially if one of the doctors prescribed an antidepressant. It is clear to me both Mark and Terry are really talented and committed to serving our patient population, but I still don't know them very well. I'm not sure that any of us know how to use their skills in our busy day-to-day work—decisions are made quickly and it takes trust to send patients to someone new. It's not entirely clear to me how it is supposed to work. If Dr. Baker asks me to check in on a patient to see how they're doing, am I supposed to tell Dr. Baker to talk to Mark or Terry? I don't think that would go over well at all!"

"Maybe it's time for us to all sit down together again and go through the SSA (Site Self-Assessment) (see **Exhibit 17-1**)," Kate suggested. "I think the process that you instituted, Maria, where we all sat around the table and tried to reach consensus on where we were on the scales was very helpful. The end result was that it gave all of us a joint vision of where we were heading and what it truly means to provide collaborative care. Perhaps going through this exercise again with one year's experience under our belt would help to take us to the next level of collaboration."

"I'd be happy to organize this," said Maria. "I've been struggling with how to measure integration and collaboration for quality improvement purposes. I've instituted some metrics (see **Figure 17-1**, **Table 17-1**, and **Figure 17-2**), but I'm not sure how well they reflect what we're trying to do. Our stats show that we're screening a lot of patients and about a quarter get an appointment with a social worker. But I wish we knew more! For example, are the patients getting better? Feeling less depressed? Why is the no-show rate so high for social worker visits? I think some of the doctors find the metrics superfluous to their work and that they don't really measure good clinical care, which is the purpose of our quality improvement efforts. I also wonder what the patients think of the whole process. Maybe the SSA process can inform our quality improvement processes as well."

PATIENT PERSPECTIVE

Maria, in her role as the QI Manager, decided that in order to get some real feedback from patients, surveys were not going to be adequate to get all of the information she really wanted to know, such as patients' feelings of stigma, comfort in accessing services, and whether patients felt they were getting better. Instead, she spoke with some of the primary care providers and asked for a few names of patients they had seen recently and referred for behavioral health services who might be interested in coming in to do a focus group. Maria and the behavioral health specialists worked together to develop a focus group guide.

The day of the focus group, Maria set out the lunch she had ordered for the group and waited for the group to arrive. She was a little disappointed when only three of the six patients she had called to participate in the group arrived. It took

I. Integrated Services and Patient and Family-Centeredness   (Circle one NUMBER for each characteristic)

Characteristic	1	2 3 4	5 6 7 (Levels)	8 9 10
1. Co-location of treatment for primary care and behavioral health care...	...does not exist; consumers go to separate sites for services	...is minimal; but some conversations occur among BHPs & PCPs; established referral partners exist	...is partially provided; multiple services are available at same site; some coordination of appointments and services between primary care and behavioral health — **6** circled	...exists, with one reception area; appointments jointly scheduled; one visit can address multiple needs
2. Emotional/behavioral health needs (e.g., stress, depression, anxiety, substance abuse)...	...are not assessed (in this practice)	...are occasionally assessed; screening/assessment protocols are not standardized or are nonexistent	...screening/assessment is integrated into care on a pilot basis; assessment results are documented prior to treatment — **6** circled	...screening/assessment tools are integrated into practice pathways to routinely assess MH/BH/PC needs of all patients; standardized screening/assessment protocols are used and documented
3. Treatment plan(s) for primary care *and* behavioral health care...	...do not exist	...exist, but are separate and uncoordinated among BHPs & PCPs; occasional sharing of information occurs	...BHPs & PCPs have separate plans, but work in consultation; needs for specialty care are served separately — **5** circled	...are integrated and accessible to all BHPs & PCPs; patients with high behavioral health needs have specialty services that are coordinated with primary care

II. Practice/Organization   (Circle one NUMBER for each characteristic)

Characteristic	1	2 3 4	5 6 7	8 9 10
1. Organizational leadership for integrated care...	...does not exist or shows little interest	...is supportive in a general way, but views this initiative as a "special project" rather than a change in usual care	...is provided by senior administrators, as one of a number of ongoing quality improvement initiatives; few internal resources supplied (such as staff time for team meetings) — **5** circled	...strongly supports care integration as a part of the practice's expected change in delivery strategy; provides support and/or resources for team time, staff education, information systems, etc.; integration project leaders viewed as organizational role models — **8** circled
3. Providers' engagement with integrated care ("buy-in")...	...is minimal	...engaged some of the time, but some providers not enthusiastic about integrated care	...is moderately consistent, but with some concerns; some providers not fully implementing intended integration components — **6** circled	...all or nearly all providers are enthusiastically implementing all components of your practice's integrated care
6. Data systems/patient records...	...are based on paper records only; separate records used by each provider	...are shared among providers on an *ad hoc* basis; multiple records exist for each patient no aggregate data used to identify trends or gaps	...use a data system (paper or EMR) shared among the patient care team, who all have access to the shared medical record, treatment plan and lab/test results; team uses aggregated data to identify trends and launches QI projects to achieve measurable goals — **6** circled	...has a full EMR accessible to all providers; team uses a registry or EMR to routinely track key indicators of patient outcomes and integration outcomes; indicators reported regularly to management; team uses data to support a continuous QI process

EXHIBIT 17-1 Site Self-Assessment (SSA)

Courtesy of Scheirer, M. A., Leonard, B. A., Ronan, L., Boober, B. H. 2008, revised 2010. Site Self-Assessment Tool for the Maine Health Access Foundation Integrated Care Initiative, MeHAF: Augusta, ME.

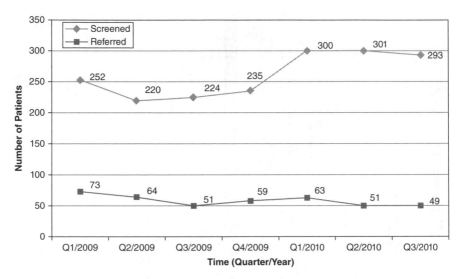

FIGURE 17-1 Number of Patients Screened
and Number of Patients Referred to LCSW

Table 17-1 Common Reasons for Referral to LCSW (Q1 2009–Q3 2010)

Reason	Number of Mentions
Adults:	
Anxiety/PTSD/Panic	61
Depression	51
Stress	50
Psych Consult or Diagnostic Evaluation	50
Chronic Disease	41
Relationships/Marital Issues/Domestic Abuse	35
Chronic Pain	21
Substance Abuse	21
Depression, Anxiety, Stress Combined	13
Children & Youth:	
Behavior	30
Anxiety/PTSD	26
School Issues	21
ADHD	20
Depression, Depression/Anxiety	17
Family Stressors/Issues	13

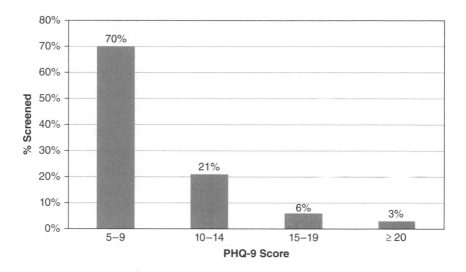

FIGURE 17-2 Distribution of PHQ-9 Scores

some time to warm up the conversation, but once the participants started talking, they were surprisingly candid. Here is some of their conversation:

Maria began with asking everyone, "How were you introduced to the concept of receiving integrated care?" Maria was met with blank stares from all the focus group participants. She quickly reworded: "How were you introduced to the concept of receiving behavioral health services?"

Susan M first responded, "If by behavioral health services, you mean my visits with my counselor, Mark, I can talk about how I was telling Dr. Appleton I had been experiencing some reoccurring headaches, and I couldn't explain them. I had stopped drinking caffeine, I thought was getting enough sleep, but they just kept coming back. She asked me what else was going on in my life, whether I had been under any stress. I paused for a second, and then I started telling her about how my husband had recently lost his job, and I was feeling that all the family responsibilities were on me. Dr. Appleton said that there was someone here that could maybe talk to me about this stress, a therapist, Mark. She brought him right into the exam room and introduced him. Mark was really nice. He said that he didn't have time to talk with me right now, but he was hoping that I would schedule an appointment with him. I have to admit I was a bit skeptical when Dr. Appleton said the word 'therapist.' I mean, I didn't want to be one of those people in therapy. However, when I met Mark he was very easy to talk to, and he introduced himself as a behavioral health consultant and explained that his role was to provide short-term support for those working through problems. This appealed to me and I was able to schedule an appointment with Mark the next week. It has been a tremendous help in getting me through the tough times. I don't know what I would have done without him."

Roberta T added, "My experience was a little different. I have been a patient of Dr. Baker's for about 2 years now. I have some pretty severe health issues, including diabetes, which I've been trying to get under control. I also get depressed. Dr. Baker has been very helpful with this, and he and I have been trying to figure out the best antidepressant. Dr. Baker thinks a combination of talk therapy and an antidepressant would be the best treatment for me; this is what all the research shows, he says. He has wanted me to go to the Rockybay Mental Health Center for the therapy. I didn't really want to go for lots of reasons. One, I will admit, is that I didn't want people to think I was crazy. Another reason is that it is pretty far from my home. Out of respect for Dr. Baker, I did call to make an appointment—and, guess what? I would have had to wait for 3 months to get in to see someone! When I told Dr. Baker this, he said I should meet with Terry, who he said was a counselor here. I made an appointment and within a week, I was able to meet Terry. She has been great. I have been meeting with her about once every other week for the past 6 months."

Jim R's experience was quite different. Jim said, "I filled out one of the questionnaires at the front. I wasn't sure what it was for or if anyone was going to read it. It asked me about my drinking. I was honest, and I said I had three to four beers a night. When I walked into my appointment, Dr. Baker went through the usual physical routine and then told me to wait while someone else came in to see me. That's when Mark walked in. He told me that Dr. Baker had sent him in to discuss my interest in treatment for substance abuse. I was so confused. I didn't know who Mark was or why he was coming to talk to me about drinking."

Maria asked, "Do you think offering integrated behavioral health is important?"

Susan immediately responded, "I think it has been great. I have come to see Mark two or three times, and he has provided some great techniques for managing my stress. I'm using them still! I didn't consider myself having a severe enough issue to travel across town to the mental health clinic. I know I would never have gone to counseling if I had to drive there. While it has been great to be able to come here, scheduling appointments with both Dr. Appleton and Mark has been a little difficult. I come at least monthly to be checked by Dr. Appleton for some other health problems I have, so sometimes I am coming here twice a week, once to see Dr. Appleton, and once to see Mark. Unfortunately, I have had to miss appointments with Mark a lot. I get here when I can, but it's not always easy. Mark has been nice enough to reschedule after I've missed. It would be great if I could get both appointments scheduled on the same day so I don't have to miss so much work."

Jim said, "I came to this group because I wanted you to know what I thought. And my worry is that by asking questions about drinking, and me talking to Mark, substance abuse is now going to be part of my record. Did you know they can charge me more for life insurance? I'm not sure if asking all of these questions is such a good idea."

Roberta enthusiastically voiced, "Terry has been a lifesaver! I still suffer from depression so it is great to be able to talk with someone about it. Another benefit to me is that Terry is helping me better manage my diabetes, too. She and I developed a plan and set some goals related to eating healthier and exercise. Whenever I see her, she follows up and asks me whether I have accomplished the goal I set for myself. It's a real motivator. She also gives me useful tips and helps me to build some self-management skills. It's funny, though, I don't think Dr. Baker is aware of this. He always just quickly goes through the same messages: 'eat better and exercise more.' Don't get me wrong; I think Dr. Baker is great at the medical stuff. He just doesn't have time to do the 'softer stuff.' I used to feel rushed with Dr. Baker. Now, I prioritize my medical issues with Dr. Baker and know that I can go to Terry for the motivation and listening ear! I think that full package is really helping me to get a handle on both the diabetes and the depression. Even Dr. Baker has noticed that I have been improving. It's Terry's and my secret about how I got there!"

After the group, Maria had lots to think about. First of all, she was frustrated that only three of the six patients who had committed to the group showed up. Second, there were some distinct differences in these patients' experiences that may highlight some of the issues the practice was having in moving fully toward collaborative care. She was looking forward to sharing the patient perspective with the staff when they convened to do the SSA.

PRIMARY CARE PERSPECTIVE

Dr. Jennifer Appleton, MPP's Medical Director, and Jim Baker, MD, MPP's other full-time physician, were meeting in the conference room during their weekly Primary Care Providers' Meeting. Lily Kowalski, the Nurse Practitioner, was not able to attend. This was just as well as it gave Dr. Appleton the opportunity to talk candidly with Dr. Baker about integration. Dr. Appleton knew he didn't fully buy-in to the LCSWs being on board and hoped to convince him to give it a better try.

In some ways staff at MPP had never been happier. The practice was finally growing. New patients and patient visits overall were way up. They had brought on a case manager, and the behavioral health providers and the staff seemed to be really gelling together as a team. Just the same, clinic operations were increasingly chaotic, no-show rates were up, wait-times were increasing, and despite their recent success in recruiting two part-time primary care providers, the clinic was struggling to keep up with the volume and provide the care patients needed.

Dr. Baker remarked, "Jennifer, I don't want you to misunderstand me, I certainly believe in the theory behind what we are doing with this Mental Health Integration Project. Given our patients' needs, it totally makes sense. But I don't think the new therapists are saving me any time or, even worse, providing much value to our patients. Have you been referring to Mark and Terry? How do you use them? Do they save you time? Do you think they are helping your patients get better?"

"I know it's not easy and that we have been really busy lately," Dr. Appleton responded, "but, yes; I depend on Mark and Terry a lot, and I think they really do help me and my patients. During our last in-service, we were told to make an effort to get to know the Behavioral Health Providers better and the types of services they could provide. Since then I have made a real effort to do this, and we have developed a good rapport. We have even been doing warm-handoffs. I really encourage you to reach out to them and experiment with how to use them best. I think they have even helped me to reduce my no-show rate with some of my more complex patients as well as help me to improve my chronic disease patient outcome measures."

Dr. Baker noted, "I know, Jennifer, your no-show rates and your diabetes measures are fantastic. I don't know how you do it. I have been referring patients out to various specialists including the endocrinologist and the psychiatrist at Metro Medical Center. The psychiatrist has been particularly helpful when I need psycho-pharm advice." Switching tones slightly, however, he continued, "But while we are speaking candidly, I think we put too much emphasis on these measures anyway. I know we are often running late and my productivity is not up to the benchmark, but I think we need to provide more holistic care. Our patients need it, and they trust me. I am reluctant to send them on to someone else. I am the one that has the rapport with them. This is how I was trained and why I chose primary care. I feel like I have developed some good strategies with patients over the past couple years. Besides, I can't tell you how often I have referred someone to Mark or Terry and the patient has just never shown up. Both of the therapists have even higher no-show rates than I do. This is why my satisfaction statistics are so low. Again, I am just not sure this integration project is working. It seems now that, not only am I responsible for clinical measures, such as diabetes and high blood pressure control, but Maria has also been rating us based on our number of referrals to the therapists, and the number of referrals that actually result in a visit with the therapist. I have to question whether these measures are improving our care as they're intended, or whether we end up referring for purposes of improving our measures! It's not that bad, I know, but all this measurement has a downside."

Dr. Appleton replied reassuringly, "Jim, I know working at a clinic like this is challenging, and you have been doing well. Don't be down on yourself, but from my perspective, the therapists are lifesavers. Most of our patients don't need medications, they just need someone to help them to come to terms with certain stressful events, develop coping skills, or perhaps figure out how they can address some of their bad habits. Even those who do need medications do much better when they have a brief series of counseling sessions along with meds. You know this literature better than I do. I think it has been great for our patients to have access to Terry and Mark. It's nearly impossible to find a counselor in the community, and even if we can find one, the patients are less likely to show up. Referring outside has always seemed like a black hole to me.

We're really glad you came on board with us, Jim. We certainly were in need of another provider, and it's tough to recruit physicians up here as you know. We want to make sure that you're satisfied. That's why when we set out with the Integration Initiative we were committed to the idea of not forcing a specific integrated model and letting all of us figure out how best to use the therapists based on our own practice preferences. On the other hand, I really think you need to make more of an effort to refer to our therapists. Mark and Terry are often free, while you have three patients stacked-up. I know you are really good at bedside manner and connecting with your patients, but I think it would free up your time considerably to let Mark and Terry do the more time-consuming, psychosocial counseling or brief alcohol interventions. It would help us overall as a practice; currently we're really struggling with the patient load."

After a moment of thinking about what Dr. Appleton had said, Dr. Baker responded, "I think that's it, exactly. I'm being asked to change the way I practice, and I'm not sure I'm totally comfortable with that. I'll admit that I became a little resentful when the therapists were asked to join the 'provider' huddle in the mornings. I just see a difference between a 'provider' and a therapist. I see myself as responsible for my patients' care. I guess I'm a little nervous that they'll go off and do something that I might not be entirely comfortable with. I know that team-based care is the wave of the future. You and Lily seem to do that very well. I'm just not there, yet."

"Well, for Lily, it was the nursing part of her training, which emphasizes team care," Dr. Appleton pointed out. "I think the therapists, too, are trained this way. In medical school, there's not that much emphasis on it. For me, it was definitely a change. It was tough at first knowing how to best use the therapists and figure out how we could best work together. They're both very open to being flexible and working with each of us to make it work. It was a lot of trial and error initially, but I've definitely worked out relationships with them both where I think we're all practicing at the top of our credentials."

Dr. Baker seemed to show a change of heart, "You know, I'd love to get some help with my no-show rate and some of my chronic disease performance measures. If they can do this, I would most appreciate it. This was a sore point in my review last month, and I am going to start leaving money on the table when pay-for-performance kicks in next year, if I don't get some of my performance measures up.

Dr. Appleton said, "I think the best idea is for us to have the therapists come to the next PCP Meeting and for us to discuss what we think has been working well and what has been challenging. Perhaps we can learn a bit more about what they are most comfortable doing with our patients and figure out some strategies for getting them better integrated with us PCPs. For some quick advice—first, I would suggest that you start referring some of your more challenging diabetic patients to Terry. She is great at working with patients to sort out why they are not taking their meds or eating according to their care plans and motivating them to be more engaged in their own care. This has led to better HbA1C scores for many of my patients, and I think it has really helped me with my no-show rates because patients are more engaged and not so embarrassed to come back. This has been especially helpful when I can get them in on the same day, perhaps as a result of a warm-handoff. Second, you should try to start experimenting more with warm-handoffs. They are great, particularly since Mark and Terry are not always that busy these days. I have developed some great routines with both of them, which have helped me to be more efficient with my patients. Instead of going into the psychosocial stuff myself, I tell patients that I have a colleague who has proven to be very helpful with other patients with similar issues and I ask whether I can bring them in the exam room so that they can meet. If either Mark or Terry is available, it is great. It eases the transition, and I think the patients feel more comfortable knowing Mark and Terry have my endorsement. If they're not available, then I walk with the patient to the scheduling desk and he or she signs up for another time with Terry or Mark. This makes the patient feel like issues are being addressed, that people care about them, and engages them in a follow-up plan. It also releases me so that I can keep on schedule."

Dr. Baker responded, "This makes a lot of sense. I will definitely try to take your advice. Let me air just one more issue. One of the main reasons I don't use the therapists is that I have a hard time communicating with them. Something happened just today that is a good example. A couple weeks ago, I referred one of my long-standing patients to Mark. The patient had scored a 17 on the PHQ-9, so based on our integration protocol, I referred her to Mark. I actually tried to do a warm-handoff with Mark, but he was not available. I was able to schedule an appointment the next day, though, and my patient agreed to see him. Well, after seeing Mark, Mark decided to refer her to the psychiatrist at Rockybay Mental Health. That was fine. Given her symptomology, I think he made the right call. When she returned for regular follow-up on her asthma this morning, I had no idea that she had been referred out. I looked really bad, the care was poorly coordinated, and I am sure my satisfaction scores are going to be low because of it. I would have liked to be consulted or informed. This is a little bit of what I have been talking about in terms of losing control over the care of my patients."

Dr. Appleton said, "That's definitely not optimal and shouldn't have happened. I think having Mark and Terry come to next week's meeting is a good way to move forward. At the top of the agenda should be discussions about how we can improve communications between the BHPs and the PCPs. One thing I have been having trouble with is getting the BHPs to do much more brief, directive summaries like 'referred out to psych-MD at MMH based on patient wishes,' and utilizing some of the alert fields in the EMR that we use all the time. This would help us to keep apprised of what they are doing. Thanks, Jim, for sharing your thoughts about integration. I really appreciate you airing all these issues. We are doing so well and things are looking up. If we can just smooth out some of these issues, we are really going to do even better for our patients."

BEHAVIORAL HEALTH PROVIDER PERSPECTIVE

Mark and Terry were hired by Maine Medical Practice nearly 1 year ago. There were several qualified applicants for the job, but the doctors, CEO, and office manager were unanimous that Mark and Terry were the best among the applicants. Although they had made the job description as thorough as possible, everyone was in agreement that it would take time to fully sort out in the practice how integrated care would/should actually work. Thus, the special qualities they were looking for in the hiring of the BHPs were flexibility and independence. Mark and Terry had both exceptional clinical expertise and were committed to working with the practice to make integration work.

Mark: "Before I came to MPP, I had been working as a therapist at the Rocky-bay Mental Health Clinic. I loved that work and the patients I saw there, but after 5 years, I just wanted to expand my professional skill set in another setting. The job description really appealed to me, and I immediately liked all the people I interviewed with here. They are all committed to doing the best for their patients, and they felt like the behavioral health side was a missing piece. They talked about their vision for integrated care. I was aware that there have been several studies showing that providing integrated care in a primary care setting improves patient outcomes for depression and anxiety, as well as being cost effective. They also talked about how some of their colleagues in other practices around the state had implemented integrated care and that it seemed to be working for them. They were honest in saying that they didn't exactly know how it would work at MPP, but that they were looking for BHPs who were willing to help them work out a strategy as they went along. I really liked the idea of being part of something new and working on a team to figure this all out. I also liked the idea of treating patients in a primary care setting with the hope that more serious mental health problems wouldn't develop, which I know could keep them out of the emergency room and hospital. That's definitely a win/win—the patient benefits and you save the system some money.

The biggest change, I think, for me was how hectic this place is! There are kids running around, the waiting room is always full—it seems that once we start our morning, we are all going nonstop until the end of the day. We have our lunch break, but often that gets filled with walk-in patients or shortened if we're running behind. No-shows are a huge deal here—if an appointment slot is left open, the practice loses revenue and we're operating on such thin margins to begin with. I think we all appreciate the little bit of breathing room that comes from one or two no-shows, but when it gets higher than that, I know that our Office Manager begins to worry. They've done all kinds of things to minimize the no-show rate, like allowing for some level of double booking and offering open access hours. My no-show rate is higher than for the doctors, which is worrisome to me. I have the sense that some of my patients don't prioritize the visit with me as they do with the doctors. For some of my patients, especially those who are depressed, I'd like to see them at least weekly for the first few weeks. I get huge no-shows, though, for these cases.

The conversation with the doctors and nurses during the day happens on the fly—if you pass in the hallway mostly. I find myself having to track down the doctors when one of my patients is coming in for a medical appointment. I want to make sure that I'm on the same page with the doctor about the patient, and I want to make sure that I get 5 minutes with the patient after she has seen him or her. Sometimes it feels like I'm stalking the doctors, just trying to get one quick minute of their time. For me, it's really important that I have a thorough record of everything I've discussed with the patient, including my impressions and what the patient and I have decided about his or her care plan. I think it's really important that the doctor endorses this. I think the patient needs to know that both the doc and I are working as a team and that we're all on the same page with the patient. But I'm not so sure that this is happening. Although we document to the same electronic record, I'm not always convinced that the doctor has read what I've written. In fact, we've had these discussions with the doctors that our notes are too long and they have to spend too much time reading them; thus, I find myself nearly stalking the doctors to give them two to three sentence updates about each patient before they're seen. So many of these updates don't happen, and I feel it's a missed opportunity with the patient. The morning huddles that we recently started have been really helpful for communication and planning for the day. The doctors, Lily, Terry, and I quickly run through our scheduled patient list for the day. We all have an idea of whether a patient might be referred to behavioral health or we provide updates of patient progress.

What I wasn't prepared for in this setting was how the doctors run the show—well, they don't actually run the show, but everything is geared to enabling them to serve their patients in the way they see fit—and both doctors seem to have a different approach to this. Thus, nonphysician staff are always trying to accommodate to their styles. Lily's not that way. She engages more with us in terms of how best to manage a patient. I feel like an equal partner in care with Lily's patients. In the specialty setting where I used to work, it seemed a far more collaborative effort. We all felt part of a team. We all did case conferences once a week where we discussed our patients and jointly problem solved. Additionally, there was the focus on 'supervision,' whereby a peer or supervisor might observe a patient encounter or simply debrief with you on a fairly regular basis. The purpose of supervision is to continue skill building, assist counselors in boundary setting, and help counselors avoid burn-out. Sometimes Terry and I are able to do this for one another, but it doesn't happen on a routine basis, and it's certainly not built into our schedules here.

It has been a learning process for everyone, including Terry and me, to identify for which conditions or for which patients we can be helpful. For some conditions that are diagnosis-driven, such as depression or anxiety, it's obvious to both the doctors and us that it makes sense that we see the patient. This is especially true for depression because we have a depression screen, the PHQ-9 that we use. We also have a protocol that suggests referral to Terry or me if the score is 10 or above. Unfortunately, the reimbursement system forces a diagnosis-driven approach, but rarely are things as clearly delineated as this. I think that the PCPs and Terry and I believe that the value of integration is in assessing the full needs of the patient. One elderly patient, I'll call her Mrs. Jones, recently lost her husband. Although generally a lively and out-going person, she was drawing into herself. This put her on a bit of a downward spiral, including with her health. Dr. Appleton realized this immediately and thought I could be helpful to Mrs. Jones and introduced me to her. Although she was somewhat resistant to seeing a 'counselor,' Dr. Appleton assured her that I would be a good person to talk with. She agreed to meet with me two or three times after her appointments with Dr. Appleton. In between appointments, I would give her a call just to check in on how she was doing. I also received permission from her to talk with her daughter. Now, she definitely has that old feistiness back, and she realizes that she has to work on reaching out to others to help her transition through her grief. I think this is a success story. Did Mrs. Jones have any 'diagnosable' mental health condition? No. Did she need some help just managing her grief and getting through a big transition period in her life? Absolutely. It's a great example of how integration can work. Dr. Appleton and I worked closely as a team to benefit Mrs. Jones. Mrs. Jones may have successfully navigated this period herself, but maybe not. And, if she hadn't, I feel certain that her health would have spiraled down quickly to the point where she may not have been able to continue to live fully and independently. As crass as it may seem, I feel sure that Dr. Appleton and I saved the health system some money by keeping Mrs. Jones' medical conditions under control during this period.

Let me also give you a growing pains story. At our practice, we do a general health history, of course. Part of that is to ask about alcohol use. Well, Dr. Baker, sent me an electronic note that she would like me to see a patient, I'll call him Mr. Cramer, for his alcohol use. I was in session with another patient at the time and responded that I would be able to speak with Mr. Cramer in about 10 minutes, if he was willing to wait in the exam room for me. From my background and from the patients I used to see at Rockybay Mental Health Clinic, when I hear 'alcohol,' I'm thinking that the patient is a heavy user, possibly abuser of alcohol. It was my fault for not reading his record thoroughly before I went to speak with him, but I didn't want to keep him waiting any longer. Anyway, I went in and introduced myself to Mr. Cramer, and I said to him: 'I understand you are interested in receiving treatment for substance abuse.' I think I nearly gave the poor man a heart attack. He was a little angry, and rightfully so. When I looked back at his health record, it noted that he had reported drinking about 3 or 4 beers at a time a few times per week. When I asked Dr. Baker why he had referred him to me, he was concerned about a problem that might be developing with alcohol. He had wanted me to talk with him more from an educational point of view and to let him know the potential adverse consequences of alcohol, especially as he grows older. As I said, a growing pains story. Dr. Baker and I clearly did not communicate well about this patient. I didn't read the chart ahead of time. I was rushed. Dr. Baker was rushed. I did not have an understanding that health promotion and health prevention were part of my purview. I'm still trying to figure out the best way to follow up with Mr. Cramer and repair that relationship.

All in all, I think integration is the way to go to maximize the quality and comprehensiveness of a patient's care. There's no guide on how to do it though. Maybe there are some better ways to overcome some of these growing pains. I think we'll get there eventually. Everyone in the practice is certainly committed to making it work; this commitment is certainly half of the battle."

CASE STUDY DISCUSSION QUESTIONS

1. How do you gain primary care provider buy-in for the new integrated approach?

   a. What can primary care providers do to become more comfortable with the change?

   b. What can the behavioral health specialists due to foster buy-in?

   c. What can clinic managers do?

(continues)

2. What does it mean operationally to go from a colocated specialty mental health practice to a collaborative and integrated approach to mental and physical health?

   a. What does it mean for patients? Please discuss the pros and cons.
   b. What does it mean for primary care providers? Please discuss the pros and cons.
   c. What does it mean for mental health providers? Please discuss the pros and cons.
   d. What does it mean for administrative staff? Please discuss the pros and cons.

3. How do you encourage mental health providers to adapt their practice to a primary care setting?

4. How do you facilitate the building of trust and credibility between primary care and mental health providers?

5. How would you go about planning for further change? What organizational transformation strategies would you use?

6. What are some concrete strategies for overcoming these organizational behavior challenges?

7. What categories of data were used by MPP to monitor their efforts in integration (clinical, operational)? How can the data be used to motivate the team?

REFERENCES

Bolestrian, S., Williams, P., & Wilkinson, G. (1988). Specialist mental health treatment in general practice: A meta-analysis. *Psychological Medicine, 18*, 711–718.

Higgins, E. S. (1994). A review of unrecognized mental illness in primary care. Prevalence, natural history, and efforts to change the course. *Arch Fam Med, 3*(10), 908–917.

Katon, W. et al. (1995). Collaborative management to achieve treatment guidelines. Impact on depression in primary care. *JAMA, 273*(13), 1026–1031.

Kroenke, K. & Spitzer, R. L. (2002). The PHQ-9: A new depression and diagnostic severity measure. *Psychiatric Annals, 32*, 509–521.

Regier, D. A. et al. (1993). The de facto US mental and addictive disorders service system. Epidemiologic catchment area prospective 1–year prevalence rates of disorders and services. *Arch Gen Psychiatry, 50*(2), 85–94.

Schulberg, H. C. et al. (1996). Treating major depression in primary care practice: Eight month clinical outcomes. *Archives of General Psychiatry, 53*, 913–919.

Simon, G., Von Korff, M., & Barlow, W. (1995). Health care costs associated with depressive and anxiety disorders in primary care. *American Journal of Psychiatry, 152*, 352–357.

Strosahl, K. (1998). Integrating behavioral health and primary care services: The primary mental health care model. In A. Blount (Ed.). *Integrated primary care: The future of medical and mental health collaboration* (pp. 139–166). New York: W. W. Norton and Company, Inc.

Appendix A

PATIENT HEALTH QUESTIONNAIRE-9
(PHQ-9)

Over the <u>last 2 weeks,</u> how often have you been bothered by any of the following problems? *(Use "✓" to indicate your answer)*	Not at all	Several days	More than half the days	Nearly every day
1. Little interest or pleasure in doing things	0	1	2	3
2. Feeling down, depressed, or hopeless	0	1	2	3
3. Trouble falling or staying asleep, or sleeping too much	0	1	2	3
4. Feeling tired or having little energy	0	1	2	3
5. Poor appetite or overeating	0	1	2	3
6. Feeling bad about yourself — or that you are a failure or have let yourself or your family down	0	1	2	3
7. Trouble concentrating on things, such as reading the newspaper or watching television	0	1	2	3
8. Moving or speaking so slowly that other people could have noticed? Or the opposite — being so fidgety or restless that you have been moving around a lot more than usual	0	1	2	3
9. Thoughts that you would be better off dead or of hurting yourself in some way	0	1	2	3

FOR OFFICE CODING __0__ + _____ + _____ + _____

=Total Score: _____

If you checked off <u>any</u> problems, how <u>difficult</u> have these problems made it for you to do your work, take care of things at home, or get along with other people?

Not difficult at all	Somewhat difficult	Very difficult	Extremely difficult
☐	☐	☐	☐

PHQ-9 Scores and Proposed Treatment Actions

PHQ-9 Score	Depression Severity	Proposed Treatment Actions
0–4	None-minimal	None
5–9	Mild	Watchful waiting; repeat PHQ-9 at follow-up
10–14	Moderate	Treatment plan, considering counseling, follow-up and/or pharmacotherapy
15–19	Moderately Severe	Active treatment with pharmacotherapy and/or psychotherapy
20–27	Severe	Immediate initiation of pharmacotherapy and, if severe impairment or poor response to therapy, expedited referral to a mental health specialist for psychotherapy and/or collaborative management

PHQ-9 and PHQ-9 Scores

Developed by Drs. Robert L. Spitzer, Janet B. W. Williams, Kurt Kroenke and colleagues, with an educational grant from Pfizer Inc. No permission required to reproduce, translate, display or distribute.

Leadership's Role for Organizational Change

By David Colton

A s the administrator of the Treatment Center for Children and Adolescents (TCCA), Jay Thompson had a lot on his mind and on his plate. At just 50 beds, TCCA was the smallest of the publicly funded state psychiatric hospitals, but it more than made up for its size because it was also the busiest state hospital, with an average of 650 admissions per year. This meant a rapid turnover of patients and a heavy caseload for the Center's limited number of staff. There were other pressures as well, such as the perennial threat of budget cuts, high staff turnover—particularly of psychiatric aides—documentation demands from insurers, and an unacceptable rate of staff injuries.

The problem confronting Jay at this moment was related to all of the above issues and more. Beginning with Philippe Pinel's decision to unchain patients at Bicêtre Hospital in 1792, there has been a long history of attempts to reduce or eliminate the use of seclusion and restraint in the care of the mentally ill. In more recent years, the use of seclusion and restraint (S/R) has been the focus of much scrutiny. In part, this has occurred in response to client injuries and deaths, as well as questions about the therapeutic appropriateness and the emotional and physical impact these interventions have on clients and caregivers. The federal government, through the Medicare and Medicaid programs, and JCAHO responded to these concerns by revising their standards for implementing S/R and setting the goal of reducing their use.

Although TCCA had recently passed its JCAHO survey, the surveyor was concerned by the Center's high use of S/R, recommending that decreasing it be at the forefront of quality improvement activities and making it clear that the next surveyor could expect to see a significant reduction in use. Jay was also getting pressure—no, make that "heat"—from his superiors in the state's department of mental health. In addition to the distinction of having the highest number of admissions for a state hospital, TCCA also had the problem of having the highest rate of S/R. Jay's superiors expressed support for him and the organization but made it clear that they expected to see tangible outcomes; in other words, reduce S/R and do it as soon as possible.

In addition to external pressure, internal forces were at work. It takes an order from a physician to place an individual into S/R, and the psychiatrists were concerned that an injury occurring from one of these interventions might put their professional licenses at jeopardy. The risk manager and the human resources director were also concerned by the number of staff injuries that were related to these interventions. The Center's Worker's Compensation insurance premium was rising, and the injury rate added to the problem of maintaining safe staffing levels.

Jay had worked his way up the career ladder in the state mental health system, starting as a psychiatric aide when he was just out of high school. While working, he attended college and earned a bachelor's degree in social work. He was promoted to a social work position and then continued his studies and attained his master's degree in social work. This opened doors to management positions, and after more than twenty-five years in the state hospital system, he had worked his way up to his current role as hospital administrator. Nonetheless, his early work experience made him sensitive to the needs of the psychiatric aides, who viewed S/R as a necessary evil: interventions that were needed to keep themselves and the other patients safe. So, although he was supportive of S/R reduction efforts, Jay did not really believe these interventions could be fully eliminated.

Jay liked to keep up with the management literature and bought into the concept of a data-driven organization, where data is used for management analysis and decision making. Several years earlier, he had hired Sue Stark as the Center's Quality Improvement Director and asked her to work with staff to identify clinical indicators that would be used to monitor performance and identify opportunities for improvement. S/R was one of the obvious areas because the data was readily available. Given the JCAHO surveyor's recommendation, Jay decided that he would make S/R reduction a QI activity and, after some thought, came up with an idea to address the problem.

Like Jay, Sue had worked her way up the career ladder, starting as a nurse and then going back to school for her master's degree in nursing administration. She was intrigued by studies such as the Institute of Medicine's *To Err Is Human*, which indicated that greater attention to the way in which clinical procedures were carried out could reduce patient mortality and morbidity. This propelled her into the area of quality improvement, which had been the topic of her thesis.

One of the first things that Sue did as the new QI director was to educate the staff on the use of data. She disseminated the seclusion and restraint data to each of the Center's four treatment units and each month met with the clinical staff to review the data and discuss how the data could be used. Because there was so much data, it was important to be able to make sense of it—for example, to see if and where there were patterns and trends. It soon became evident that more S/R interventions occurred in the late afternoons and evenings, when the kids were out of school. The younger the child, the more likely he or she would be placed in a restraint hold, whereas, the older the child, the more likely he or she would be placed in seclusion. Use of S/R increased when admissions increased. And although a few kids with multiple interventions skewed the data, it was also apparent that use was high throughout the Center, with one in every four children being secluded and/or restrained.

The psychiatrists and psychologists were also interested in how the Center compared to other mental health facilities in treating children and adolescents. JCAHO collected such data through its ORYX program, and the National Association of State Mental Health Program Directors also collected the data through its NASMHPD Research Institute. This data indicated that, in contrast to other facilities, the Center used S/R at a higher rate. Sue used the psychological term "cognitive dissonance" to describe the clinical staff's reaction to this information. When they saw how poorly the Center compared, they came up with a variety of excuses to explain or defend the status quo. For example, the clinical staff indicated that because these databases included both for-profit and not-for-profit hospitals, it was like comparing apples to oranges. However, Sue found that another state hospital, which served the same population, had a similar bed capacity and a similar number of admissions, yet had less than half the number of S/R interventions. Because of this data, it was hard to refute the fact that the Center faced a serious challenge.

Such was the situation when Jay called Sue Stark into his office to share his idea for a QI project to reduce seclusion and restraint. "What I want to do," he explained, "is to create a quality improvement team. They'll be given the task of identifying things we can do at the Center to reduce seclusion and restraint. We can prioritize the list of actions they come up with and begin working on them one at a time in order to plug away at the problem."

Sue could tell that Jay was excited about the idea, but she had some reservations. She herself was an enthusiastic supporter of QI teams, but she wasn't so sure this was the best way to approach the problem. Sue knew that organizations that were successful in reducing and even eliminating S/R engaged in multiple activities rather than one at a time. This fostered a process of cultural change. An organization's culture is its internal identity based on norms, practices, shared values, beliefs, and assumptions. In regard to S/R reduction, successful organizations moved from a culture of external control, in which treatment providers know best, to a culture in which the role of staff is to help empower the patient. Because these changes are often threatening to staff, the change process requires strong leadership from management. And because cultural change is a long-term process, leadership must be unwavering in its commitment.

In her review of the literature, Sue also found that leadership's beliefs and values were the most important factors influencing the organization's ability to reduce seclusion and restraint. For example, S/R reduction rarely occurred in psychiatric hospitals where the administrator believed that S/R was a legitimate treatment intervention or, at best, a necessary evil. On the other hand, the psychiatric hospitals with the best results had administrators fully committed to the goal and process of S/R reduction. Sue was aware that Jay was still in the first camp, seeing it as a necessary evil, and therefore she was concerned that he was unprepared to provide the level and kind of leadership needed to guide a process of cultural change.

Unfortunately, the Center's past efforts suggested that her worries might be founded. Two years earlier, the Center had rolled out a training program with great fanfare. Every employee had been required to attend a series of training sessions and the initial results had been promising. However, once the project was over, the training was not sustained. Given an annual turnover rate of 25%, none of the staff hired in the following two years—nearly half of the psychiatric aides—had been exposed to the training.

And then there was the reward program from earlier in the year. Jay decided that to recognize staff efforts, the treatment unit with the lowest number of seclusions and restraints for the month would earn a pizza dinner for its staff. For a number of reasons, Sue had openly expressed concern about that approach as well. For one, this created a climate in which there were winners and losers, and she had known that staff would quickly get discouraged when they were repeatedly on the losing end. Additionally, this approach did not recognize successful treatment; a newly admitted child may initially display a lot of aggressive behavior requiring a lot of S/R before treatment effectively reduces the aggression. It came as no surprise to Sue that this project lasted only a few months and was quietly phased out.

Sue was concerned that Jay's latest idea might be another short-term, quick fix that would not achieve sustained results. As Jay expanded on his plan, Sue tactfully (she hoped) tried to introduce some suggestions: "It would be helpful if the Center had a clear vision about what it wants to attain in regard to seclusion and restraint reduction and, ideally, a strategic plan to guide these activities."

"Our vision is to get S/R down to the lowest level possible" he responded somewhat defensively, "and as far as a plan, that is what I am hoping we can develop as a result of this activity."

"To assure I understand what your expectations are," Sue continued, "you want the team to use their work experience to identify problem areas and to make recommendations as to what we might do to address these problems. It will be important to clarify whether or not staff are free to explore all the issues, even if it may not initially appear that we can resolve the problem. For example, from my experience, this QI team will probably say that we don't have enough staff, even though, because our number of positions is fixed, it is a resource issue we have virtually no control over."

Jay concurred and also explained that he wanted Sue to serve as the team's facilitator, providing guidance for the process, but not participating in the actual content of the discussion. Jay and Sue also talked about the makeup of the team and agreed it would be best to keep it small—no more than six members. They agreed on a psychologist, a nurse, an activity therapist, and three psychiatric aides. Sue also got a commitment from Jay to initiate the process by meeting with the group to directly articulate his expectations.

In all, the QI team met a total of eight times over a 2-month period. Sue found the group to be very focused and dedicated to their task. As the group identified issues and concerns, she wrote them on a blackboard. Discussions typically ensued about each issue, and the information she wrote on the board needed to be refined and rewritten. After each meeting, Sue drafted minutes for the group to review along with the list of issues, which grew in length the more times they met. By the sixth meeting, the group felt they had identified all of the relevant concerns and they spent the last two meetings making final revisions (see **Exhibit 18-1**). The QI team asked to meet with Jay and his executive team in order to

Human Resource Management:

1. Occasionally, staff attempt to use accrued leave but cannot because of staffing shortages. Some have gotten to the point that they have lost annual leave and compensatory time. In those cases, provide the employee with money for time that would be lost or extend the time in which they can use their leave.

2. Reevaluate the need for straight 8-hour shifts and the impact this has on change-of-shift meetings and issues related to patient safety. (For example, having enough staff available to monitor children when in their rooms during change of shift.) Otherwise, pay staff overtime for attending change-of-shift meetings.

3. Salaries need to be adjusted to ensure that individuals with seniority are paid more than staff with less experience. Hiring new employees at salaries greater than the pay of more senior staff contributes to low staff morale.

4. Most employees are willing to work when needed, but sometimes this is not always possible. Management has declared that there will be no mandatory overtime. Therefore, management needs to provide alternatives.

5. Tighten up hiring practices and listen to hiring managers' recommendations regarding the suitability of an applicants.

6. Conduct an employee-satisfaction survey and use the information to improve the quality of work life at the Center.

7. Identify exemplary staff who can function as mentors and provide an increase in pay for those who serve as mentors.

8. Make review of a new employee's performance an agenda item for shift supervisor meetings.

9. Create a system in which staff who have prevented use of S/R can be identified and provided a monetary bonus.

10. Increase the monetary bonus for not using sick leave.

Staffing:

1. To ensure staff and patient safety, when staffing is lower than recommended levels, do not accept admissions and, if need be, buy beds in the community.

2. To ensure patient safety, when staffing is lower than recommended levels (for example when there are employees on light duty), lower the bed capacity.

3. To ensure there is no favoritism in approving leave, appoint one individual to assume responsibility for scheduling direct-care staff.

4. Create a "crisis management intervention team" composed of staff with advanced training and skills who can provide support to unit staff during a crisis intervention. Provide a monetary bonus to those employees.

EXHIBIT 18-1 QI Team's Concerns and Issues *(continues)*

Staffing (continued):

5. Adhere to scheduling guidelines to ensure that there are adequate numbers of shift supervisors on duty, especially on weekends and holidays.

6. Make the state department of mental health aware that efforts to reduce S/R are in part dependent on staffing levels and use results of staffing study (item 8 below) to support request for more psychiatric aides and nursing positions.

7. Increase the pool of part-time psychiatric aides and ensure that these employees understand they are needed to work on weekends, evenings, and holidays.

8. Complete a staffing study to compare recommended and required staffing levels (standards) to actual staffing levels at the Center.

9. Identify light duty staff who can drive patients to medical appointments, get money from the cashier's office, etc.

10. Create a list of administrative and administrative support staff available to drive kids and staff to local medical appointments.

11. Allow staff to periodically change shifts for brief periods in order to enhance working with staff on other shifts. This might reduce burnout and the accompanying lost time associated with call-ins.

Staff Development:

1. Break orientation into two parts so that new staff has time to spend on the units, working with kids. This will help them relate to the training they receive.

2. Enhance S/R reduction training by increasing the amount of time available for new staff to learn and practice verbal interventions and skills other than holds.

3. Revise orientation so that there is a greater emphasis on the skills new employees need in order to work with patients and to reinforce the type of interactions the Center supports.

4. Realign duties of the shift supervisors so that they serve as mentors to new employees (for their shift but across units) during an employee's first month at the Center. Additionally, assure that mentoring (from a supervisor or senior staff) is provided during the employee's first year of employment.

5. Ensure that training opportunities are provided consistently and that a system is established to ensure that staff can attend training.

6. Provide a monetary incentive for staff based on obtaining training to enhance their skills.

EXHIBIT 18-1 QI Team's Concerns and Issues *(continues)*

Programs and Treatment:

1. Provide weekend and holiday activity therapy services. As part of this process, evaluate the amount of time AT staff spend in planning and preparation versus providing direct services.
2. Evaluate the possibility of gender specific units, particularly for the adolescent program.
3. Transporting kids to medical appointments takes staff away from the Center and is extremely difficult to do when staffing levels are low. Given that the Center's mission is to provide short term, acute stabilization, complete a retrospective review to determine the number of outside medical appointments necessary versus those that are desirable but could be deferred.
4. Identify approaches to ensure that a patient's treatment plan is implemented consistently across shifts.
5. Evaluate the need for the community integration activities that AT staff carryout. This takes them away from the Center with small numbers of children and appears to be inconsistent with the Center's short-term, acute model of care.
6. Evaluate the possibility of creating an MR/autistic unit.

Environment:

1. Install sound-dampening materials on the units, particularly in the day areas.
2. Change the furnishing in the bedrooms so they are safer.
3. Convert one or more seclusion/time-out rooms into a "sensory room": a room where kids can go to calm down but which is made into a comfortable, inviting environment, rather than a bare, sterile setting.

Communication:

1. More face-to-face communication between management and staff at all levels—particularly during stressful periods.
2. Ensure participation of all disciplines during change-of-shift meetings and during weekly treatment review in order to enhance communication within treatment teams.
3. After the QI workgroup and the executive team meet, share the information with all staff and ask for their input so that the process is inclusive.

Leadership:

1. Provide support for monthly treatment team meetings, across shifts, to encourage communication and teamwork.
2. Create a process whereby managers can spend 5–7 days each year working with direct care staff on the units.
3. Reinstate change-of-shift meetings that allow the majority of staff from the two shifts to meet.
4. Provide support for an employee-recognition program.

EXHIBIT 18-1 QI Team's Concerns and Issues *(continued)*

present and discuss their recommendations. They wanted to use this meeting to answer questions and discuss how the Center should proceed.

Two weeks after their last meeting, the QI team met with the executive committee. In addition to Jay, this group included Dr. Weston Blake, the medical director, Dr. Charles Simpson, the psychology director, Anna Dupre, the nursing director, Renee Gaston, director of social work, and Al Lindy, the chief administrative officer. The QI group had asked Lesley Duggins, the psychologist on the team, to present their findings. Dr. Duggins began by describing the process and then asked the executive team if they had any questions about the QI team's findings. And that's when things began to fall apart.

The QI team had expected a lively discussion about the issues they had identified. Instead, they were met with an uncomfortable silence. Finally, Dr. Duggins again asked the executive team if they had any questions and again there was silence, which was broken only when Dr. Blake, the medical director, noted that there was a lot of information to take in. That's when Sue realized the information was new to the executive team; they had not received advance copies and had not had time to absorb the information! The QI team was clearly disappointed. They had spent a lot of time and energy on this project and expected a lively exchange. "Perhaps," Sue interjected, "we should give management more time to review and think about these recommendations. Could we set a date for another meeting?" Here again there was disappointment, because the executive team could not meet with the QI team for nearly a month. This connoted to the QI team that the project was of low importance to management.

The QI team decided to meet again to process what had happened. Sue was concerned it would become a "gripe session" but understood the group's ire and frustration because she herself shared these feelings. And although the team did vent their disappointment, they talked about how to improve communication with management, which was one of the issues they had identified in their analysis. Sue left the meeting feeling more positive about the process, but, as she was to find, these feelings were premature.

At the next meeting, the executive team did not ask a lot of questions. Instead, they focused on the recommendations they felt were out of the Center's control, such as not accepting admissions when staffing levels were low. State regulations required the Center to accept all admissions, regardless of the resources that were available, and therefore the organization did not have the legal authority to stop admissions. Consequently, some members of the executive team questioned why these actions were even recommended. Sue had to remind them that the QI team had been charged with exploring *all* issues and possibilities, regardless of feasibility. However, it was evident, based on their roles and responsibilities, that the executive team members thought that many of the recommendations were not helpful or doable. This placed the QI team on the defensive because they had to justify each of their recommendations. This meeting concluded with Jay stating that the executive team would meet among themselves to further review and discuss the list of recommendations.

Two weeks later, Jay called Sue into his office. Jay shared that he was disappointed with the process. Although he felt that there were some usable recommendations, for the most part he did not feel that the QI team did what he had wanted it to do. "This is not the product I thought we would get," he confided to Sue. "We may be one of those kinds of organizations where QI teams just don't work." Sue asked him what would become of the recommendations. Jay handed her a copy of the list, which the executive team had revised, and she noted that more than half of the recommendations were deleted. Jay told her that the executive team would continue to discuss the remaining recommendations to see what could be done. Finally, Sue encouraged Jay to send the QI team a memo or email thanking them for their work, and he promised that he would do so.

A month later Jay had still not written the thank-you letter, so Sue stopped by to chat with Jay's secretary and used the occasion to ask her to remind Jay about it. The letter was sent out a week later. To his credit, Jay did ask the personnel director to look into a number of the human resources issues, such as appointing one of the supervisors to do all of the scheduling, and he asked Al Lindy, the chief administrative officer, to find funds for more part-time staff. Sue recognized that this was reflective of the organization's management culture: a few baby steps rather than a comprehensive, strategic approach to solving problems. Sue wondered what the next "big idea" to reduce S/R would be. Three months later, Jay announced a total personnel reorganization, with the psychiatrists having direct supervision of the nursing staff. A year later, the details of that plan still had not been worked out.

CASE STUDY DISCUSSION QUESTIONS

1. Identify the internal organizational factors that create opportunities and threats to TCCA's goal of reducing S/R.

2. In health services, managers often have a clinical background. In what ways might that prepare them for a role as an administrator and the assumption of a leadership position within the organization? How might that hamper them in that role?

3. If you had been in Sue Stark's position, what would you have done in response to the executive team's reaction to the QI team's recommendations? For example, what could she have done differently to foster a better reception and ultimately use of the recommendations?

4. Based on the Case Study and Exhibit 18-1, what communication problems do you think might exist in this organization? What would you do to address these problems?

5. Jay's reservations about eliminating use of seclusion and restraint appear to have influenced his willingness to take bold, decisive actions. Describe a situation you have been in, in which your values, beliefs, and biases have significantly influenced the decision-making process. What can an administrator do to better assess his or her own position and how it might influence his or her management style and ability to provide leadership?

6. Some would argue that cultural change is too nebulous to define, let alone actually influence. And even if you can influence the process, it may not turn out the way you want it to, and it may consume more resources than you have available. Explain why you would agree or disagree with this position.

Mending Relationships After a Communication Breakdown

By Roger F. Hogu

Harry Long was fuming! "That witch!" he thought to himself. Harry had just learned that Mary Jones, a fellow manager in the pediatric clinic, had offered a position to Christina Duncan, his new medical records staff. It had taken an entire year to fill the vacant position in the medical records department. During this year, Harry had to work 60–70 hours a week to keep up with the department's work volume. How could Mary do this to him?

At 39-years old, Harry was an interesting character with a storied and eclectic professional life. He had difficulty deciding his career path, and his educational pursuits reflected his indecisions. Along the tortuous course to his current job, Harry had earned degrees in biology and sociology and held positions in both the private and public sectors. He even tried his luck as an entrepreneur. Having failed in this last venture as a hardware store owner, he obtained an insurance license and worked as a general agent until the birth of his first son. Harry decided at this time that he needed a stable position with a great benefits package to meet the needs of his family. So 5 years ago, he accepted the position as the Health Information Manager within Baptist Memorial Health's (BMH) outpatient division.

"When will Christina transfer to the Pediatric Clinic?" asked Renee Crooks, a friend and coworker with whom Harry was attending the organization's quarterly leadership meeting. These sessions brought together all middle-level managers for an update on the state of the system. The stupefied look on Harry's face cut the conversation short. "I am sorry!" Renee cried, "I thought you knew." "No, Renee, I had no idea," Harry replied; "How could she?" "Please don't tell Mary I said anything," begged Renee, "Please!"

The day dragged on for Harry as he thought about the past year and his relationship with Mary. As a cost-cutting measure, BMH had adopted a new employment policy that created several barriers to hiring new employees. Obtaining approval to hire for a vacant position required several levels of signoffs and justifications. Harry felt betrayed by Mary. He thought that positive relationships existed among the midlevel managers at the organization—a camaraderie of sorts. Harry could not let this affront go unanswered.

The next day, Harry arrived at work early. Sitting at his desk with his head in his hands, he recalled his conversation with Anna Arias, the human resources generalist, when he filled out the request for the medical records position, "Mr. Long, I truly understand your situation," she said, "but your requisition for a FTE has to go through an approval process." "The position was approved in the budget," Harry replied, "Are you sure?" "I am sorry but these are the rules! It's going to take a little time. I have to send the documentation to your supervisor; if she approves it, then it will be forwarded to the CFO for review." The "little time" turned out to be 1 year.

Compounding the cumbersome process of hiring a new employee, the starting salary for staff in the Health Information Management (HIM) department was the lowest in the system, matching that of the general maintenance staff. Harry had always found it challenging to retain good employees. Historically, the more able candidates used the HIM department to get a foot in the door at BMH. Once hired, they would inevitably transfer out of the department. For every posted position, Harry received dozens of applications from unsuitable candidates—unemployed administrators, nurses, medical assistants, and the sundry of professionals attempting to join BHM with the goal of eventually transferring to a more desirable position within the system.

One year earlier, Harry had hired Christina, a very capable 23-year old who had recently been laid off from an upper state hospital's HIM department. Christina had it all—intelligence, experience, a great work ethic, with an easy-going personality. In other words, she had all the attributes Harry was seeking in a candidate! She was even familiar with the software applications used at BMH.

Christina was a good fit in the HIM department. Even though she had health problems that required frequent physician visits, Harry was glad to accommodate Christina's schedule because she was an outstanding employee.

The news of Christina's transfer took Harry completely by surprise. Harry soon learned that Mary Jones, the pediatric clinic manager, had actively recruited Christina with the promise of a higher salary. He planned to address this matter with Christina as soon as she arrived to work.

At 9 a.m., Harry walked to Christina's work area poorly hiding his dismay of the situation and asked, "What is this I hear about you transferring to another department?" Turning beet red, Christina apologized profusely. "Mary asked me; please forgive me!" she implored. "I wanted to tell you, but I was told not to say anything until the transfer was finalized. I accepted the position only because it pays more than what I earn in this department." Looking back, he now saw that Christina had avoided him for more than a month. The usually talkative and upbeat employee had been quiet and withdrawn, and he never bothered to ask her if she needed help with whatever was causing this unusual behavior.

It became clear to Harry that he was the last one to learn about this transfer! How could he have missed it? Ellen Temple, the clinic's administrator, both Harry's and Mary's boss, knew full well this had been going on, yet no one had approached Harry to apprise him of the situation. He felt betrayed because he had shared with his peers on numerous occasions how difficult it was to get the HIM department position filled. In addition, this course of action went completely against the organization's culture.

Harry's challenge was to find a constructive way to communicate his displeasure with the situation to Mary and Ellen. He knew he had to move past his feelings of betrayal and sense of loss in order to achieve a solution to his dilemma.

He first tried to understand Mary's frame of reference. Harry had attended various BMH leadership development classes, and one point discussed in all the sessions was to show empathy for others and avoid passing judgment. This was not easy! Harry's first thoughts were identifying problem areas: 1) the poor management style displayed by both Ellen and Mary, 2) the possible broken relationship between Harry and his peers, 3) the breakdown in the communication flow, and 4) the conflict arising in response to Mary's actions.

Harry requested a meeting with Ellen to address the issue that caused him the most distress, his exclusion from the transfer decision. Christina had already accepted the position, and Harry did not intend to create a barrier for her. He truly cared about his staff and often encouraged them to engage in furthering their education so they could take advantage of growth opportunities when presented.

Seated in Ellen's office, Harry attempted to communicate his concern without provoking a confrontation. "Although probably unintentional, I was not notified that Christina was transferring from my department. As you know, Ellen, BMH's policy is that there be interdepartmental communication prior to approving employees' transfers," Harry stated. Ellen looked confused and replied with a pitch of surprise in her voice, "Harry, are you telling me you were not notified?" Harry nodded yes. Ellen replied, "I will clarify this. I will speak to Mary right away. I am sorry, Harry, this is awful. I didn't ask Mary if you had been told about this—I just assumed. This situation is delicate, and I will need your support to fix it." Harry hesitated a moment then answered, "Ellen, you know how stressed and unhappy my staff has been, I cannot ask my employees to go through this again." "Well, Harry, let me think about this; I will get back to you tomorrow," replied Ellen.

Harry had always known Ellen to be an honest and forthright individual, and this conversation had reminded him not to assume the worst of others. With his previous feeling of being betrayed, Harry had concocted a conspiracy theory that now made him feel silly and a little embarrassed. "How on earth could I have thought such a thing!" Harry thought. He had always prided himself in remaining calm in such situations.

The following morning, Ellen called Harry and Mary into her office. Mary had arrived first and, as Harry walked in, the two women turned toward him. "I didn't know," started Mary, "I didn't know I was supposed to tell you!" Mary had worked as a bedside nurse for 15 years, and she had no supervisory experience prior to her current position. Attending leadership classes helped a little, but she often felt overwhelmed. Mary continued in an emphatic tone, "I really needed an assistant for my department. Our referral coordinator is on family leave, and senior administration has received several complaints from the physician specialists."

Harry contained his frustration, exhaling loudly. "Mary," he said, "I know it seems overwhelming at times, but you can count on our support with whatever you need. Remember that you have to keep the referral coordinator position open. By law, you cannot terminate an employee on family leave." Informing Mary of something she may not have known cemented his reputation as a team player. Ellen smiled and turned to Mary: "Now, Mary, until Harry can hire a new employee, some of the HIM department's duties for the pediatric clinic will have to be taken over by your staff. That will depend, of course, on work volume. I will arrange for a temporary relief person to float in the HIM department until then."

Leaving Ellen's office, Harry knew he needed a permanent solution to the problem. The solution came to him in the middle of the week; he would request salary adjustments for HIM employees, which would help him compete for and retain his employees. He knew this solution would be difficult to achieve, but he was determined. His counterpart in one of BHM's other hospitals gave him the idea. "Reclassify your employees, Harry," suggested Diane, "My employees do the same jobs as yours but get paid 25% more. You hire medical records clerks. I hire health information management technicians. You should do the same."

Harry brought Ellen the job descriptions for both positions and described in detail how the functions of his medical record clerks matched those of the health information management technicians. In fact, in some cases, the qualifications of the medical record clerks exceeded that of the technicians. Ellen was supportive of Harry's solution.

Budget time was right around the corner. Harry contacted Anna in HR to determine the new salaries of his employees, assuming the adjustment was approved. He would need these figures when he prepared his department's budget. Not long after, Human Resources called Harry to request the names of his employees. He hadn't said anything to the staff because there was always the possibility that the salary adjustment would not be approved by the CFO. However, Harry remained hopeful imagining the joy in his employees' faces when he would announce their raise.

CASE STUDY DISCUSSION QUESTIONS

1. What are the causes of the communication breakdown in the case study? Assess the flows of communication in the organization.

2. Do you approve of the way Harry handled the issue? Why or why not?

3. What would have been the proper procedure for Mary to recruit Harry's employee?

4. Using Herzberg's Two-Factor Theory and Adam's Equity Theory, explain Christina's choice. How should have Cristina handled the job offer?

5. Which conflict-handling mode did Harry use to resolve the issue? Why did he use this mode?

6. Put yourself in Harry's position, how would you have resolved the situation?

7. Assess Ellen's handling of the situation. Was it appropriate? Why?

Too Busy To Care

By Susan J. Kowalewski

THE SITUATION

Mercy Hospital is a 642-bed hospital in an urban city in the northeastern United States. The hospital is a nonprofit facility and began operations in 1949 with major renovations completed in 1984 and 2008. Mercy Hospital's mission statement reads that "Mercy Hospital is an institution dedicated to providing quality patient care with unrelenting attention to clinical excellence, patient safety, and an unparalleled passion and commitment to assure the very best health care for those we serve in our community and its surrounding area." The hospital recently rolled out a new marketing campaign titled "Our Patients are #1."

There are 6 hospitals located within a 50-mile radius of Mercy. Two local colleges offer 4-year nursing programs, graduating 160–180 nurses each year. However, this number falls short of what is needed by Mercy and the other area hospitals to sufficiently staff their nursing needs. Due to nursing shortages across the United States, nurses (and those individuals who work with them in providing care) work under stressful conditions.

This case presents aspects related to staff stress (and how they cope; or don't cope), employee roles, diversity, and communication. Health care needs to be delivered in a team approach; requiring individuals from different backgrounds and experience to work together to provide quality care in a supportive environment.

THE CASE

Lori, a 36-year old Caucasian patient diagnosed with Guillain-Barré syndrome was admitted to Mercy Hospital 4 weeks ago. Lori's disease is a serious autoimmune disorder that causes paralysis. As such, Lori is bedridden, unable to move her body below the waist and both arms. In addition, she is experiencing facial Bell's palsy. Lori is dependent on healthcare providers for feeding and assisting with her bodily functions.

On a particular evening, the hospital's general medical floor is very busy. All the beds are occupied, and the unit is one nurse short-staffed. At 8 p.m., Lori rings the call button to request assistance with her feeding. Jaeda sighs when she sees another call bell light up. How will she manage all these patients that require so much assistance! Jaeda is a 54-year-old African American licensed practical nurse (LPN). She has been employed by Mercy Hospital for more than 30 years. Jaeda has a reputation for being a hard worker, but at times exhibits a bad attitude. During the last three years, she has filed four grievances against her nurse supervisors and two physicians related to race discrimination; one grievance was determined in her favor, the other three in favor of the physicians and one nurse supervisor.

It took Jaeda more than 10 minutes to respond to Lori's call for assistance because of her need to obtain pain meds from the pharmacy for the patient in room 101. When she arrived in Lori's room, Jaeda could see that she was in distress and immediately began helping Lori with her needs. Within 3 minutes, Jaeda received 3 more alerts of calls for assistance and told Lori she would be back as quickly as she could. Ten minutes pass and Lori is ready to continue eating but can't reach the call button. After another 15 minutes, Lori is able to place pressure on the call button to request assistance. Lori continues to press the call button every 10–15 minutes. Finally at 10 p.m., Jaeda returns. Lori has now gone without eating for 2 hours. Lori complains about the lack of attention Jaeda is providing her. Jaeda shouts, "We're short-handed and I can't do everything! You are 50 pounds overweight and missing one meal would be in your best interest anyway. I only have 2 hands and the nurses don't do anything!" This upsets Lori, who begins to cry and hyperventilate.

Maria, the 29-year old Hispanic nurse supervisor for the unit was just returning to the floor after meeting a few of her friends in the cafeteria to celebrate earning her MSN degree earlier in the week. As Maria reflected on the celebration, she was happy that she joined Mercy Hospital 2 years ago. She had made quite a few friends—more than at the hospital she worked prior to coming to Mercy. As Maria walked down the hallway, her attention is drawn to Jaeda's shouting and Lori's crying. She quickly moves down the hallway and enters the patient's room. Assessing the situation, Maria tells Jaeda, "That's enough, leave the room and wait for me at the nurses' station." Jaeda begins to leave but abruptly turns and starts shouting, "We're always short-handed and I end up doing the work of three people. You don't do anything to change things. Just because I'm black, you can't order me around! It's always transport this patient to radiology, empty that patient's bedpan, and answer that call. It never stops!"

Maria calms Lori and asks her to recount what happened. Lori explains that she was waiting to be fed for 2 hours This is unacceptable, she's ill, not feeling well, and then this happens. Maria asks if she wants to talk to the patient advocate or Director of Quality Assurance. Lori tells Maria that she will consider her suggestions and will let her know the next day. Maria returns to her office, bypassing the nurses' station, to think what she needs to do to rectify this situation.

Maria determines that there are a number of alternatives on how she could/should handle this issue and the care rendered to Lori. As she begins to think about the situation, the following concerns become apparent:

- This is not the first time that there have been attitude issues with Jaeda. She has a letter of reprimand dated 4 years ago in her personnel file for insubordination. Maria has heard that there were other instances prior to Jaeda transferring to her unit 6 months ago, but only one incident was documented.
- Maria is concerned that Lori received below expected standards of care in her unit—the unit she is responsible for managing.
- Is Lori going to file a complaint with the patient advocate or Director of Quality Assurance? That's not going to look good for her unit, Jaeda, or herself.
- Could Lori file a negligence/malpractice claim related to the poor/lack of care she received?
- Should Maria address this issue tonight (immediately) with Jaeda or wait until the next day?

- Mercy Hospital has had a shortage of nursing staff for over 4 years, there has to be a method of addressing this issue with Human Resources—patient care is becoming an issue due to the nurses and LPNs being exhausted and stressed.
- Jaeda has filed previous grievances regarding race discrimination; Maria wonders whether she will say this was the issue with this incident.

CASE STUDY DISCUSSION QUESTIONS

1. Are there additional issues that should be considered in this case?
2. If you were Maria, how would you handle the situation with Jaeda?
3. What issues in the case relate to:
   - diversity
   - conflict
   - stress
   - communication
4. Describe the organizational culture you think Mercy Hospital has.
5. How would you explain the motivation of the employees at Mercy Hospital?
6. How do you think Maria handled the issue at the time that it occurred? Did she have any alternatives?
7. How do the following organizational behavior theories (Theory X/Theory Y, goal setting theory, and status characteristics theory) relate to the case?

Post-Merger Impacts within a Health and Social Services Centre in Quebec

By Carole Lalonde and Eva Jarosová

D uring the period 2004- 2005, a health and social services centre in Quebec, Centre Ste-Clothilde, was merged with two neighbouring centres, Centre Vilmont and Centre St-Andrews. The decision to merge the three establishments into one was part of the reform undertaken by Quebec's ministry of health and social services (*Ministère de la santé et des services sociaux*) in an effort to improve continuity of services among the various health service centres, provide greater accessibility for the communities they serve, and control the costs attributable to duplication of services. After the merger, the newly combined health service centre became one of the largest of its kind, both in terms of human resources and budget. No jobs were lost during the process as the entire staff of the three institutions was integrated into the new organization. In addition, the centre took on transregional responsibilities and has since become an essential resource for other health service centres in many highly specialized areas of expertise. It has a very good reputation and is the envy of the executive directors of neighbouring facilities. "We are now one big family and we must work together for the well-being of the people of this region," declared the new executive director, Mr. Fillion. The changes that Mr. Fillion must implement are the result of a policy decision taken by the health ministry and have thus been imposed on the staff of the three facilities.

The executive director of the new combined centre, Mr. Fillion, had been the director of Centre Ste-Clothilde, one of the three merged centres. The former directors of the two other centres, Mr. Bédard and Ms. Desgroseillers, have assumed senior management positions within the combined centre. Mr. Bédard is now director of professional services and Ms. Desgroseillers has become the director of clinical programs for the combined centre. While disappointed by the merger, with which they did not concur, the two former directors nonetheless wished to continue their careers within the new organization and were ready to work with the new executive director to create a dynamic and innovative organization.

It is a matter of public record that Mr. Fillion had considerable influence on the decision-making process that led to the merger, particularly through his political contacts with the health minister of the time. Mr. Fillion had previously held a highly placed position in the government bureaucracy and had established ties with a wide network of political contacts. Many professionals and service providers in the health and social services sector believed that Mr. Fillion was the main beneficiary of the merger because he was named executive director. In fact, Centre Ste-Clothilde had essentially absorbed the two other centres. Furthermore, the new combined centre created by the merger is called Centre Ste-Clothilde and the two other centres have, in a sense, lost their unique identities; no effort was made to find a new name to represent the new organizational structure. Mr. Fillion has a reputation as a master strategist in terms of his analysis of the situation outside the organization; however, within the organization, he is viewed as intransigent, authoritarian, and moody. His close collaborators never know what attitude to adopt in his presence. His management style is by turns quite collegial and very "dictatorial." Most of his collaborators eventually came to distrust him, while still seeking his approval. His character seems at once fascinating and repellent. He knows how to develop big ideas and elicit support, yet at the same time can be hurtful and "abrasive" toward the people he works with. From the perspective of the board who appointed him, Mr. Fillion was the best qualified person to assume the executive director's position after the merger.

Mr. Fillion began his career as an administrator in the education sector, first as the principal of a secondary school, then as assistant director at the college level. Politically active, he worked within a political party and was chief of staff to a government minister for 5 years. Moreover, he has maintained the valuable network of contacts from his years in politics. Before becoming executive director of

Ste-Clothilde, he had accepted the position of president of the board of directors for a healthcare organization in the Montérégie region, an elected and unpaid post.

Mr. Bédard is trained in the health sciences. He worked as a nurse and then became director of nursing care in a hospital centre. He was later named the executive director of St-Andrews, one of the three health and social services centres involved in the merger. He is ambitious, but also knows how to work as part of a team. Concern for quality health services is one of his central priorities. Thus, before the merger, Mr. Bédard headed Centre St-Andrews, which was closed following the merger and the staff relocated to Centre Ste-Clothilde. "He (Mr. Fillion) has been very shrewd throughout the merger process. I ran a nice little team that was quite tight-knit. It was an exciting challenge for me to lead that team. But hey, now we have to help the staff accept the change." Although he had some difficulty accepting the merger, Mr. Bédard was among the first managers to back the new director.

Ms. Desgroseillers has an impressive resume within the health and social services system. Very committed to community and social concerns, her training is in social work. Early on in her career, she became the director of a centre for troubled youth, where she made her mark. Her management style is very collegial and personable. In general, both her staff and her colleagues hold her in high esteem. Moreover, she has built a solid reputation in the health and social services sector. Many of her peers would have liked to see her continue her career as executive director. Before the merger, Ms. Desgroseillers was director of Centre Vilmont, which was closed following the merger and the staff relocated to Centre Ste-Clothilde. "He (Mr. Fillion) has contacts in high places and the health ministry probably saw no need to maintain a free-standing health centre in Vilmont as the population living there is generally perceived as quite comfortable and well off." Of the two directors whose facilities were closed, Ms. Desgroseillers was clearly the most saddened by losing her prior status as director and the most suspicious of Mr. Fillion's intentions.

It was in this context that in 2006–2007, two years after the merger, Mr. Fillion decided to take stock of the results of the merger and determine to what extent the leadership's goals for integration had been met. He called in a consulting firm to conduct an analysis on the post-merger impacts, contacting the firm's senior consultant, Mr. Louis Gauthier, to discuss the project. Mr. Gauthier's firm is well known to managers in the health and social services sector and has an excellent reputation. Himself a former manager in the sector, Mr. Gauthier knows its inner workings and had previously been brought in as a consultant in the context of similar changes.

The first meeting included Mr. Gauthier, Mr. Fillion, and Mr. Bédard. Ms. Desgroseillers did not participate in this first meeting. Over lunch, the two directors discussed their needs and expectations with Mr. Gauthier. One of their major concerns was the quality of services, both in terms of management and service to the public. They also hoped that the entire staff was committed to the organization.

Mr. Fillion showed great enthusiasm about working with Mr. Gauthier, for whom he had great respect. Mr. Bédard shared those sentiments, if less intensely. Mr. Gauthier felt flattered by so much praise, but asked to be more specific on his role and the role played by Mr. Fillion in this project. Mr. Gauthier aims to clarify mutual expectations about the course of this project.

Mr. Fillion: We have so many needs and you can be so useful to us!

Mr. Gauthier: I am honoured by your confidence and encouragement, Mr. Fillion. It will be my pleasure to work with you. If you want me to be really useful to you, we should define the specific mandate under which I will work.

Mr. Fillion: Okay. How should we proceed? What do you suggest?

Mr. Gauthier: Well, I'm interested in organizational change management and we could start by conducting a large consultation with the staff of all the teams to find out their opinions of the post-merger situation. We could then analyze the current situation and I could make recommendations at the end of that process.

Mr. Fillion: Okay, that sounds fine. We need someone like you to tell us how the various teams are doing and what they are saying about the current management. It will be great to get a better picture of the situation.

Mr. Fillion gave him complete freedom to establish the parameters for his work within the organization. "I'll let you put all this in writing," he said. "We'll have another meeting when your proposal is ready." It was thus the consultant who prepared the project proposal and suggested how the consultation should proceed; the executive director made very few changes to the document. During their discussion over lunch, Mr. Gauthier had noted the management team's initial goals in forming a single integrated organization. These three objectives were to 1) to develop a new organizational structure that promotes cohesion and coordination of programs and services, 2) ensure appropriate guidance for the staff (in terms of supervision, motivation, recognition, etc.), and 3) develop a sense of belonging to the same organization (in terms of support for the organization's values, culture, and mission, etc.) Several ad hoc committees were created to try to harmonize practices and agree on a common vision about providing services to the community. This "post-merger" integration work took two years and revealed two major difficulties: 1) a larger than anticipated disparity in professional practices and access to services among the merged institutions, and 2) latent opposition among the former staff of Centre Vilmont, which took the form of a lack of acceptance of the current rules at the new facility. Integrating this information into the description of the mandate, Mr. Gauthier proposed to assess how well the management team's initial goals had been met, using appropriate tools and methods. "This is great! What you suggest is really interesting." Mr. Fillion cooperated fully with the consultant and supported his work. It was agreed from the beginning that regular update meetings would be held to share the consultant's findings and make adjustments as needed. Mr. Fillion essentially gave the consultant and his team a free hand in conducting the consultation process. He placed complete trust in him and was eager to see the results. Everything seemed to be off to a good start.

Very shortly after this agreement, Mr. Gauthier began the consultation process. Over a period of 6 months, Mr. Gauthier and his team conducted interviews with the entire staff of the centre. They also collected documentation about the process, the progress toward achieving goals in the various units, and the operations of the centre. The first groups of employees and managers who met with the team were rather reticent about participating in the consultation process. It should be noted that Mr. Gauthier and his team had not been formally presented to the staff and, at the time that the first meetings with employees were held, they had not been informed of the management's reasons for bringing in a consultant They were quite skeptical of the process Mr. Fillion had undertaken and wondered if it was another attempt to control them.

> **Employee:** It is just another of the director's whims. Just what is he trying to find out? Since when is he interested in us?
>
> **Mr. Gauthier:** I understand your mistrust, because you don't know me, but I'm here precisely to help improve things and to better understand your concerns, with your help. If you don't talk to me, there's not much I can do. I can't raise the upper management's awareness of your experience as professionals. You can count on my discretion. I will not identify anyone in my report. Of course, you can choose not to tell anything, but I think it would be a missed opportunity to make some changes, don't you think?

For the consultant and his staff, this attitude spoke volumes about the climate of distrust that seemed to prevail between the administration and the clinical staff.

Faced with this reticence and the quasi-refusal to participate in the consultation process, the consulting team began to worry about whether they would be able to complete the project.

To overcome the staff's reticence, Mr. Gauthier was very reassuring, explaining that the content of their meetings would remain confidential and anonymous. He showed that he was sympathetic to their worries and concerns. The consultant's attitude, and the empathy and sincerity he showed for the staff's concerns, worries, and disappointments, as well as the empathic ambiance he created during the meetings, finally led the employees to open up more and to participate more widely. Indeed, in spite of the marked reticence at the beginning of the project, the process elicited a high level of participation, reaching a participation rate of 70%, which was considered excellent under the circumstances. Once the consultants had passed the initial "test" of the first few meetings, everyone wanted to meet with them. They gradually built an excellent reputation within the centre through their ability to listen and their knowledge of the health and social services sector. During a brief meeting with Mr. Fillion, Mr. Gauthier reported that the process is well underway, but did not specifically mention his initial concerns about the staff and their apparent view of Mr. Fillion's management style. He did not think it was useful to address it that time, preferring to continue the process of investigation. Mr. Fillion was still very positive and enthusiastic about the consultant's work and reiterated his trust in Mr. Gauthier.

As they continued their analysis, Mr. Gauthier and his team increasingly noticed the tension that existed between the administration and the staff in general. It seemed that the way the merger had been managed had created much bitterness and disillusionment. Quite negative comments were made about the executive director, who was seen as very controlling and attempting to centralize authority. Both employees and managers felt that they were not taken into account, creating a ripple effect throughout the working climate. Furthermore, many of them had still not accepted the merger process. The staff of one of the merged centres, Centre Vilmont, believed that, with respect to the other two centres, theirs had a unique identity in terms of management style, the characteristics of the community it served, and the range of services offered. Indeed, many members of the staff held on to a strong but vague longing for their former autonomy. The demographics and socioeconomic condition of the community served by Centre Vilmont were in fact quite different from those served by Ste-Clothilde and St-Andrews. The management style of the former director, Ms. Desgroseillers, had been very open, collegial, and focused on human resources. The employees had felt that they were involved in decision-making and that their work was appreciated and valued. This desire to maintain Centre Vilmont's distinct organizational identity was very clearly expressed by the employees; however, Ms. Desgroseillers was more reticent, feeling torn between her loyalty to the new organization and her thwarted ambitions as executive director. From the point of view of Centre Vilmont's employees, Mr. Fillion was an opportunist who had compromised their identity as an independent organization. They were far from being committed to the new organization, which Mr. Fillion consistently referred to as a "big new family" in all his speeches. In short, many employees had experienced the merger as the loss of organizational identity for their smaller entity, which had a friendly working environment and a strong sense of belonging. In addition, the closure of some service locations had created crowding and a lack of space in the workplace, adding to the bitterness related to the merger.

Beyond getting a better idea of the prevailing mood at the centre based on the feelings expressed by the employees, Mr. Gauthier and his team gathered as much factual information as possible. They reviewed all aspects of the operations: the management tools in use (including the organizational chart); the systems for coordinating activities; the mechanisms for recognizing work performed by the various units; each units' operational plans and goals; their main achievements, efficiency, and productivity and so on. The team observed that although official management structures had indeed been put in place, there was no effective coordination among the working units. Goals and objectives were not clearly defined and there were many grey zones in the descriptions of responsibilities allocated to each unit, to the point that everyone simply tried their best to get things done. Fortunately, the employees reported that they could count on collaboration and support from their colleagues in order to complete their work. They had the impression that the unit leaders did not have any latitude and simply followed orders from above. Overall, however, the performance of the various units and programs was quite good. For example, the ratio of the hours worked to the number of services delivered and the ratio of hours worked to number of clients seen were above average compared to other facilities in the same category.

Mr. Gauthier also noticed the tension within the management team itself, particularly between Mr. Fillion and Ms. Desgroseillers, as illustrated by this brief but emotionally charged exchange:

> **Mr. Fillion:** So, Ms. Desgroseillers, what do you say? Are you going to stop mothering your employees? Isn't it about time to step up and assert yourself more?
>
> **Ms. Desgroseillers:** I think we must understand people and be empathetic to what they are experiencing. I don't want to rush them.
>
> **Mr. Fillion (angrily):** Well, that's just great. Just go right on playing mommy!

After this exchange, Ms. Desgroseillers left the meeting in tears, casting a chill over other participants. The meeting continued, however, and a few minutes later, Ms. Desgroseillers returned and joined gradually to the discussion. Mr. Gauthier is a silent witness to all this. He takes note of this unfortunate incident. Not knowing whether or not to share his perceptions to the management team or Mr. Fillion himself in private, he decided not to talk at this time of the incident, preferring to continue the investigation within the organization.

Mr. Gauthier and his team completed their analysis of the entire organization in light of all the collected information. One of the main findings was that the integration goals that the executive director had been pursuing since the merger had been only partially achieved. Among other factors named in the analysis, the executive director's centralized leadership style was identified as a problematic factor, both in terms of working climate and the independence of the various departments. The two former directors of the merged centres, who now held senior management positions, did not feel that they had the required latitude to spearhead important projects or to create a feeling of belonging among the members of their respective teams, which would motivate them to improve organizational performance. It appeared that the executive director was burying himself in the details of budget management and going behind the directors' backs to get information about the conduct of the internal affairs of each department. This tended to undermine the directors' actions and make them look bad in front of their employees, which added to the oppressive organizational atmosphere. In short, there seemed to be no real mutual trust among the members of the management team.

Based on the indicators collected to describe the organizational culture, Mr. Gauthier noticed that the employees identified with their professional group first and only secondarily with their section or department. Thus, the nurses identified with the professional nursing group, social workers with social workers, and doctors with doctors. Some employees had a more multidisciplinary view and identified with the section in which they worked. For example, the professionals and service providers in the youth care section identified with that section, no matter their profession, and had a sense of belonging within that group. However, very few employees or unit heads expressed a real sense of belonging to the organization as a whole. The employees stated that they did not know what the organization's major strategic goals were, because they had never been told about them. Each had their own way of defining the main objectives of the organization and also showed great devotion to the clientele they served.

Once the meetings with the various teams and department managers were completed and the information-gathering process was over, Mr. Gauthier prepared his report. To maintain objectivity and be free of undue influence, he considered it best not to have the executive director read it in advance, especially since some parts of the analysis were far from favorable toward him. At the end of the project's mandate, he submitted the report, which contained a set of recommendations intended to:

- consolidate the operational structure
- develop staff's sense of belonging to the new organization
- improve channels of communication in order to favor two-way communication (top-down and bottom-up)
- suggest ways to develop a shared leadership around core values of the organizational mission
- introduce new measures such as communities of practice to energize and stimulate innovations and team spirit

The executive director invited Mr. Gauthier to present the report to the Board of Directors. The director also organized a special meeting of all staff to give Mr. Gauthier the opportunity to present the report. There was broad consensus in favour of the proposals in the report. Everyone concerned recognized the accuracy of the organizational analysis put forward and was satisfied with the consultants' work. The set of recommendations constituted a veritable strategic action plan for the organization, based on a process of organizational development and designed for the long term. Everyone, including Mr. Fillion, were delighted with the report's recommendations and optimistic about the future. The staff showed their gratitude to Mr. Fillion for having allowed the process to be undertaken.

Shortly thereafter, Mr. Fillion met with Mr. Gauthier to ask him to oversee implementation of the recommendations in the report, as a continuation of the previous project. Again, Mr. Gauthier was given free rein. He prepared an operational action plan, which he asked to discuss with Mr. Fillion and the management team. Approximately one week later, Mr. Gauthier submitted his proposal to Mr. Fillion; however, he noticed a change in Mr. Fillion's tone and attitude.

Mr. Gauthier:	Here is the operational plan based on the report that I submitted last month. It contains a number of measures related to the recommendations in the report.
Mr. Fillion:	Many of the actions you propose are not really necessary. I would like you to remove some items, because we are already doing some of them and others are a waste of time.
Mr. Gauthier:	I don't understand. I thought…
Mr. Fillion (sternly):	Let's focus on concrete actions, if you don't mind.
Mr. Gauthier:	Okay. If that's what you decide to do.
Mr. Fillion:	That's right. I'm the one who decides.

Whereas a few months earlier Mr. Fillion had endorsed the entire report, he now discarded some of the report's central recommendations out of hand, saying they were not relevant. Mr. Fillion felt that his management team was already working on many of the issues raised in the report and it did not seem appropriate to him to undertake an organizational development process that involved such profound changes in management style. "You have to be firm to lead an organization like ours," he said.

However, Mr. Fillion identified a few well-defined projects within the action plan that he asked Mr. Gauthier to be involved in. These projects were not among the most central or strategic listed in the report, leaving the consultant under the impression that the main recommendations had been taken off the table. After the meeting, Mr. Gauthier was puzzled, but did not reopen the discussion with Mr. Fillion concerning the deeper reasons that might have explained his change in attitude and behaviour. He allowed ambiguity to hang over the concrete follow-up of the report and over the organization's future direction.

The executive director, while letting the consultant continue his work, became increasingly unavailable for update meetings with him and did not seem in a hurry to move forward with many of the proposals in the report. He seemed to be occupied with other things, but no one really knew where he was heading or what his goals were for the organization over the short and medium term. Since Mr. Gauthier's report had been submitted, very little concrete progress has been made toward resolving the problems identified during the consultation. Mr. Gauthier was quite disconcerted and the other directors started to complain. It was the same old tune, as far as they were concerned. They were not surprised at this turn of events, as they had become accustomed to similar situations in the past. They deplored such situations, but felt powerless to resolve them. They were sorry that Mr. Gauthier, whom they respected, was caught up in the current quandary.

A few weeks had gone by when a meeting was called by the executive director. The meeting was held at a resort, making it less formal than regular management meetings. Before the meeting officially got underway, various members of the management team informally shared their impressions and unease concerning the follow-up to the strategic action plan submitted by Mr. Gauthier and the fact that Mr. Fillion seemed to be ignoring it.

Ms. Desgroseillers: How do you feel about it? Things haven't been going as planned with Mr. Fillion, have they?

Mr. Gauthier: Well, let's just say that things have taken an unexpected turn. I really don't know quite what to think.

Director of Finance:	Mr. Fillion is a bit of an odd case. He never ceases to surprise us.
Ms. Desgroseillers: **(apologetic and resigned)**	The way he acts makes no sense to me. He never intended to go ahead with the proposed changes. It was asking too much of him. He'll never change. That's just the way he is.

When Mr. Fillion arrived, everyone quit talking and the executive director took control of the meeting. No one raised the misgivings, which, a few minutes earlier, they had all been discussing. During the meeting, in spite of the fact that he had asked Mr. Gauthier to lead the meeting, Mr. Fillion frequently interrupted him, making him look bad and creating such a chill in the proceedings that no one else dared speak.

Mr. Gauthier:	To begin, I would like to briefly review the recommendations presented in the report as well as the planned actions. First…
Mr. Fillion:	Well, let's not waste time. All that is all well and good, but we have to get things done. Anyway, I'm not sure that your proposals are relevant.
Mr. Gauthier:	But it was my understanding that we had agreed to follow up on the concerns shared by the entire staff of the centre and…
Mr. Fillion:	That's just philosophizing. I'd like to hear from our two new management interns. So, what do you think of all this?
Intern 1:	Well, I don't really know what to say. I guess you're right…
Intern 2:	I just want to fit into the organization and contribute by meeting expectations…

In addition, Mr. Fillion unilaterally presented two newcomers to the management team who would be advising him on a new strategic action plan for the organization. The two people in question were trainees, with no real power over what should or would be done in the future. Nevertheless, Mr. Fillion seemed to give them symbolic, informal authority. Mr. Gauthier found this particularly humiliating, and other participants in the meeting shared his impression but kept quiet. A few months later, the two individuals were hired as members of upper management.

The meeting broke up somewhat abruptly, with Mr. Fillion leaving the room hastily; no one knew what to make of the follow-up to the report and action plan. The attendees are saddened by what had happened and Mr. Gauthier went home seething with anger. The executive director and the consultant had progressively less contact over time. They continued to have occasional contact on professional collaborations for several years without raising the question of the follow-up to the action plan.

CASE STUDY DISCUSSION QUESTIONS

1. How would you describe the organizational climate at Centre Ste-Clothilde two years after the merger? What is the broader context in which the change process took place?

2. How did Mr. Fillion fulfill his role as leader of the transformation process after the merger?

3. What were the distinctive characteristics of Mr. Fillion's leadership pattern?

4. What were the main weaknesses of the management team meeting at the resort? How would you describe Mr. Fillion's influence on the meeting?

5. If you were Mr. Fillion and you were truly willing to implement the action plan based on Mr. Gauthier's recommendations, how would you prepare and lead the management team meeting to ensure that it was effective? How could you foster more collaboration within the management team during the meeting?

6. What provoked the changes in the client–consultant relationship that led to a rejection of the consultant's suggestions? Did Mr. Fillion, the executive director, change his management style? Did he sincerely want the consultant's help? Was he disappointed by the consultant's report?

7. Why didn't the staff and managers dare speak up about their concerns? Did they fear reprisals? How would you describe the communication methods?

8. What do you personally think about this case? Do your own ideas concerning leadership, power, and communication influence your analysis of the case?

Conflict at the Academic Medical Center: Productivity Levels

By Carolyn Massello and Thomas Massello

PART ONE

Caroline Summer is a newly hired data analyst for an academic medical center (AMC). Jack Burke, the executive assistant to the chief of staff, has called Caroline into his office for an assignment.

"Caroline, I need you to look at the productivity of individual surgeons in each specialty and make recommendations based on your analysis." Caroline hesitated for a moment, wondering to herself what Jack would include in his consideration of "productivity," since productivity is a performance measure that includes both effectiveness and efficiency.

After a moment of thoughtful consideration, Caroline asked, "What specifically are you looking for? Productivity would include looking at how many cases they perform and how efficiently they are performed. What is the cost of our input versus the cost of the output—that sort of thing? Do you want to know how much revenue each surgeon generates compared to the salary he or she draws? Do you want to include how much each procedure costs us in the form of physician compensation compared to how much each procedure gets reimbursed? Do you want a ranking of how many procedures are performed by each surgeon sorted by specialty? If you can be more specific on what type of outcome and what level of detail you're after, I can get started on this right away."

Jack mulled this over for a minute or two, and then stated, "At this time, I would just like to know the caseload and salaries of each surgeon sorted by specialty. I want to know who our most productive surgeons are."

Caroline said, "I can have this information and my recommendations on your desk by the end of the day." As she left, she was thinking about what specific data fields she should pull before she starts to analyze the data. She would need to know number of cases completed, salary, and specialty, for sure. She wondered if the seniority of the surgeon would affect the results, so she included age as well.

Jack watched her leave and recalled his conversation earlier that morning with two of the newest surgeons. They were very stressed and complained that they felt they were being taken advantage of by the older surgeons, who appeared to be getting by without contributing much to their departmental workload. It just didn't seem equitable to them, and they were frustrated and angry. Jack assured them that their efforts were certainly appreciated and thanked them for their hard work. But it made him wonder if their complaint was valid. He knew he couldn't go to his boss with the complaint without data to back it up. He would know soon enough whether he needed to elevate their concerns.

Back in her office, Caroline prepared her database query to sort by specialty, caseload, salary, and age, in that order. When she had her printout, she began to look at the results to make meaning out of the data. She noticed that the youngest surgeons do the most cases, but the oldest surgeons are paid the highest salaries. She decided to check with Human Resources to see how the surgeons are compensated. She contacted Jenna Turner, the HR compensation specialist, who told her that the salary is strictly by seniority—not productivity—with a 1.5% raise across the board every 2 years.

CASE STUDY DISCUSSION QUESTIONS

1. Do you think the compensation policies are equitable?
2. What does equity theory tell us concerning its impact on motivation and productivity?
3. What, if any, recommendations would you make for changes in the compensation policies?
4. Discuss the organizational consequences of each recommendation, along with the consequences of making no changes.

PART TWO

Three years have passed since a new productivity pay component was added to the AMC's compensation system. Jack Burke, executive officer to the chief of staff, was perplexed. Despite giving bonuses to surgeons to increase their case-loads, the AMC is struggling with decreasing revenues and increasing costs. Jack called data analyst Caroline Summer for her assistance. When Caroline arrived, Caroline noticed that Pat Jurgins, the HR director, was present. Jack said, "Since we instituted a compensation policy change a few years back, the surgeons have been given a 'performance pay opportunity' of up to a 25% annual bonus based on the number of surgical cases performed in the previous year. Our caseloads are up; however, our bottom line hasn't improved. In fact, it's gotten worse. What went wrong? Could you two please revisit this issue and get back to me?" Caroline said, "Pat, let me pull some data and then you and I can meet to discuss what I find."

Caroline Summer was curious about what she might discover as she returned to her office to revisit the "productivity of surgeons by specialty" assignment to see if there is an improvement in surgeons' productivity. However, this time, Jack Burke has asked that she also include reimbursement revenue in her data pull to see if caseloads increased and, if so, whether revenues increased. Sure enough, when she pulled the data, she noticed an increase in the number of cases performed, but a decline in revenue. Closer analysis indicated a marked increase in the number of small cases being performed, but a decrease in the number of large (more highly reimbursed) cases. She also noticed that the more junior surgeons who had previously been identified as being most "productive" were now completing even more cases. It appeared that every surgeon had shifted their focus to completing many quick, easy cases to take advantage of the performance bonus. She dialed Pat Jurgins' number and arranged to meet.

CASE STUDY DISCUSSION QUESTIONS

1. What went wrong?
2. What recommendations would you make?
3. State the consequences that might ensue from each of your recommendations.

Budget Conflicts: Who Will Win?

By Carolyn Massello and Thomas Massello

Ginny Vaughn, the Chief Operating Officer (COO) of one of the city's hospitals, has called a staff meeting of all clinical department chiefs because she has received a task to cut operating costs by 10%. This means the hospital must cut $10 million just to break even. More cuts would be necessary to begin making a profit. The hospital has been running "in the red" for the past 3 years. Only through the benevolence of a wealthy donor has the hospital escaped closure. However, the donor has indicated an unwillingness to continue supporting a hospital that cannot balance its budget and is forcing the hospital to fend for itself. Vaughn announces that the Chief Executive Officer (CEO), Ben Hope, has said these cuts are absolutely necessary in order to keep the doors open for another year. Management understands this will cause hardship in light of already decreased profits and increased need for care at the facility.

The clinical department chiefs begin to discuss ways to attack the issue. The physical therapy chief tentatively suggested that all budgets should be cut by 10% to be perfectly fair. The pharmacy chief quickly offered to take a straight 10% cut as long as everyone else did the same. However, many chiefs (including internal medicine, orthopedics, and surgery) immediately interrupted and insisted their departments could not survive with any further cuts and stated that the cuts must come from the other departments. The pharmacy chief backed down and withdrew his proposal. The physical therapy chief, who was feeling very uncomfortable when the discussion turned into an argument, announced that he'd go along with whatever everyone else decided. The discussion had quickly become quite heated and nonproductive, so Vaughn interrupted and promised to provide the chiefs with the Department and Line Item Profit and Loss Worksheet within the hour. They were quiet for only a few moments and then resumed their animated discussion on which departments would bear the brunt of the budget cuts. One idea offered was to simply delete each line item that was experiencing a net loss of $2 million or less because that would add up to $10 million. However, that brought objections also. Ginny Vaughn again interrupted the heated discussion by announcing they had 10 days to present their ideas for bringing the hospital in line with this new tasking, and then she adjourned the meeting.

The clinical department chiefs returned to their departments to hold staff meetings to discuss ideas for budget cuts. Needless to say, the chiefs were very unhappy.

CASE STUDY DISCUSSION QUESTIONS

Role-Play: You will be assigned the role as either a department chief or a staff member for one of the clinical departments. Using the assigned conflict-handling modes, role-play your part.

Limited English Proficiency: Managing Beyond the Words in Long-Term Care Settings

By Carol Molinari and Mary Helen McSweeney-Feld

Rising Sun is an assisted living facility located in a suburb of a major Southeast city. The for-profit facility is part of a well-known chain of assisted living facilities with nonunionized staff. The regulations for assisted living facilities in the state Rising Sun operates are based on a social model of care, in which residents are relatively independent and autonomous and, thus, capable to choose services in their care plan to fit their needs.

Rising Sun serves a diverse clientele in terms of ethnicity and religion. About 10% of the residents are Asian with limited English proficiency (LEP). These residents speak one of three Asian dialects: Korean, Mandarin, or Cantonese. There are several members of the direct care nursing staff who speak one or more of these languages, but they only work during the daytime. In addition, approximately one-third of the direct care workers are Latino and speak Spanish. However about one-fourth of these direct care workers have limited English proficiency, thus restricting their ability to effectively communicate with non-Spanish-speaking clients and staff.

Recently, the corporate office of Rising Sun revised the organization's mission and vision statement to reflect its commitment to provide culturally sensitive and competent health services. It was noted that senior management took this strategic step to demonstrate the organization's response to the changing demographics of the senior market with the intent to attract more diverse elders to its facilities. However, the corporate office did not strategically plan for the needed investment to provide 24-hour translation services to its residents with limited English proficiency. As such, Rising Sun only had limited translation support from some staff members and family member volunteers to offer to its LEP residents, and a majority of these individuals were available only during the daytime. Moreover, the LEP among some of Rising Sun's Latino direct care staff create language barriers that have interfered with the delivery of care to its residents. There have been documented incidents where LEP Asian residents have misunderstood the verbal communications of both Latino and non-Latino caregivers, and these episodes have resulted in growing mistrust and conflicts among the staff and residents. Rising Sun's Director of Nursing, Mrs. Ryan, has asked the corporate office's human resources department for cultural training for her direct care workers so they can better communicate with the Asian residents, but no action has been taken yet on this request.

Mrs. Kim, a native Korean, has recently become a resident of the Rising Sun facility. Although Mrs. Kim is 88 years old, suffers from macular degeneration in both eyes and Parkinson's disease, which affects her balance and her ability to walk, she is a fairly strong and independent person. However, due to her limited English proficiency, Mrs. Kim has not made many friends or developed relationships with other residents. Mrs. Kim's family visits regularly, always bringing home-cooked Korean dishes for her. Occasionally, Mrs. Kim's family takes her home on weekends to visit her grandchildren. Her family members speak fluent English, and they serve as translators for Mrs. Kim when she needs to communicate to the facility's nursing staff.

Overall, she appears to be in a good psychological state and enjoying her stay at Rising Sun. After returning to Rising Sun late Sunday evening from a weekend visit with her family, Mrs. Kim decided to take a shower before retiring. When stepping out of the shower and bending over to pick up the towel that had fallen from the rack, Mrs. Kim lost her balance and fell to the floor. Although a little shaken from the fall, she managed to get back on her feet. Mrs. Kim did not push the call button in the bathroom for help, as she was embarrassed about the incident. Instead she telephoned her daughter to let her know that she had a "little accident" in the bathroom, but nothing to worry about. After the call with her daughter, Mrs. Kim watched her favorite TV show and then went to bed. The next morning, Rosa, the direct care worker assigned to Mrs. Kim, came into her room to assist her with dressing and taking her daily medications. Although Rosa and Mrs. Kim have a workable relationship, each finds it difficult to fully understand the other. Rosa is from Central America with a very heavy Spanish accent and Mrs. Kim has very limited English proficiency. Rosa immediately noticed that Mrs. Kim's left arm and knee and both hands were bruised. Rosa asks Mrs. Kim what happened during the night that caused the bruises. Mrs. Kim, still embarrassed by her "little accident" and having difficulty translating the experience, responds that she was "hit" when she went to the bathroom. Rosa looks for the nursing employee who speaks Korean to ask Mrs. Kim for more details about her bruises. Finding that the nurse is on vacation and concerned that Mrs. Kim may have been abused by a staff member during the night shift, Rosa reports to her supervisor, Ana Burke, Rising Sun's Assistant Director of Nursing that Mrs. Kim was "hit."

Ana Burke recently joined Rising Sun and is new to a supervisory position. She spent over a decade as a nurse working in various skilled nursing facilities, but this is her first management role and with a for-profit assisted living residence. Since she arrived a month ago, Ana has received several reports of arguments between direct care workers and the facility's Asian residents, but it has been difficult to determine who is at fault because of the language barriers. Upon hearing Rosa's report, Ana goes to Mrs. Kim's room and asks about the bruises on her arm, knee, and hands. Mrs. Kim, confused by her questions, repeats that she was "hit" in the bathroom. Ana quickly becomes worried about possible abuse by the evening direct care worker, Miguel. Fearing that Mrs. Kim's family may see the bruises and suspect that the staff is abusing their family member, Ana contacts Miguel to ask whether he was in Mrs. Kim's room the previous evening. Miguel responded that he had looked in on Mrs. Kim and asked if she needed anything. Mrs. Kim had responded "no." Miguel also related that no resident had pushed the call button the previous evening requesting assistance from him. Ana called the other nursing employees on staff the previous evening to confirm whether or not Mrs. Kim had pushed the call button for assistance. All responded that no requests from Mrs. Kim had been received.

Still concerned that this may be a case of elder abuse, Ana felt pressed to make a decision to protect her job and to minimize the potential risk of a lawsuit to the organization. Without consulting Ed Gordon, Rising Sun's care coordinator and primary contact for the residents' family members, Ana decides to suspend Miguel pending an investigation in the hopes of averting a formal complaint from Mrs. Kim's family. Later in the day, Ana relates the incident and her decision to suspend Miguel to Ed, pursuant to the organization's policy on episodes of this type. After hearing the story, Ed contacts Mrs. Kim's daughter to tell her that her mother may have had an argument with a direct care worker and that the staff member has been suspended pending an investigation. The daughter and son-in-law visit the facility later that evening. The family members talk to Mrs. Kim in Korean and find out that Mrs. Kim slipped and fell in her bathroom but was too embarrassed by the incident and confused by the questions asked to actually report the facts of what happened the previous evening. The family met with Ana and Ed the following day and related that Mrs. Kim had fallen and was not "hit" in the bathroom. While the incident was resolved within 24 hours, many of the LEP care staff remained worried. They feared that what happened to Miguel may happen to them.

CASE STUDY DISCUSSION QUESTIONS

1. Who is/are responsible for this dilemma? Explain.
2. Given the current limited translation support for residents by several daytime staff, discuss reasons why these staff may not be providing culturally and linguistically competent care to LEP residents.
3. Discuss ways to enhance staff's culturally sensitive communication with LEP residents.
4. When a language problem occurs with a resident that is noted by the direct care worker, propose a process that would help clarify and resolve the problem early.
5. Given the communication challenges posed by LEP clients and staff, how would you advise the supervisor to reduce the recurrence of this type of communication problem?
6. Discuss why cultural competence can be an effective strategic marketing tool to attract culturally diverse senior residents.

Discord in the Doctors' Domain

By Carole Paulson

Dr. Amy O'Donnell, an internist, was enjoying a cup of coffee in the doctors' lounge when her colleague, Dr. Jon Fisk stormed in, seething, "Did you see the email this morning from Fred?" Fred Jones, MD, was the chief medical officer for Lansdorf Health System–Southern Region, a large multispecialty physician practice. He was appointed medical director approximately a year ago when Lansdorf underwent a reorganization that resulted in many physicians being reassigned as directors of regional centers' medical and surgical departments. "Can you believe the memo states that the number of referrals to physicians within the system are too low, and we are to increase them by not referring patients to specialists not employed by Lansdorf—no ifs, ands, or buts about it? You know that I have established great professional relationships with many of the specialists in our community who are not in Lansdorf's network. They provide excellent care to my patients and always make sure I am in the communication loop regarding the patient's care."

"Are you kidding me?" exclaimed Amy. "Where does Fred get off sending out an email like that? Besides, he can't force us to keep our referrals within Lansdorf's network, can he? I was taught in medical school to do the right thing by your patients, and that means referring them to the doctors you trust to do the best job by them."

"There's more," quipped Jon. "Yesterday a few surgeons told me that they are not getting anywhere on their equipment requests. They need new surgical tables for bariatric cases and updated equipment for performing knee arthroscopies. When they try calling the new CEO, Dave Howard, to set up a meeting to discuss these issues, his secretary keeps putting them off."

"You know where all the money's going now—the heart clinic. We can kiss goodbye to any additional funding for our department in the foreseeable future," stated Amy flatly.

"I'm concerned," Jon said resignedly. "It just seems like ever since the reorganization, they've taken away all of our decision-making and just hand down 'edicts' for us to follow. Now we're supposed to take mandatory training for implementing the new EMR system. Where am I supposed to find time to do that? And I'm not convinced that the amount of money they're spending on it is worth it!"

At that moment, Dave Howard, MBA, Lansdorf Southwest's CEO, entered the lounge. After a few pleasantries, Dave asked Amy and Jon, "Would you be interested in participating in a panel discussion the local TV station wants to tape about the upcoming hospital expansion and new heart clinic and what it means for patient care and access? Both of you have high community recognition with your large practices, and it would put a good face on the project… you know…emphasizing primary care but with highly specialized acute care. You know that's where the money is for the system! We need to portray to the public how we work as a team to bring the highest level of care possible to the community."

Amy gulped just as Jon blurted out, "Dave, why don't you ask Fred Jones? He's the biggest cheerleader of the heart clinic!"

CASE STUDY DISCUSSION QUESTIONS

1. In a multispecialty system such as Lansdorf, identify general attitudes among physicians, both positive and negative, that can develop toward leadership.

2. Explain the physicians' perceptions of the motives of Lansdorf's administrators.

3. Regarding group dynamics, discuss the benefits and problems of multispecialty group practices. As an administrator, discuss strategies that will promote positive group interactions.

4. Explain why clinicians and administrators may develop conflicts regarding the operation of a health system and what strategies can be used for overcoming these conflicts.

Smyrna University Hospital Department Of Internal Diseases: Finally Walking Side By Side

By Gülem Atabay and Şebnem Penbek

SMYRNA UNIVERSITY

Smyrna University was founded as the fourth university of Turkey and the first university of the Aegean region, in accordance with the decision of the "Turkish Ministry of Education" with the requirement of law number 6595 in May 1955. The rapidly growing university was not only eliciting the well-educated workforce of the Aegean region but also it was the *only* research and education institution that contributed to the commercial, health, social, and cultural development of the Aegean region. Soon after the establishment of the Turkish Higher Education Council in 1981,[1] the university had separated into two universities.

[1] The Council of Higher Education was established in 1981. It is a fully autonomous supreme corporate public body responsible for the planning, coordination, governance and supervision of higher education within the provisions set forth in the Constitution (Articles 130 and 131) and the Higher Education Law (Law No. 2547). It has no political or governmental affiliation. At present, there are 139 universities in Turkey, 45 of which have foundation status: www.yok.gov.tr

While the Smyrna University continued its academic activities under the same name, a new government university named September University[2] was founded in 1982. This new university was the second state university of the Aegean region and founded with faculties that were transferred from Smyrna University.

Since 1982, Smyrna University has played a vital role during the establishment and development of the new universities. It played a fundamental position in education for the Aegean region, and in 2001, the university had become the guarantor for the foundation of the first private university in Izmir. Today Smyrna University represents Turkish universities in the "500 Leading Universities of World," and according to the evaluation of "University Ranking by Academic Performance," it is the fifth leading education institution in Turkey (http://www.hurriyetegitim.com/kurum/1004015144/izmir/onlisans-lisans/ege-universitesi.aspx).

Soon after the founding of the Smyrna University, it started its first academic year (1955–1956) with 90 students. Today, more than 50,000 students are educated in 11 faculties, 8 institutes, 13 vocational schools, 1 state conservatory, and 26 research centers. There are more than 3,200 academicians and 4,000 administrative staff employed by the university.

SMYRNA UNIVERSITY FACULTY OF MEDICINE AND HOSPITAL

Smyrna University Faculty of Medicine[3] was one of the first two faculties of Smyrna University, which was founded in 1955. During the early years of its foundation, education for fundamental sciences was conducted in several buildings, prefabs, and temporary structures around Bornova,[4] where other sub-units of faculty, including internal diseases, child care, and chest diseases were continuing education in buildings belonging to various hospitals around the city. In 1971, the university was moved to its permanent campus, which was located in Bornova, and since then, Smyrna University Faculty of Medicine has

---

[2] September University was founded on July 20, 1982. Seventeen previously founded institutions of Smyrna University and other various higher education institutes were affiliated to the university in the same year. The number of its academic units reached 41 by 1992. Presently September University owns 10 faculties, 5 schools, 5 vocational schools, 5 graduate schools, and 5 institutes: www.dcu.edu.rr

[3] Smyrna University Faculty of Medicine will be abbreviated as faculty for the rest of the case.

[4] Bornova is one of the counties of Izmir, which is located very close to the city center.

been maintaining its academic, research, and healthcare activities in this campus. In 1981, the university had restructured its academic activities as a result of the Higher Education Law numbered 2547 (Official Gazette No: 17506; Date: November 6, 1981; http://www.resmigazete.gov.tr/default.aspx).[5] With this new regulation, all departments of Smyrna University Faculty of Medicine were grouped under three major scientific divisions. Under each division were included major medical departments. The organizational structure of the faculty is demonstrated in **Appendix 26-A**.

Beside its academic activities as a medical school, the faculty has been sustaining healthcare services under the name of Smyrna University Faculty of Medicine Hospital (www.egehastane.ege.edu.tr). All of the academic staff in the university are, at the same time, working as physicians in the Smyrna University Faculty of Medicine Hospital. Therefore "Smyrna University Hospital" is often referred to as a "university hospital" whose duties are well ahead of just patient care as:

1. **Medical Education**: Training current and future doctors and resident physicians, and provide clinical education.
2. **Research Center**: Creating new knowledge through conducting basic science and clinical investigation.
3. **Patient Care**: Delivering comprehensive healthcare services to patients through one or more hospitals.

As a result of all these duties, Smyrna University Faculty of Medicine Hospital always keeps in track with the recent development in patient care and treatments. Today, the healthcare services are operated in three different hospitals stretched through the campus as:

1. Smyrna University Faculty of Medicine Children's Hospital
2. Smyrna University Faculty of Medicine Adult's Hospital
3. Smyrna University Faculty of Medicine Oncology (Cancer Care) Hospital

The future physicians who completed their theoretical "clinical education" are then tasked to work as interns in the university hospital. Among these interns who preferred to continue their career in internal diseases will be the future members of Department of Internal Diseases of the "adult hospital" of the university.

---

[5] Date of enactment: November 4, 1981. Published in the Turkish Official Gazette No: 17506; Date: November 6, 1981. For the full body of act, see the official site of Turkish Official Gazette http://www.resmigazete.gov.tr/default.aspx. Please refer to http://www.cepes.ro/services/pdf /Turkey3.pdf for the English translation.

Department of Internal Diseases (DID)[6] has been developing patient care services since 1958, and today it is operating in 4 different buildings stretched through the campus with 52 academic staff, 100 medical staff, 65 nurses, and 370 employees. DID was the largest clinic of the hospital and, moreover, in terms of academic members, it would not be an exaggeration to compare the department with the other faculties of the university. The place of DID in the organizational structure can be seen in Appendix 26-A.

INTERNAL DISEASES DEPARTMENT NEEDED A NEW HEAD, EARLY ELECTIONS, AND AN UNEXPECTED CANDIDATE: PROF. DR. SELIM

Since the establishment of the DID as a separate department under the Medical Sciences Division,[7] there were nine individuals elected in succession for the head position. Prof. Dr. Selim acted as vice head for the Department of Internal Diseases during the illness of the ninth head, Prof. Dr. Gurhun. Unfortunately, the illness was so deleterious that Selim's temporary agency position had lasted for nearly a year. In that trial period, he had found that he was ready for responsibility and that there was much to be done in the DID. Acquiring the head position would enable him to impose his ethical codes on the team of DID, including patients, nurses, residents, and medical staff. After the mourning of Prof. Dr. Gurhun, Prof. Dr. Selim decided to stand as a candidate for the head of DID. However, he had discovered that people were ready to protest and were not very pleased with his candidacy. There had been one other candidate, but Selim won the race with a one vote margin.

This large department had been managed by Prof. Dr. Selim since 2002. He felt at home there, having spent time in DID as a physician, an academician, and a manager simultaneously for most of the time. He had been working in the faculty since his graduation from the Smyrna University Faculty of Medicine in 1981. His admirable commitment to the faculty was not only because he had been a member of the faculty for 30 years but it was also because his father—the mayor of Izmir in 1955—was the one who signed the foundation protocol and worked hard to establish the university in its early years.

---

[6] The name of the "Department of Internal Diseases" will be abbreviated as DID for the rest of the case.

[7] As mentioned in the text, previously the faculty had been restructured with law number 2547 and all academic activities were grouped under 3 major divisions.

Both the local and national press had started to talk about the changes in the DID of Smyrna University Hospital. What was happening there? In order to evaluate the antecedents and consequences of this change under the supervision of the new head, a meeting was arranged with Prof. Dr. Selim.

When the meeting started it was nearly 7 p.m. in the evening. Although a tired man, who would not be able to speak for more than 30 minutes was expected, Prof. Dr. Selim was standing with an inspiring smile and was full of vim. He greeted the interviewers warmly and made sure that everybody was comfortable in this hospitable room. The room was elegant and cozy, with one of the walls decorated with photos of previous department heads. He offered tea and cookies and smoothly gave permission to record the whole interview, which took nearly 2 hours.

As of 2011, Prof. Dr. Selim had been continuing his third period as DID's head. Since his first days, he spent hours walking around the patient rooms, talking to them and listening as they poured out their grievances. He nearly spent all his time at the hospital. He said, "We are more than physicians. The white coat we wear means treating all patients equally, regardless of their status, race, gender, and any other features." Patients were not his only concern; he also stayed in touch with students, academics, and medical and administrative staff of DID. It sometimes took him nearly an hour to reach to his office from the other end of the "20 meter" corridor that leads to his own consulting room, because on the way he answered any question directed to him, shook each hand offered, and listened to any problems without any refusal. He stated that it was very important for him to be in touch with everybody around him believing that he could learn important details about the department that might have been missed through formal communication. For example, in one of his long walks, Prof. Dr. Selim felt completely helpless with what he heard about a promising young lady: she had abandoned her medical education in her second year due to some financial problems. This event triggered Prof. Dr. Selim, and a charitable fund was established in the faculty that supported the education of poor students. With voluntary contributions from the doctors, nearly 230 students received scholarships from this fund in the last 10 years. However, each scholarship student was required to work for faculty where needed according to their academic programs and competencies. Some worked in the library and others helped the administrative staff with new technology such as computers, thus these students were aware that they received this scholarship in return for their efforts.

THE MAIN PROBLEMS OF DEPARTMENT OF INTERNAL DISEASES: WHEN PROF. DR. SELIM HAD ACQUIRED THE HEAD POSITION

In the very early days of Prof. Dr. Selim's promotion as head, there were several problems to be addressed at the DID. The staff, even the doctors, avoided Prof. Dr. Selim, choosing to walk in the opposite direction when they saw him. By doing this, they were barring the most important communication channel that Prof. Dr. Selim prefers, face to face. Besides, no one had taken the responsibility for what they did. The problems were all around but nobody had tried to solve them. Therefore, DID was unable to find solutions and fell into a vicious circle where the same problems repeatedly emerged.

On the other hand, everybody was complaining to one another about a variety of problems at DID. Whether from habit or not, nurses, employees, and doctors—thus, nearly all members of DID—were complaining about each other. Some were trivial but some were destructive to their relationships, such that personnel were criticizing and comparing working hours, attendance periods, reward systems, promotions, and so forth. Academic promotion of some physicians had been delayed for years for personal reasons in the department. Although the procedures and requirements for the promotions must follow the faculty laws and regulations, these rules were ignored in most of the cases. However, according to Prof. Dr. Selim, any kind of academic appellation could not be under the control of one person; rather, it depended on the merit of that person who decisively and worked hard for it. Thus the academic promotion of doctors could not be directed by personal closeness to the head, or value attributed to their "surnames" by the society.

Another challenge faced by Dr. Selim was in financing the department. The Turkish government allocated a determined amount of financial funds for hospitals. Each hospital then allocated those financial funds among departments. However, the financial funds that had been designated to DID had never been a sufficient amount to maintain Prof. Dr. Selim's ideal department. The overall physical structure of the DID was not sufficient to satisfy contemporary health services. The patient rooms were inadequate to meet the moderate hospitalization services, and the equipment supplied to the administrative and academic staff was so limited that it was even slowing down the daily routine of the department. The assistant doctors, doctors, and nurses were not allowed to use the printers in the department to print their educational materials, such as academic papers, due to the limited amount of paper supplied to DID which was to be used for routine administrative activities and for patient reports.

THE CONSEQUENCES OF MANAGEMENT ALTERATION AND LEADERSHIP STYLE: THINGS STARTED TO CHANGE AT DID

This section summarizes significant phrases from the interview with Prof. Dr. Selim that highlights the work he did at the Department of Internal Diseases.

The professor's agency position for one year was a great chance for him to draw up his road map. During this period he saw the deficiencies of the department. Therefore, the main concern of Prof. Dr. Selim was to make radical changes in the department when he decided to be a candidate for the head position as the overall management principles were not overlapping with the working and ethical principles held by Prof. Dr. Selim. As soon as the professor became the head of DID, his main concern was showing the deficiencies of the current state. Organizational members were no longer seen as negative factors; rather they were the solution centers. This new role model, who was fair, hardworking, devoted, and open-minded, started to inspire the whole department. The winds of change were felt at all levels of the department. At the end of his first year as the head, the number of complaint petitions had started to decrease, and in the last 9 years, no petitions were forwarded to head of the DID. As it was mentioned earlier, for some of the academic promotions, the faculty laws and regulations were ruled out; however, during those 9 years, no one had lost any academic promotion due to a conflict of interest or personal reasons.

With Prof. Dr. Selim, they started to feel free to visit the head office whenever something went wrong within the DID, knowing that the door was always open to them with a genuine listener behind it. He allowed the organizational members to take active roles in decision-making processes and kept communication channels open all the time. He aimed to raise the awareness of organizational members about improper applications. Therefore, members of DID were ready to take responsibility for their mistakes, believing that problems needed a solution for the well-being and success of DID. At last they were walking side by side in the corridors. The best example of the positive effects in the DID could easily be seen from the latest newspaper account entitled "Halil Ibrahim Library Lends Books to Patients in DID at Smyrna University Hospital." An employee named

Halil Ibrahim was distributing books to patients in DID at the end of working hours from his "mobile library." He had been working as a sanitary in DID for 15 years when Prof. Dr. Selim became the head of the department. He tried to distribute books and newspapers to patients in the past but he could not continue with his limited income. Soon after he shared his idea with Prof. Dr. Selim, he was given a book cart where he could place books and walk around the corridors easily. Prof. Dr. Selim also started a second-hand book campaign for the Halil Ibrahim Mobile Library. With this campaign, all nurses, doctors, academicians, and even patient relatives brought books to him. There was no such service in any other department of the faculty; moreover, not in any other private or public hospital around Izmir. All these examples were major indicators of the multidimensional effects of all staff, from the head to the janitor, on the development of organizations with effective projects and valuable staff contributions.

Soon after he started to work as the head, he began to look for new financial resources for the department, although it was not his area of responsibility. The initial funds raised were used to meet the daily administrative needs of the department. Thus, for example, scarcity of paper for both assistants and administrative staff was no longer a problem for the department.

As mentioned earlier, in DID, the patient rooms had not been meeting the requirements of modern physical health conditions, with 6–8 beds in less than 20 square meters and a communal toilet on each floor. In fact, this is the leading problem of the Turkish healthcare sector. Thus, as of 2007 in Turkey, the total number of doctors per 100,000 people is only 123. However, this number is 567 in Italy, 330 in France, and 287 in Armenia. On the other hand, the total number of patient beds per 10,000 people is 25 (http://www.biyoetik.org.tr/files/hekim%20sayisi%20yetersiz%20mi.pdf:19.09.2011), which means that in Turkey the attainability and fair distribution of healthcare services was very limited. The need of beds for patients was a more tremendous problem for university hospitals where nearly 60–70% of all teaching hospital patients entered because of serious illnesses that required long-term treatment (Yiğit, & Ağırbaş, 2004). Therefore in order to increase the number of patients treated, the hospital administration preferred to increase the number of patient beds per room. However, on the other side, this increase decreased the quality of healthcare services supplied to patients. As mentioned above, Smyrna Hospital was one of those university hospitals that experienced the similar patient bed problem because of the huge gap between supply and demand of healthcare services in Turkey. Probably the solution found for rooms has been the leading contribution of Prof. Dr. Selim to both DID and the Faculty of Medicine. Prof. Dr. Selim's offer for two-bed patient rooms with air conditioning and a private toilet had initially increased the tension in the academic committee at those days where the general belief was to hospitalize as many patients as possible regardless of the number of nurses and health conditions. In Turkey the majority of the hospitals tried to increase the number of patients treated and therefore, regardless of the insufficient healthcare services due to the inadequate number of doctors and nurses they employed, they chronically invested in increasing the number of beds. However, Prof. Dr. Selim interpreted that, "I always believe the number of nurses is the main determinant of the number of patients as each person deserves the best condition for hospitalizing."

With the help of donations and different sources of financial aid, DID started to make modifications in patient rooms. At each stage of construction, the professor had asked for the assistance of end users of these modifications. During the construction of new patient rooms, he always collaborated with the organizational members, knowing that they were the ones who would work under renewed conditions. For example, for the location, ergonomics, and decoration for nursing centers, he held long discussions with the nurses and modified the existing centers according to the feedback he received from them. Soon after they had started to renovate the patient rooms, the microbiology department complained to the Dean about the modification, accusing the DID of causing infection for hospitalizing patients. The unavoidable fallout of such modifications like the smell and dust, and chemicals such as paints and polishes were impeding the hygiene of the entire building where DID operated. Prof. Dr. Selim stated, "I am sure that they were all right about their complaints. Although we have taken all the necessary precautions, the dust and the noise spread around had bothered the other departments. Especially the microbiology department was very sensitive to it, as they were operating on the ground floor of our building." The Dean, who considered that the arguments of Prof. Dr. Selim were reasonable, had not taken any legal action about the complaints of the microbiology department, and the renovation continued. This was the very best proof of the administrative support given to Prof. Dr. Selim for his longstanding efforts to transform DID into an enhanced place for both patients and healthcare staff.

The hospital administration assigned additional rooms for DID in the existing building. However, all these rooms needed similar modifications. As mentioned earlier, due to insufficient financial position, DID had to raise its own funds for the modification of these rooms. This time the required fund was reasonably more than the hospital could support on its own, therefore Prof. Dr. Selim had talked to the rector about his ideas and got the permission to take this subject to the Izmir representative of the governing political party. By chance, the Izmir representative was trying to contact Prof. Dr. Selim for a health problem at that time, and he promised to help him; although his heavy schedule did not allow him to head the fundraising drive himself. Prof. Dr. Selim continued to search for other sources of donations and contacted two of Izmir's philanthropic families. Both agreed to help Prof. Dr. Selim and did more than they promised to do at the very beginning of the project. One of these families granted to help him just because Dr. Ali Selim, Prof. Dr. Selim's father, was the person whom the family admired. Prof. Dr. Selim added that "There again I felt the admirable inheritance I took over from my father. Thank god I had those wonderful traces and the powerful shadow of my father in my life." So the modification of patient rooms was finished and ever since then the DID had been operating in two floors with facilities that best suit proper health conditions and the demands of patients.

> ...then the rooms were ready to meet the proper health conditions. Thus, there was no doubt that we made a successful change! But it was just the beginning and unfortunately the easiest part of an organizational change. I am very sure that all those changes might turn out to be a waste of time, energy, and money if the staff would not appreciate the things done in the department. That was the newest and the most difficult problem of our department that I had experienced. When I acquired the head position I also acquired the team that I have been working with. They were sharing the vision and principles of the previous head and they were far away from adopting my principles and sharing my desire for change.

As Prof. Dr. Selim stated, in Turkey, in governmental bodies, when you acquired a position you also acquired the staff. Thus, the managers were not involved in the decision process of hiring and selecting the people they were going to work with. Furthermore, they had to choose among candidates that were sent to them whenever a position had to be filled. However, he believed that sustainable development could only be achieved if and only if the new structure of the DID was internalized by all members of the department. So he kept in touch with the organizational members, listened to them, and tried to be a solution partner for problems in DID.

Despite the insufficient HR policies discussed above, the head nurse, Alaz, was his instant counselor and best supporter during those hard days. He vaguely recalled their first meeting and how he tested her personality and compatibility with his ethical codes.

> *There was no doubt that Alaz was a very young "head nurse"; however, she was the one whom I was looking for. The smile on her face and the light in her eyes gave me an instant impression of an honest personality. Her wide sense of perspective under different circumstances and sense of justice soon justified my first thoughts about her.*

Thus the harmony between them had triggered Prof. Dr. Selim to think of transferring daily routine businesses to the control of the head nurse. From then, only strategic projects and/or complex problems related to DID were discussed with the DID's head. DID was no longer a place where "the head orders and the rest obeys." Prof. Dr. Selim said that:

> *Her existence in the head nurse position made me feel comfortable because from the "director's chair" things might have been blurred or you saw them only from the point that they were shown to you. Soon after I delegated the leading of a reasonable amount of daily routines to Alaz, I realized that by doing this I was both indirectly kept in touch with the nurses and their problems, and caught any detail that may have been missed if I had worked alone. Finally, I have created an organizational climate of my dreams that was very supportive and open to new ideas for better conditions.*

Prof. Dr. Selim was not *only* executing the administrative duties, rather he was a full-time physician and an academician. He carefully considered university education and its major objectives. Education could be achieved through transferring knowledge, encouraging the students by developing their competencies, and enlightening the exact nature of attitudes and behaviors. The first two could easily be done by words, but the latter could only be achieved by example.

The following quotation from the interview proved that Prof. Dr. Selim was the follower of the opinion mentioned above:

> *Today we are living in the age of technology, where everybody could easily access knowledge. So, successful educators or managers helped their followers to use the knowledge and transfer it into competencies that distinguished them from others. I have been working very hard to make DID a better place for all stakeholders. We renovated the rooms, redesigned the job descriptions, reorganized the working conditions, and reapplied the rules and principles of the hospital. The best thing about all those changes is that, this team is ready to survive in this new system. Thus if I leave the position today, without any question, they will allow the sustainability of "new DID." This is not because I established a perfect system; rather it is*

all about the cooperation and coordination. My major role during this great transition was distributing justice and sustaining the fair progress of the change. Today, I am very pleased with the atmosphere we finally achieved. However, I now started to think that there is a life outside the walls of this clinic, which is very precious. I have been devoted myself to DID but doing this caused me to miss the life out there.

CASE STUDY DISCUSSION QUESTIONS

1. Using the "Lewin's Force Field Analysis," illustrate the change process in DID.

2. Analyze the change process of DID according to the most appropriate model(s) of a "Planned Organizational Change" giving examples from the case.

3. According to John Kotter, there are eight pitfalls to be avoided for the success of a change program. Discuss whether Prof. Dr. Selim made any of these mistakes, supporting your answer with examples from the case.

4. Discuss the leadership practices of the Prof. Dr. Selim during the change process of DID. Which leadership theory (theories) do you think best describe(s) his leadership style?

5. According to the major concerns and definitions of an organizational change process, what may happen to DID if Prof. Dr. Selim is not a candidate in the coming election?

REFERENCES

Ankara Medical Chamber—health policy commission. (March, 2007). Insufficient number of doctors in Turkey! Retrieved from http://www.biyoetik.org.tr/files/hekim%20sayisi%20yetersiz%20mi.pdf:19.09.2011

Ege Üniversitesi. Retrieved from http://www.hurriyetegitim.com/kurum/1004015144/izmir/onlisans-lisans/ege-universitesi.aspx. Accessed October 30, 2012.

Ege Üniversitesi. Retrieved from www.egehastane.ege.edu.tr

Official Gazette. Higher Education Law numbered 2547. Official Gazette No: 17506; Date: November 6, 1981. Retrieved from http://www.resmigazete.gov.tr/default.aspx

Yiğit, V. and Ağırbaş, I. (2004). Effect of Capacity Use Ratio on Costs in Hospitals: An Application in the Ministry of Health Tokat Maternity and Child Care Hospital, *Hacettepe Sağlık İdaresi Dergisi, 7*:2.

Appendix A

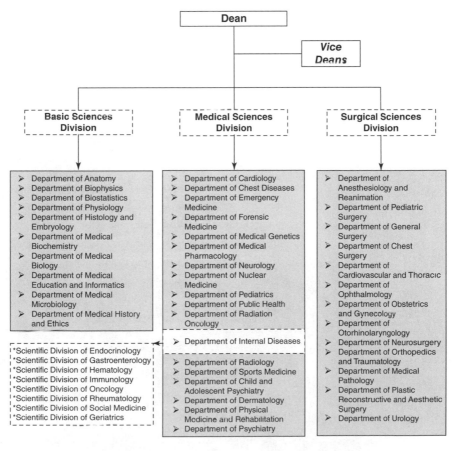

Dean	
	Vice Deans

Basic Sciences Division

- Department of Anatomy
- Department of Biophysics
- Department of Biostatistics
- Department of Physiology
- Department of Histology and Embryology
- Department of Medical Biochemistry
- Department of Medical Biology
- Department of Medical Education and Informatics
- Department of Medical Microbiology
- Department of Medical History and Ethics

*Scientific Division of Endocrinology
*Scientific Division of Gastroenterology
*Scientific Division of Hematology
*Scientific Division of Immunology
*Scientific Division of Oncology
*Scientific Division of Rheumatology
*Scientific Division of Social Medicine
*Scientific Division of Geriatrics

Medical Sciences Division

- Department of Cardiology
- Department of Chest Diseases
- Department of Emergency Medicine
- Department of Forensic Medicine
- Department of Medical Genetics
- Department of Medical Pharmacology
- Department of Neurology
- Department of Nuclear Medicine
- Department of Pediatrics
- Department of Public Health
- Department of Radiation Oncology
- Department of Internal Diseases
- Department of Radiology
- Department of Sports Medicine
- Department of Child and Adolescent Psychiatry
- Department of Dermatology
- Department of Physical Medicine and Rehabilitation
- Department of Psychiatry

Surgical Sciences Division

- Department of Anesthesiology and Reanimation
- Department of Pediatric Surgery
- Department of General Surgery
- Department of Chest Surgery
- Department of Cardiovascular and Thoracic
- Department of Ophthalmology
- Department of Obstetrics and Gynecology
- Department of Otorhinolaryngology
- Department of Neurosurgery
- Department of Orthopedics and Traumatology
- Department of Medical Pathology
- Department of Plastic Reconstructive and Aesthetic Surgery
- Department of Urology

Location of "Internal Diseases Department" within the Organizational Structure of Smyrna University Faculty of Medicine

Bionix Diagnostics' Organizational Culture and Business Imperatives

By Clifford R. Perry

BIONIX AND ITS CORPORATE CULTURE

On July 1, 2010, shortly after celebrating her 20th year with the company, Juliana Mitre, Bionix Diagnostics' chief executive officer and chairman, proudly announced record company financial results at the annual meeting in Ft. Lauderdale, Florida. Mitre had just completed her 4th and most successful year in this top post, and was beaming with pride over the outstanding results she publicly attributed to employees and her top leadership team who spearheaded the performance of Bionix's 4th strategic business units. The company easily exceeded analysts' earnings expectations and literally blew the cover off their estimates of margins and revenues and their projections of cash flow for the coming fiscal year.

At the same time, the company also announced that employee wage dividends and management bonuses, while not yet distributed, would reach record levels this year. These payouts would once again demonstrate the company's commitment to profit sharing, which formed the cornerstone of its pay-for-performance culture. Just as important, Mitre's public recognition of employee and management contributions would reflect Bionix's company values and its reputation for acknowledging and celebrating outstanding employee performance. Positive reinforcement was a key motivation strategy at Bionix, and the company culture and organizational behavior it shaped continued to produce outstanding financial performance.

STRATEGIC DIVERSIFICATION TO ACCELERATE GROWTH

One of Bionix' business units, the Dylan Medical Instrumentation Division, located in upstate New York, contributed significantly to Bionix's increased operating earnings and margins during the past year. Two years ago, Juliana Mitre had personally negotiated the difficult acquisition of Dylan, then a NYSE listed manufacturing and marketing company, because she believed that Dylan could contribute to Bionix's long-term profitability goals. Dylan was recognized as an industry leader that develops and produces sophisticated diagnostic medical devices used by biomedical and research professionals. The $2.2 billion acquisition of Dylan, although considered expensive by some Wall Street analysts, was a good strategic fit and complemented the three other business units that formed the new Bionix Diagnostics company. Mitre stated during the announcement to the press: "I firmly believe that Dylan Medical's company values that vaulted it to the annual survey list of *Business Magazine's* 100 Best Companies to Work For are similar to Bionix's and will make Dylan a seamless fit with our extended company." As Mitre would soon learn, however, her assumptions about values and cultural fit were based on a cursory corporate intelligence report filled with scanty anecdotal evidence that, as she would later admit, could not have been further from reality.

Over the years, Dylan had successfully established itself as a determined and respected competitor as a medical diagnostic systems provider within the healthcare industry. Its patents, R&D capability, and reputation for fast-to-market production helped to establish its brand leadership as a manufacturer of technologically innovative, highly reliable biomedical analysis devices. Its earnings margins were the envy of the industry. In particular, the company was best known for its highly profitable X-omatic D-Laser Computer, a reliable, cost-effective diagnostic instrument used in the detection and diagnosis of various lung related ailments and diseases. Currently, the D-Laser Computer enjoys a 32% market share, well ahead of its primary competitor, Bradley Systems, Inc.

DYLAN'S D-LASER COMPUTER CONTRIBUTION SHORTFALL

Although Dylan's contributions to Bionix's recent annual financial performance goals were significant, the large Dylan division that designed and manufactured the D-Laser Computer fell far short of its annual performance targets. This highly successful flagship product used in health clinics and doctor's offices throughout the Northeast failed to meet profit contribution commitment targets. Division performance and profitability targets are taken very seriously at Bionix, and continued variances are not acceptable. Juliana Mitre was known for her impatience and determination to replace managers who failed to deliver. Bionix's pay-for-performance culture demanded accountability. In fact, she frequently stressed that "Bionix's commitment to increasing shareholder value is paramount to our success as a company." It was clear that remedial action was required, and quickly.

The shortfall has been pinpointed to significant X-omatic D-Laser Computer equipment reliability problems, and the subsequent conflict within Dylan's operating units resulting from the efforts to resolve these problems. The conflict was escalating and was now not only inhibiting progress toward resolving the reliability problem, but was taking on a life of its own.

While determining the precise impact on profitability caused by the D-Laser Computer problem, Miter used the following table of performance results during a Bionix financial planning session to illustrate the impact this situation had on Dylan's overall financial performance.

REPUTATION AT RISK

The recurring set of technical problems with the D-Laser Computer scanning and recording mechanisms have required field servicing, causing downtime lasting 2–3 days. Hospitals and clinics are threatening to return the D-Laser Computers, begin litigation against the Dylan Medical Instrumentation company, and purchase similar diagnostic equipment from Bradley Systems, Inc. The situation was reaching a very high profile and was recently covered in Bloomberg's Market News. It stated that "while Bionix's acquisition of Dylan has apparently

Table 27-1 Dylan Medical Instrumentation Division—Three Year
Financial Results

	2008 ($M)	2009 ($M)	2010 ($M)
Revenue	$532	$534	$518
Gross profit margin	37.4%	36%	34%
SADA expenses	167	165	161
Operating income	31	26	23
Net income after tax	38	27	25
Net margin	5.6%	7.2%	5.1%
Total assets	524	54	504
COGS	n.a.	n.a.	n.a.
Total equity	332	341	310
Return on equity	11.5%	15.0%	7.9%
Operating cash flow	36.1	38.5	24.7
R&D expenses	24	23	23
Employees (thousands)	2.5	2.6	2.7

paid off, some Northeast regional hospitals have migrated to rival Bradley Systems products in response to alleged quality control problems with Dylan's diagnostic equipment."

Since Dylan had built its reputation on being an ISO 9001 certified manufacturer of high quality products and had recently received a prestigious customer service award from the leading trade publication covering the medical device industry, the negative publicity in the press and failed attempts at resolving the source of customer complaints were having a serious impact on the assumed harmony, cooperation, and teamwork previously enjoyed by employees and management within Dylan Medical. Frustration and blame fixing were emerging almost daily.

Gregg Johnston, vice president of Dylan's Manufacturing and Service Division, felt responsible for high priority action "to determine the causes of this significant reliability problem and to turn this profitability situation around, and quickly." Gregg has responsibility for the Apparatus Division, the Distribution Center, and the Customer Equipment Service Division (CESD). Johnston was recruited personally by CEO Juliana Mitre shortly after the Dylan acquisition based on his industry reputation for leadership, problem-solving by fostering teamwork, and expertise with problem business turnaround situations.

When he joined the Dylan team, Johnston was enthusiastic and upbeat with his vision for his division, the heartbeat of Dylan Medical: "The work ethic and culture I find in our division positions us for unbeatable productivity and quality competitiveness within our industry and will form the basis of teamwork, collaboration, and trust that will significantly increase the quality of worklife throughout our division."

Johnston, together with James Wright, VP of Dylan Administration, and Frank Lopez, VP of Dylan Marketing, report to Dylan's president, Kathryn Mendes. While Wright and Lopez had been with Dylan only a few years, Mendes joined Dylan as an electrical engineer the year before Dylan issued its IPO and progressively moved up the ranks. After the acquisition, Juliana Mitre appointed her president of Dylan Medical.

THE ORGANIZATION

The design and manufacture of all Dylan Medical's equipment is done within its large-scale Apparatus Division located within a few miles of its corporate headquarters. This division is headed up by George Bay, a stern nuts-and-bolts former mechanical engineer who got his degree during night school while working for Dylan for 25 years. Reporting to George is Tim McDough, director of Quality Control; Evan Groth, Manufacturing Engineering; and Sue Chavez, senior manager of Product Design. While McDough and Groth did not like confrontations, Sue Chavez was known to "lack sensitivity and diplomacy" when dealing with other Dylan managers. In addition, Jim Langworthy is the director of Manufacturing, Production, and Inventory Control; and Fran Homberg is the director of Human Resources.

The Customer Equipment Service Division reports to Roger Felston, a tough-minded hot-tempered manager who rose through the ranks as a service engineer.

Felston, who harbored a lot of company resentments, was known for his "quick temper and quick-to-blame" attitude, but otherwise was a crackerjack manager who earned customer respect for quickly responding to their equipment service complaints.

Bay and Felston report to Gregg Johnston, who gave both a lot of autonomy. Carlos Rios who has been recently promoted to director of the Distribution Center also reports to Johnston, although he was still on probation until he proves that he can handle his new enlarged responsibilities. He was tentative in his decisions and displayed a risk-averse disposition during his first few months as director. All three reports are soon scheduled to formulate leadership development plans required of all high-level managers at Bionix Diagnostics. It is Johnston's responsibility to enable, guide, and encourage the professional development of these managers: "I am committed to provide leadership development opportunities for my direct reports that will ensure their future success and contributions to Dylan Medical."

ACTION, ASSERTIONS, AND EMERGING ISSUES

When news of this recurring field problem affecting Dylan's largest customer base reached Dylan's president's office, Johnston was summoned and agreed to provide a comprehensive report detailing the source of the problem, and, more importantly, its remedy. He immediately formed a small task force to investigate.

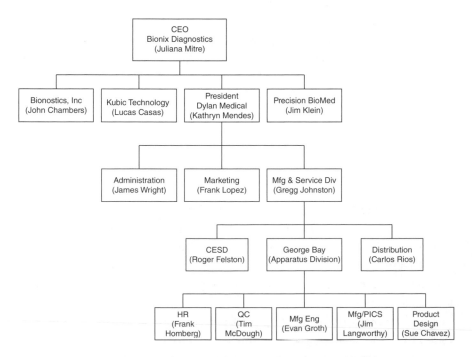

FIGURE 27-1 Bionix Diagnostics Organizational Chart

After a series of interviews with Bay, his direct reports, and Felston, it became apparent that there was serious conflict among the Apparatus Division, the Customer Equipment Service Division, and the Distribution Center. Roger Felston, who was in direct contact with the irate customers, was feeling heat that he felt was unfair to his team, which had recently been recognized for excellence in repair processes based on Malcom Baldrige Quality Standards. Felston claimed that Bay's Apparatus Division was responsible for producing inferior quality resulting in the D-Laser failure in the field, subjecting his unit to respond to repeated D-Laser Computer system breakdowns. Additionally, Felston suggested that McDough's Quality Control group was not adequately inspecting the D-Laser from Manufacturing for reliability beyond the minimal warranty period. Felston also hinted that Carlos Rios's transportation unit within Distribution was lax at implementing safety procedures to ensure the safe delivery of these ultra-sensitive D-Laser Computers. George Bay, although he would not state it publicly, agreed with Felton's assertion about Rios's transportation unit.

Because he felt his annual performance appraisal and subsequent bonus were going to be in serious jeopardy, Felston has gone on record with his riff with George Bay in the Apparatus Division and his commitment to identify root causes of this serious D-Laser breakdown problem. Felston said, "The manufacturing unit and its managers need more focus on improving the performance circle of cost, quality, and cycle-time, and less on developing a leadership style of managing upwards, scapegoating, and other stuff." Bay's resentment, on the other hand, was based on Felston's failure to recognize the Apparatus Division's recent award in Six Sigma Quality and its ISO 9001 quality management system certification.

The task force's interview process also revealed that within the Apparatus Division there was significant conflict between organizational subunits. This was particularly disturbing to George Bay: "We need to realize that we're on the same team and stop quibbling and conjecturing about others' faults." For example, the Quality Control Unit was pointing fingers suggesting the reliability problem originated in the materials department within the Manufacturing unit. Meanwhile, Manufacturing Engineering claimed that the Product Design unit was not designing a D-Laser Computer based on specifications amenable to well-designed, cost-effective, reliable product manufacturability.

In addition, the series of problem solving interviews revealed there was more conflict among four of the five Apparatus Division operational units.

For example, Jim Langworthy, the surly manufacturing manager who was recently removed from probation for insubordination, is accusing Sue Chavez's Product Design unit of designing an electronic control board internal to the

D-Laser Computer that has unnecessarily complex assemblies and ultra-thin plastic components that make it difficult to reliably manufacture. "Design is pretty straight-forward if you don't care about the cost constraints and quality demands of manufacturing" was a favorite mantra of Langworthy. McDough in Quality Control agrees with Langworthy and reports that his team has had frequent rejects when testing the control boards. Upon retesting, however, they report that some of the boards passed inspection. In a counter argument, Chavez claims that Evan's manufacturing technology team constructed a control board assembly fixture that can subject the board's circuitry to pressure that can negatively affect its feedback function. She also has asserted that Langworthy's obsessive focus on labor efficiency and cost control is jeopardizing the integrity of the circuit board assembly process. Chavez has told him "the work time standards for careful assembly need to be increased or the insertion of the safety control integrated circuit in the small delicate electronic subassembly board will possibly default." He neither acknowledged her warning nor made any change that would jeopardize his commitment to cost control.

THE REPORT AND THE DILEMMA

The company report that documented the various dimensions of the D-Laser Computer reliability problem and the various internal conflicts reducing both productivity and profitability was a disappointing surprise to Dylan's president, Kathryn Mendes, and to Bionix' CEO, Juliana Mitre. Both realized that conflicts among managers were generally coproduced by operational and management issues that can have a paralyzing effect on a company. And yet, Bionix Diagnostics had prided itself on the effectiveness of its organizational culture toward shared values and objectives, and its ability to problem solve and collaborate as a highly motivated and results-oriented team. Its chairwoman has been often quoted: "With commitment to collaboration, teamwork, and shared values, Bionix's serves customers with quality and provides employees with opportunities to succeed and professional fulfillment."

Bionix's new acquisition, Dylan Medical, was now the cause of serious concern, and Juliana Mitre was determined to get to the bottom of the behavioral and operational problems. The impact of the repeated field breakdowns of the D-Laser Computer system on Dylan's profitability and Bionix's reputation was her most serious crisis since her appointment as CEO. The impact of this crisis was escalating, and the financial and reputation damage was building. Perhaps more serious was the revelation of considerable conflict among managers and within operating units. The apparent lack of teamwork, insufficient leadership, and a breakdown of shared company values was creating possible career derailments for both Kathryn Mendes and Gregg Johnston. Bionix's corporate headquarters was losing its patience with both executives. "Our commitment to outstanding financial performance while developing leadership and maintaining adherence to company values is paramount to our success," concluded Juliana Mendes's presentation at the annual meeting in Ft. Lauderdale on July 1, 2010.

CASE STUDY DISCUSSION QUESTIONS

1. Elimination or significant reduction of organizational conflict at Dylan Medical is necessary for personnel development and operational goal attainment at the Manufacturing & Service Division.

   - What are the characteristics of superior leadership, high performance teams, and motivation enhancement programs that can neutralize or surmount performance obstacles at Dylan created by ill-conceived organizational policies, procedures, or processes?

   - Use examples such as poor hiring practices, short-sighted operating objectives, inadequate professional development programs, ill-conceived or unfair performance appraisal and compensation systems, and inadequate consequences for failure to adhere to company values.

2. Discuss various approaches to identify elements of organizational conflict within Dylan's Manufacturing & Service Division and within the Apparatus Division. Can these approaches be used to formulate organizational interactions in terms of possible reasons or causes that can be analyzed and lead to prescription and ultimate resolution?

The Struggle for Power at Midwest Hospital System

By Tracy H. Porter

Midwest Hospital System, a large 500-bed hospital, with 5 satellite locations and over 5,000 employees, will be seeking a new Chief Executive Officer as Mr. Tom Jones, the current CEO, retires by the end of the year. Since the announcement of Mr. Jones' pending retirement a few months ago, there has been a level of intensity within the organization due to many interested candidates jockeying to be considered for this most desirable position. Over the past month, two candidates have risen to the forefront as the top contenders for Mr. Jones' job—Donna Harvard and Steven Evans.

Donna Harvard currently serves as CFO of the health system and has worked her way up through the ranks during the past 20 years. Harvard, with an MBA, has been the genius behind the company's financial success in recent years and possesses a thorough understanding of the inner workings of the organization. Recently she completed a second graduate degree in healthcare administration and has spent numerous hours trying to learn about the system's various clinical departments, which are the only areas she feels somewhat at a loss. Those who support Harvard for the CEO position describe her as "a true professional with a deep understanding of the needs of the hospital in both the short and long runs." The current CEO had been overheard saying that "Harvard is the candidate with the most experience with regard to running a hospital." Still, the lack of clinical experience may be an issue, and when Harvard is questioned on this issue, she states, "I will trust the health system's medical staff to handle that part of the job. I won't tell them how to do their job if they don't tell me how to do mine."

The second candidate, Steven Evans, is relatively new to the healthcare industry, receiving his medical degree 2 years ago. Evans is less experienced than Harvard, but as a physician, he appeals to the system's medical staff. Many believe his medical training and other credentials will be valuable assets for the CEO position. Evans' supporters state that "he is the only candidate who is capable of understanding the central purpose of the institution." However, during his time with the health system, Evans has only worked in the Emergency Department with little or no experience with the business side of health care. When questioned on this topic, Evans relates, "I went to medical school so I am confident I can learn the business side of running this hospital. It will only take a short while for me to bring myself current on that information." In addition to being a physician, Evans is also well liked within the hospital. This is clear as he walks through the hospital with everyone greeting him with a smile and handshake. One of the nurses was overheard saying, "Everyone loves Dr. Evans. He isn't the type of person who thinks he is better than us. He is just one of us."

It has become apparent to Mr. Jones that there is an apparent divide between the clinical and the nonclinical sides of the health system. The clinical members of the organization see the administrators as "clueless people who have no real grip on the central focus of this hospital. They (administration) are here to support us but often they think they are more important than they actually are." The nonclinical (administrative) members of the organization see the clinical employees as "not focused on the bottom line and lacking any sense of fiscal responsibility." An "us against them" mentality has become the main thrust of choosing the best candidate. Mr. Jones wants the Board of Directors to make the right decision about who should succeed him. Which candidate should he recommend to the Board? Which candidate would be best for the health system's future?

CASE STUDY DISCUSSION QUESTIONS

1. French & Raven introduce five bases of power: Coercive, Reward, Legitimate, Referent, and Expert.

    1. **Coercive Power:** The ability to force someone to do something that he/she does not desire to do.

    2. **Reward Power:** The ability to grant another person things that person desires or to remove or decrease things the person does not desire.

    3. **Legitimate Power:** The ability to the ability to administer to another certain feelings of obligation or the notion of responsibility

    4. **Referent Power:** The ability to administer to another a sense of personal acceptance or personal approval.

    5. **Expert Power:** The ability to administer to another information, knowledge, or expertise.

    Which of French and Raven's power bases does each of the candidates exhibit?

2. How do you believe the clinical and nonclinical employees view the power of each candidate?

3. Based on what you have learned about each candidate, which individual would you choose as the new CEO? Why?

EMR System: A Blessing or a Curse?

By Tracy H. Porter

For the past 3 years, Mark Emmitt, COO of a small rural hospital system in the Midwest, has been actively striving to improve the efficiency of the organization's processes and procedures. Part of his changes is the introduction of an electronic medical records (EMR) system to improve patient care and reduce costs. EMR's are a way for physicians to organize patient medical records, which are integrated within the hospital system and allow for physicians and nurses alike to access and input all information through their computer.

Since its inception, the hospital's medical records have been charted using pen and paper. Many of the hospital's medical staff have been with the hospital since graduating from their residency programs and have little or no experience with computers. Since arriving at the hospital, Emmitt has enjoyed an easy, professional relationship with the medical staff. He sees his position as one of support for the clinical staff's needs. Emmitt has avoided interfering in the hospital's clinical issues and focuses his attention on the efficient running of its operations.

Emmitt has spent many months researching the benefits and challenges associated with implementing an EMR system. He has sought out colleagues at other hospitals across the country that have implemented EMRs and found mixed results. While some had negative comments, many had positive results after the "learning curve." Emmitt compiled his research without the use of a committee to save time, his and others. He presented his finding to the hospital's CEO and Board of Directors, who accepted his recommendation for implementing an EMR system wide. It never dawned on Emmitt that the clinical staff would not be thrilled with this "time saving" electronic tool, so he proceeded to purchase the hospital's EMR system. When the physicians and nurses heard about the purchase of the EMR system with an anticipated installation date in 2 months, they were angry. In addition, a comprehensive "how to" manual was placed in each of their in-boxes with optional training sessions being offered the month before the equipment would be installed. It was made clear to all clinical staff that the hospital's governing board had approved this system-wide change and as such, everyone (no exceptions!) was expected to begin working on the system as soon as it was installed. Physicians had varied responses to this directive from administration. Some ignored the forthcoming change, others became very angry and vocal with Emmitt after they found out he was the lead of the change, others resigned from the hospital in protest. One of the more vocal physician protestors said, "I do not use a computer in my private or professional practice and I see no reason to begin now. Computers are too complex, add extra work, and I don't have the time or desire to learn." The implementation of the EMR system dominated the conversation in the hospital's physicians' lounge:

Dr. Young: Who does he think he [Emmitt] is to decide this without consulting us?

Dr. Hopkins: I think he has lost his mind with this EMR idea and how much do you think all that equipment will cost the hospital?

Dr. Young: Millions!

Emmitt entered the lounge and was overwhelmed by the physicians' concerns regarding the EMR system. He could not get a word into the conversation and resigned to just listening to their complaints.

Eventually, Emmitt was allowed to leave the lounge and returned to his office. He began to rethink his decision when he saw a pile of messages on his desk from the nursing staff stating the same concerns as the physicians. He began to seriously question the way in which he handled this change.

CASE STUDY DISCUSSION QUESTIONS

1. What communication problems do you see in this case?

2. If you were Emmitt how would you have communicated this change more effectively?

3. What motivation would the medical staff have to implement EMR's? How can Emmitt aid in this motivation?

4. Given the present situation how might Emmitt correct his relationship with the medical staff?

Enriching Jobs at Midwest Hospital System

By Tracy H. Porter

Midwest Hospital System has been a central part of the city's infrastructure since 1900. Over the years, the hospital had expanded to a 500-bed hospital with 5 satellite locations and over 5,000 employees. During this time of growth, many of the long-standing policies and procedures utilized to run operations had become antiquated and inefficient.

When Donald Stewart took over as Director of Administrative Services, he knew things needed to change. When it first opened decades ago, Midwest was the only hospital in the region. Now there were four hospital systems in the area. Competition was fierce so running an efficient organization was more important than ever. Stewart's first challenge was the Business Office. He noticed that productivity per worker had steadily declined in recent years even with the implementation of electronic billing. While touring the department, he noticed many employees appeared stressed and disengaged from their work. He knew that he needed to talk with the Business Office employees to hear their perceptions of what was working (and not working) within the department.

Stewart's first appointment was with Mary, an employee celebrating 20 years with the organization.

> **Stewart:** Mary you have been with us for a long time. How do you think things are working in the Business Office? Do you have any concerns or recommendations for improvement?
>
> **Mary:** I am not aware of any problems. I just come in and do my job.
>
> **Stewart:** Why do you think staff's productivity has gone down recently?
>
> **Mary:** Again, I just do my job and have done this job for many, many years. I don't bother anyone and they don't bother me.
>
> **Stewart:** Where do you see yourself in this organization in the next 5 years?
>
> **Mary:** Still sitting in this same chair performing my current job. The same thing I do day in and day out. It is mindless work.

The conversation Stewart had with Mary was repeated with several other employees within the Business Office. It was obvious to Stewart that the Business Office employees lacked motivation. Stewart set about to determine what the problem was within the Business Office. He requested that Human Resources survey the employees using a motivating potential score (MPS)[1] to find out what could be done with the current situation. The survey results reflected that the employees were bored with the daily repetition of their jobs, which caused them to make careless mistakes requiring a high percentage of others' time redoing their work. Their jobs required stuffing envelopes for the monthly bills to patients. Primarily this was done in an assembly line format, and there was very little deviation from this format. Many of these employees had been in their current positions for over 10 years and during this time had quietly gone about their duties.

Stewart had heard about a technique called "job rotation" and decided to try it out. Previously each worker specialized in a particular aspect of the billing process at the hospital. The previous director felt this approach made each worker a specialist in their job. Anxious to try out this new technique, Stewart asked for volunteers to exchange jobs one morning a week. The plan was for the workers to "learn as they went along." This initial program turned out to be a tremendous disaster, with the number of mistakes and work slowdown only becoming worse. Those employees participating become more stressed than previously. After one week of this pilot project, Stewart decided to rethink his decision.

---

[1] The central premise of the MPS draws upon the core job characteristics and looks to determine which of these characteristics might be the reason behind the lack of motivation.

On the second round, Stewart decided to be much more methodical with regard to the "job rotation." Just as was previously done, he asked for volunteers to exchange jobs one day a week. However, this time the job rotation was done in pairs, which allowed for job enlargement. The pairs consisted of an "expert" worker or one who had been in the position previously and a "new" worker or the one being trained in the position. This approach was a tremendous success and after a brief learning curve productivity increased across the board, mistakes decreased, and the workers' morale appeared substantially better.

CASE STUDY DISCUSSION QUESTIONS

1. Was the MPS survey the appropriate tool to determine the motivation problem within the department?

2. How does job variety affect motivation within the context of this case?

3. How did the "job rotation" program enrich the jobs at Midwest Hospital Systems and perhaps increase motivation?

4. What lessons should Stewart learn from the process of bringing "job rotation" into the organization?

"Poof" You Are Now in Management: A Case Study in Leadership

By Tracy H. Porter

Kelly Brown has been a dedicated nurse within the Midwest Hospital Systems for 10 years, and during these years, she has been well respected by her peers. After many years as a floor nurse, Kelly was given the promotion to head nurse of the surgical unit. Initially, the announcement of her promotion was greeted with "well-deserved" among the nursing staff. This was in line with expectations as the surgical unit was known to be a tightly knit group of dedicated nurses who spent a great deal of time together both in and out of the hospital.

Prior to Kelly's promotion, a great deal of mistrust had developed between the nursing staff and those in administrative positions. Over the past few years, the nurses felt they were being taken advantage of by administrators as their workload increased, overtime was cut, and no salary adjustments had been made in 3 years. On numerous occasions, the nurses had complained about their working conditions to the previous head nurse, Mildred, without success. The nurses viewed Mildred as never being able to rectify their problems. For example, when the nurses received a memo from administration telling them they would be asked to work 10-hour shifts instead of the standard 8-hour shifts, Mildred simply told the nurses, "What do you want me to do? They didn't ask for my input." When the nurses heard that all overtime was being cut immediately, Mildred once again simply shrugged at the nurses who complained. Finally, when the nurses loudly complained to the lack of raises in years, Mildred simply responded that times were difficult and the nurses needed to be patient until the economy was more stable. During this time, the nursing staff came to mistrust Mildred's explanations and felt she had become "one of them"—an administrator. After a few years, Mildred tired of the complaints and decided to retire.

During these years, Kelly had been one of the gang and actively complained about the lack of support from Mildred. She routinely voiced her distrust of anyone in an administrative position and only added to the "us against them" culture that had developed within the surgical unit.

Therefore, when Kelly's promotion was announced many nurses publicly congratulate her, but behind the scenes, it was a different story. Several nurses were heard muttering, "How could Kelly become an administrator?" Another nurse told Kelly, "Just remember who your real friends are and remember to take care of us. Don't do what Mildred did and become one of them." Several other nurses took the opportunity to gain Kelly's ear and asked:

1. Can overtime be changed so we (the nurses) can decide when and how often we need to work?
2. Can salaries be raised to account for the 3 years of no adjustments? Retroactively?
3. Can vacation time be extended?

One of the senior floor nurses was overheard to say, "Now that Kelly is in this new position, perhaps we can make some of the changes around here that we have all been complaining about for years!"

CASE STUDY DISCUSSION QUESTIONS

1. What are the potential advantages and disadvantages of the present situation for Kelly?
2. If you were Kelly, how do you believe this promotion would affect your relationship with your coworkers?
3. What hurdles will Kelly face in her new role as a leader? How should she overcome these hurdles?
4. Will it be possible for Kelly to be seen as a leader within the surgical unit?

Is This Person-Centered Planning? Change Management in a Mental Health Center

By Doris J. Ravotas

onald Simpson looked at James Spada with exasperation and whispered, "Can you believe this? Yet another hoop to jump through!"

"Yeah." said James, "Do you remember the days when a psychotherapist could just listen to people's problems and help them out just like we were trained to do? Now, you have to justify every decision you make, limit your sessions, and on top of that now we have to prove that we are 'person-centered.' Give me a break! Psychotherapists are 'person-centered' by definition."

Donald and James were sitting at a mandatory meeting about person-centered planning for supervisors from throughout the state mental health system. They had been colleagues for over 15 years, first as psychotherapists at Phillips Health Center and now as parallel outpatient psychotherapy supervisors since Donald's promotion at Phillips and James's move to Blackhawk Mental Health Center a couple of counties away. They had both seen many changes in that time, particularly since the rise of managed care, including limits on sessions, limits on who can be treated in county mental health centers, and constantly changing standards for documentation and justification of services. In fact, documentation had become a very time consuming aspect of their jobs and that of the psychotherapists that worked with them. Now, there was a lot of buzz about person-centered care, but neither one of them could figure out what the buzz was all about or how it was different from the work that they and their staff did every day.

The state legislature had recently passed a law mandating that all services in public mental health institutions must show evidence of person-centered planning, or funding would be cut to those institutions that did not do so. The state mental health system was scrambling to educate all of their administrators to make sure that changes were in place within the next year. This training focused on the major tenets of person-centered planning and suggested changes in documentation that would serve as a warrant to state auditors that person-centered planning was happening in that clinic. It also laid out a timeline for administrators to follow: Training and new documentation templates must be completed within 3 months (by March 1st) and used for the next 3 months following that. Six months from now (in the month of June) state auditors would travel to each mental health center and observe how each unit has incorporated person-centered planning into their work, offering a seal of approval or placing the center on probation and suggest revisions in their process.

Donald and James were not the only skeptics in the room, but as outpatient psychotherapy supervisors, they were at a distinct disadvantage. They both had heard about person-centered planning from their colleagues who work with consumers in developmental disability services offering day programs, work programs, and skills-in-living programs. They knew that members of the ARC (a powerful grassroots advocacy group of parents of cognitively challenged individuals), usually parents of consumers with developmental disabilities, frequently advocated for services that were based on the preferences and dreams of those consumers. However, incorporating someone's "dreams" into an activity program or work program certainly seemed more applicable than trying to do this in one-hour psychotherapy sessions for consumers that have the types of severe problems that were now the norm in outpatient psychotherapy clinics.

The morning training didn't seem to give them much to challenge their skepticism. The importance of person-centered planning was stressed with examples of consumers in state institutions and foster care who were denied preferences of leisure activities or visitors with the explanation that it was not agency policy. The trainer pointed out that these preferences could be part of an ongoing treatment plan based on the consumer's goals for their lives. Examples were also given about work programs and day programs that failed to consider the input from consumers. Instituting person-centered planning completely changed some of these programs for the better with much happier and engaged consumers. Yet, Donald and James still failed to see applications to their outpatient clinics as these examples did not apply to their type of settings and very few outpatient psychotherapists actually treated individuals with developmental disabilities. Also, if truth be told, they both still found themselves irritated by the relatively new term of "consumer." The term had a materialistic bent and clashed with their training as outpatient therapists where they learned to treat "clients."

Yet, there were a few things that did perk up James's ears. One was the mention that the National Alliance on Mental Illness (NAMI) was also heavily involved in supporting the legislation for person-centered planning. NAMI is a grassroots organization made up of consumers and family members of consumers with severe and persistent mental illnesses. These were just the type of consumers that the outpatient clinics were now mandated to treat. This was another big change in outpatient mental health work. When James started as a psychotherapist he treated women with depression and couples with marital problems (the kind of clients that he was trained to treat). Now those minor problems would not qualify for treatment in most mental health centers. To be treated in a public mental health center a person must have an increasingly severe form of mental illness. Even though most of the psychotherapists on staff were struggling with how to treat these new types of clients, he had one employee, Cathy Arps, who specialized in this work and ran a group for families with a member who was newly diagnosed. She helped some of the parents set up the local NAMI group. Perhaps she had some ideas of how this might apply to their work in the outpatient clinic.

The other thing that James heard is that many consumers were given services because that is what services were available rather than services that were based on how that consumer wanted to change his/her life. James pondered this. Was it possible that the staff in his clinic were not giving the consumers enough input?

The afternoon was spent reviewing the timeline for action and the values of person-centered planning that are emphasized in the PCP (person-centered planning) state guidelines based on the law. They stressed that the PCP process must:

- Work toward achieving the consumer's dreams, goals, and desires for their life through developing goals and objectives based on those dreams, goals, and desires.
- Develop, initiate, strengthen, and maintain community connections and natural supports that will assist the individual in accomplishing his/her dreams, goals, and desires.

- Support the consumer choices within the PCP planning meeting of:
  - Who will attend the PCP meeting
  - What will be discussed at the meeting
  - Where the meeting will take place
  - How needs and goals will be addressed

The planning meeting with all of the above elements had to be completed by the time the consumer was seen for the fifth time by the treating individual or team in the mental health center. Both Donald and James snorted at this last point. After all, without reauthorization of treatment, outpatient psychotherapists weren't allowed to see consumers for longer than six sessions! This would mean that the planning meeting could happen very close to the end of the time that the state gave them for treatment. Certainly, no one thought through how these new regulations would fit in with the old regulations. It was clear, however, that the documentation from the planning meeting must prove that the parameters of person-centered planning were met.

At the end of the day, James looked at Donald and said, "So what do you think you are going to do?"

Donald shrugged and said, "What can you do? I am going to meet with the outpatient staff and tell them that we are going to have to comply with this new way of doing things and then figure out how to get some new paperwork forms together."

FIRST THREE MONTHS: BLACKHAWK COUNTY MENTAL HEALTH CENTER

When James Spada returned to work, he started the next staff meeting at Blackhawk Mental Health Center with the announcement about the new state mandate. He said, "There is a new law in Michigan that we will have to comply with. We have to change the way we make therapy plans to match the values of person-centered planning." He was met with a group groan.

Lorraine Van Buren, an MSW with 30 years of experience exclaimed, "Not again, why can't those bureaucrats be satisfied with at least one thing?! First, it was all this extra documentation for managed care, than the whole idea that every goal has to be in 'measurable' terms (like life can really be measurable!), then having the client sign off when they are already so overwhelmed. Can't those people in Lansing just let us stop writing already and do our job!"

Dion Jones spoke up next. He also had been a psychotherapist for many years as a licensed counselor. His expertise is in family and marital counseling, and he had been having a hard time adjusting to the change in the type of clientele over the years. "What are we supposed to do? Miracles in six sessions with people with persistent illnesses like schizophrenia? We are supposed to get people hearing voices to tell us their 'dreams'? Then what, hallucinate with them?"

James looked around the room. Most of the staff were nodding in agreement. He knew this was not going to be an easy change. He let a few other people with similar sentiments talk and then he said, "Okay, I can't say that I am thrilled with this change either and I agree that we seem to have an ongoing slate of changes, but you know what they say, 'the only constant in life is change.' And I have to say that I don't think some of these changes are all that bad. Hasn't helping clients write measurable goals helped us to measure the successes that we are having? That certainly got us praise in our last yearly report. In fact, Lorraine, you are fantastic at this and have really gotten even difficult clients engaged with the process."

James went on, "I am afraid that this person-centered planning is now the law of the land and we are going to have to figure out how to address it. Why don't we spend some time in these meetings getting to understand the concept and our mandates and then see how it would actually fit into outpatient therapy work. Dion, I know that you have been working with one of the day services programs in the Developmental Disabilities Division on behavioral plans that could be used within the intensive day services as well as at home by parents. I know that our Developmental Disabilities Division do this kind of planning. Have you been involved in any of this person-centered planning?"

Dion thought for a minute. "Not really," he said, "usually they call me in when they already know that they need a behavioral program. I have heard them talk a little bit about it though and come to think of it they seem positive about it—but of course, day program work is very different than outpatient psychotherapy."

"No argument with you there," said James, "This whole thing started in developmental disability circles and when I was at this meeting sometimes I thought that there hasn't been much thought given to how you do this planning when you offer the kind of services that we offer. Dion, would you be willing to talk to some of the people that you know in day services, to see what they say about this process? We could spend some time next week talking about what you found out." Dion nodded.

James turned to Cathleen Arp, whom he had been thinking about at the state meeting. Cathy was a relatively new master's level psychologist who probably had more training on the treatment of people dealing with persistent mental illnesses than anyone in the meeting due to changes that have recently occurred in some training programs. This difference in training had the odd effect of those with the most actual experience having the least training for working with the most prevalent type of consumer in outpatient treatment. Cathy loved working with consumers who had some of the most challenging problems and she had a great deal of zeal for her work. Being the "new kid on the block" though, she often was relatively quiet in staff meetings and, true to form, she hadn't said a word yet on this subject. James asked, "Cathy, what do you hear about person-centered planning from your association with the local NAMI group?"

Hesitantly, Cathleen said, "I actually have heard a lot about it. As some of my family members get more involved with NAMI, they get educated on some of the latest trends and they are very excited that treatment could be more tailored toward their dreams for their own lives and/or that of their family members. I have tried to incorporate some of this into my own planning sessions with consumers. I try to listen very closely."

"Don't we all," Lorraine said under her breath.

"Now wait a minute, Lorraine." said James, "Let's listen to how Cathy feels that this approach is different." He turned to Cathy and asked, "How is this different than the way we were all taught to listen in our training?"

Cathleen began to respond by saying, "It is something about prompting the person to really tell you what they want out of their life, what their dreams are…" when she started to talk about dreams she looked at Lorraine who released an audible sigh, "I don't know…I guess I am just not good at it, I was only trying to do what the families had told me."

James could see that Cathy had been intimidated by Lorraine, and he wished that Lorraine could be a little more charitable to her. "Sometimes, we are much better than we think we are at a skill, the families and consumers you work with must have felt they could trust you with these ideas to bring them to you. Could you ask one of the family members you work with to come to one of our meetings in a couple of weeks and talk to us about their perspective?"

"Sure," said Cathleen, "I have a family member who might be willing to help us out."

"Okay," said James, "then this is what I would like us to do. We have 3 months to make this change and then 3 months to practice and revise our process. I want to use those first 3 months to research this idea, the mandate from the state, and decide how this might work with what we currently do and make sure that it goes along with our individual philosophies and styles of psychotherapy. There were some resources suggested at this state meeting, I will look them over and next week try to explain what I found. Dion will also bring the information that he has from the day program. The week after that, Cathy will hopefully be able to have one of her family members come. After that we will begin the task of figuring out how we can make this change in this department, how to document it, and how to keep the quality of our work up. I must ask all of you to keep an open mind and to take this task seriously. I don't think it would do us any good to just say we are doing this without a clear picture what it is and a plan on how we will do it."

So, the outpatient psychotherapy department of Blackhawk County Mental Health embarked on a journey of discovery about person-centered planning and how they might be able to fulfill the state requirements and maintain quality services. Dion reported that day services had been doing person-centered planning for about 6 months, and in that time, they had seen increased motivation from almost all of their consumers. They said it took a while for consumers to realize they were actually being asked for their input on daily activities because in the past they would be asked, but only within certain choices. It took some activities that were "out of the box" to convince the consumers that the staff was really looking for their input. Finally, one of the consumers said that he wanted to learn to play the guitar. The staff made time in the day to take him to guitar lessons. With that step, his social skills began to blossom (one of the overarching reasons for day programming). They did have some problems with consumers that had little experience thinking for themselves and some people who had outlandish goals—to become a state senator or a rapper—but even then they were usually able to take the goal and work on some step toward it (like helping to organize an event at the center or learn to rap in front of others). Most of the staff listened with interest when Dion was talking, but some of the same concerns regarding this being a different type of a program and a different kind of client were raised in the meeting.

When Cathleen had approached one of her family members to come into the outpatient meeting the family member felt she might do better by finding someone with experience in person-centered planning through NAMI. The NAMI group was able to find Andrew, a consumer who was an outpatient client in another mental health center.

Andrew mesmerized the outpatient staff with his tale of the many years that he has been in and out of treatment. As a consumer dealing with a severe case of schizophrenia, Andrew heard voices almost all of the time. He had lived with his parents for over 30 years, and his parents brought him in for day services, work services, and living skills services, but all of these services were frightening to him due to the voices and he never wanted to be a part of them. Medication had helped somewhat, but he still heard some voices that interfered with his concentration, and he couldn't bring himself to be involved with services that he was bored with. He had been referred for outpatient therapy several times to learn behavioral skills to deal with the voices, but again he saw no reason for this. Finally, he had been referred to a psychotherapist a year ago who started asking him about what he liked to do before he got sick and if he would like to do any of this again. He admitted that he loved to go fly fishing with his father who taught him how to tie flies. He was surprised when the psychotherapist said that he could learn how to ignore the voices enough to enjoy tying flies again and enjoy some quiet days of fishing with friends. He started to learn the behavioral techniques needed to deal with the voices and eventually, with help from his therapist and his case worker, joined a local fishing group where a couple of older men took him under their wings. He smiled broadly when he said that because he can now battle the voices for about 2 hours, he has been able to teach some of his new friends some of the fly-making tricks that his father taught him.

Most of the staff in the room were moved by Andrew's presentation, both for the role that person-centered planning had played in his life and for the impact that psychotherapy techniques had on his skills in dealing with a persistent mental illness. They started to see some possibilities.

After Andrew left, several staff members brought up their thoughts about doing this type of treatment, stating they could see how person-centered planning worked in this situation. Dion ventured forward and said, "I have to say that one of my problems with person-centered planning is probably not with that at all, but what I realize is that I don't know that much about treating people with persistent mental illnesses. That is really the frustrating part of my job. I was trained, as most people were in my day, to treat depression, anxiety, and relationship problems in basically healthy individuals. I have been able to adjust this to my work with families with developmental disabilities, but I always feel like I am spinning my wheels with people who have persistent mental illness. To tell you the truth, when I was in training, the thought was that psychotherapy doesn't work with those people."

There were head nods all around the room. James realized that some of their resistance to person-centered planning might have to do with this earlier change in their roles as psychotherapists. He said, "How many people would be interested in some continuing education about treating people dealing with persistent mental illnesses?" Several people raised their hands. "Ok, I will look into what might be the possibilities."

James was true to his word and approached his supervisor about the training. Training was one of the things on the cutting block of the budget, but finally after a couple of weeks, James was told that the agency would pay for a local professor from the clinical psychology department to come in and do some training with the outpatient department as a whole.

By the time that James knew about the possibility of training, the staff had reviewed more about the values and concepts behind person-centered planning as well as discussed how this would really fit into their work. James announced that the training for working with those with persistent illnesses would not be for a few months and therefore, they would need to work on person-centered planning approaches and templates before having the training in hand. He passed out their present template for treatment planning and the major points from the state meeting that would be important to incorporate into their planning. He asked all of the staff members to put some thought into how that template could be transformed as a guide to incorporating person-centered planning into their work while serving as a warrant to the state that they were indeed doing person-centered planning. He said they would be going through the forms and changing them together over the next few weeks. Several of the psychotherapists said that they were still not sure what they were doing, but they all agreed to give it a try.

The next few weeks brought a great deal of discussion about the topic. Lorraine brought up that the state's insistence that person-centered planning would need to "work toward achieving the consumer's dreams, goals, and desires for their life" in the limited amount of time they had was ridiculous. "Aren't we setting them up by allowing them to have these gigantic goals (like to be the president or a doctor or something) and then us having to whittle it down to something that is doable? You notice that there is no suggestion of extra time to do this."

Cathy said, "I agree with you about time and having to whittle it down, but when you get down to it, isn't the basis of any of these big life goals small steps that we are good at helping people with? Things like overcoming fear and anxiety or self-doubt, learning people skills, taking chances, these are the things that people with persistent mental illnesses need to work on just as much as other people, and if we are honest that becoming president will take a very long time but we could help you with some of the skills you would need to do that, wouldn't they benefit from the journey?" James was thrilled that Cathleen seemed to be moving from being the scared new kid to taking her place as a member of the group.

In the end the staff agreed that because the "dreams, goals, and desires" were a linchpin in person-centered planning that it should be placed at the top of the template right after the demographics. To address the amount of time it would take to address the presenting problem, the dreams, and goals, and the formulation of a plan to address both, they asked if they could have a brief "temporary" treatment plan with immediate concerns leading to concrete plans. They could then work under that initial plan until a more formalized plan emerged. This plan had the effect of seeing their initial work as part of the process, but keeping in mind that the consumer might want to change their work based on their life goals. James said he didn't see anything wrong with this idea, the state mandated that the person-centered plan be completed by the fifth meeting.

Part of that initial treatment plan would be the preparation work for the person-centered plan. A philosophical discussion about the best ways to work with consumers in this process produced the thought that most people could be asked about how their presenting problem (whatever brought them in) interfered with the dreams for their life. This would connect their immediate experience with their ideas for the future. Because most of the therapists recognized that this motivational work would take some time they proposed that the person-centered plan be completed during the third or fourth session rather than the second or third, which they had done with their earlier treatment planning. This was acceptable within the structure of required documents and it launched them into a discussion about setting up a system of therapy that would be a step model. The therapist and consumer could work on a specific goal for the 6 weeks that they were given for treatment without appeal and then the consumer would be given a hiatus from psychotherapy in which they could practice new skills (perhaps with the help of a case manager for some consumers). The consumer would later return to therapy for another specific goal. Some of the staff were opposed since it didn't seem like "real" psychotherapy to them. But those who were interested knew that the regulatory group in the state did seem to approve of "serial" treatment rather than treatment that continues over several months (and the formal process to continue therapy past 2 months was quite timely). They decided that they would bring these up as possible strategies when they met with the professor about treating those with persistent illnesses.

The outpatient staff then reviewed the other patient-centered planning parameters and noticed that some of the parameters referred to what they thought of as the consumer's logistics on how the planning would occur. This got them talking about the actually person-centered planning process as spread out across two sessions rather than just one. The first session (and even sessions before that) would lead up to the session in which goals and plans were finalized by getting the consumer's ideas on: 1) who they want involved in the process, 2) who will attend the PCP meeting, 3) what will be discussed, and 4) where the meeting will take place. The decision was made to put these sections early in the template so that it was prioritized before setting up the formal planning session.

These questions, however, were not added without discussion. Many of the therapists expressed some discomfort with having additional people in the planning session. Cathleen stated, "I have to admit that even though I am now working with families, it still seems strange to me. As a psychologist, I was really trained to work on people's ego strength individually."

Lorraine jumped in and said, "As far as I am concerned, it is about time that we pay attention to people's support system. That is what social work is all about!"

Dion nodded, "I don't see how you can help anyone make changes without including their family and/or other supports. This is a powerful part of every person. I wish we would do this even more." He pointed to the last parameter for person-centered planning. "Look at this last statement; 'develop, initiate, strengthen, and maintain community connections and natural supports that will assist the individual in accomplishing his/her dreams, goals, and desires.' This should be a very big part of our business, let's put a section in here that says something like natural supports the consumer will develop or strengthen and then the same for community connections. Where would we be without the communities that we are a part of?"

Lorraine agreed, "I try to get all of my consumers talking about this—it will be nice to actually have it on the form rather than implying that people are just examining their navel. But, I want to get to this whole thing about where the meeting will take place. Now this, I think, is ridiculous; with our busy schedules are we really able to be rushing around to Timbuktu? Come on!"

James piped in on this one. "I agree with you Lorraine, but there are some choices that are right here, what about a checklist that says, 'therapist's office, group room, day program,' and maybe something like 'alternative.' That way you could accommodate a consumer in an unusual situation. Like one who lives in a group home and their disabled roommate is one of their biggest support people. I think it would be nice to be a little flexible here, but we definitely cannot be going out to everyone's home. I think that we would have to tell people that we could only consider alternatives if they are reasonable and could fit into our schedule."

So, the person-centered planning elements were incorporated into the old treatment plan and they had a discussion on how they would approach the elements in the actual planning process. However, two sections of the original form were left to discuss. These were both at the end of the original form and it was unclear how they would fit in with the new format. One was the actual goals and objectives for the plan with steps toward accomplishing those goals and objectives. The state had made a big deal of the importance of goals and objectives and they all went through training on how to develop measurable goals. Even though many of them were disgusted by the time it took for them to develop this skill, most of them developed respect for the practice. Yet, it was a little difficult to see how this fits into person-centered planning. After all, consumers have a difficult time developing goals that they can accomplish.

There was quite a bit of discussion about how these very specific goals could fit into a plan based on an individual's global dreams, goals, and desires for life. Finally, Cathy returned to the idea that the goals would be specific steps toward the global dreams and that the document would move from the very general to the very specific. They all agreed that this made the most sense and they left a few lines for explanation about the connection between the two.

The final section in the document was the diagnosis. Most of the psychotherapists felt like the diagnosis was out of place in this document. "I think that this is particularly a problem with those people with persistent mental illnesses that we see," said Cathleen, "Here we are trying to build them up with the skills they do have and have them make all these plans and then they have to see this descriptor that lays out all of their major challenges in daily life. It is very discouraging."

"I agree," said Dion, "I often work with consumers about what their diagnosis is, but after they get some perspective and learn to trust that I will work with them on what is important to them. This is way too much to do in a few sessions: get people through a crisis, help them define plans for their future, set clear goals, and help them understand a diagnosis."

"No kidding," Lorraine said, "we all know that the diagnosis is really there to justify that they need services—it often isn't helpful at all."

This discussion went on for a long time, but finally James said, " I have to say that I certainly understand what you are all saying and this whole diagnosis thing this early in treatment goes against the strength-based approach. Unfortunately, we are stuck with this. Our guidelines clearly state that the diagnosis must be in here. Managed care won't pay for the services without the diagnosis. It is just one of the things that we aren't going to be able to change. On the positive side, I believe we have a plan. I would like to have someone I know in Lansing look at this and make sure that what we plan on doing will work to demonstrate that we are within the law."

FIRST THREE MONTHS: PHILLIPS COUNTY MENTAL HEALTH CENTER

Donald Simpson at Phillips County Mental Health Center also met with the out-patient staff within a week after the state meeting on person-centered planning.

He started out with, "As you all know I just got back from the big meeting about person-centered planning. The long and short of it is that there is now a state law mandating that we all have to show that we do person-centered plan-ning, which basically just means that you ask the consumer to be involved in the process."

"Well, who doesn't do that, we are psychotherapists for heaven's sake," said Virginia Allen, a licensed counselor who has been a psychotherapist for about 15 years.

"The big push is for self-determination," continued Donald, "making sure that the consumer owns the process."

"Well, I am all for that." said Morningstar Frank, "I don't think that many of the people I work with have a sense that this is 'their' treatment."

"That's because they are all dealing with really bad mental illnesses," Samantha Billings interrupted Morningstar out of frustration.

"I think that if we worked more closely with them we could help them take ownership," Morningstar snapped back.

"How can you work closely with someone who isn't thinking straight?" asked Virginia.

Morningstar had received her MSW about 10 years ago, but she had worked in psychiatric hospitals for almost 20 years before that and had a soft place in her heart for consumers who had to deal with persistent mental illnesses like schizophrenia, bipolar disorder, or personality disorders. She was always shocked at how little most therapists knew about treating consumers with the most severe problems, but she also knew that she had a lot to learn.

Samantha Billings, on the other hand, received her master's degree in coun-seling psychology 4 years ago. She did receive some training in working with consumers with severe disorders, but she prefers to work with children and adults who have trouble with anxiety or relationship problems. She just feels uncom-fortable with those people with severe problems and has been a little shocked how many of them show up on her case load. She wants "real" therapy where she can see the results.

Donald ignored the conflict and went on. "So we are going to have to change our paperwork."

Everyone groaned.

Samantha quickly bristled, "How can it be that I have been here less than 4 years, and every time we turn around, the state wants something more from us?!"

James wasn't surprised at the anger. More than one of the psychotherapists had confided in him that the constant change in demands was wearing on them and they had thought of doing some other type of work. "I know, I know…" James said, "but that is the way it is in a public mental health center. Luckily, the people in the day programs for the treatment of developmental disabilities are already doing this so I am planning on going over there and seeing what we need to do. How about if I send you all some of the material that I got from the state so you can all take a look at it? I don't think this will really mean too much of a change for us, if we aren't trying to invent the wheel. I will do the legwork on this so don't worry. I frankly don't see that this is a whole lot different than what we have been doing."

Although James intended to go over and talk to Marilyn Stephens, the supervisor in the day programs on the developmental disability side of the mental health center within a few days, the demands on his time took over, and it was over a month before he talked with her about their practices.

Marilyn said, "Yes, we have been doing person-centered planning for about 6 months. It is a simple idea to include people in their own planning, but we have had to work hard on not imposing what we think is best for them and really engage them in the process."

"I can see that with your clientele, Marilyn," said Donald, "but these types of things are built into psychotherapy. Would you mind giving me the template you use for your planning sessions?"

"Sure," said Marilyn, "feel free to use anything you need from it."

When Donald received the template from Marilyn, he took a look at it. He was surprised to see that not only did the template include some of the language from the person-centered planning meeting he had been to, but he also saw a similar structure to the kind of treatment planning they did in outpatient, starting with consumer information and ending in clearly defined goals. He quickly forwarded it to his staff to use as their new person-centered planning template.

Every once and a while, Donald wondered how the staff was feeling about the new template for treatment planning but no one had complained about it so he figured that everything was going well, and he didn't see the urgency of bringing it up in their staff meetings. After all, there were always plenty of more urgent topics to deal with. However, one day he was doing a routine audit that he conducted on a quarterly schedule. He started to notice that there were quite a few blank spaces in the person-centered plan. When he looked more closely he realized that many of the sections that were blank clearly did not apply to outpatient therapy. They were things like "Leisure activities to pursue in the day program," "Needed assistance in daily living skills (toileting, feeding, hygiene)," even something called an "evacuation score"—he had no idea what that was. He became embarrassed that he hadn't looked more closely at the form and vowed to adjust it or find a new form before the staff realized his mistake. He was surprised to find that some therapists had actually put some answers in these slots in the form and wondered how they could fill out something that had little to do with psychotherapy. Moreover, some of the staff seemed to be using the old treatment planning form that didn't have any mention of person-centered planning. He knew that he needed to make the point that everyone must use a person-centered planning form as soon as he found one that would work well or they would be losing some funding.

He began to wonder what James Spada was doing back at the Blackhawk County Mental Health Center. Coincidentally he received a call from a mutual friend telling him that James was using a person-centered planning template that was already approved by the state. Donald called James who explained how he had used definitions of person-centered planning from the state to engage the employees in a plan to adjust their practices, which led to developing training in needed areas and ultimately developing a person-centered planning template that is now used by all outpatient psychotherapists to guide the planning process.

Donald carefully viewed the state definitions of person-centered planning, the training developed by James, and the template developed by the Blackhawk outpatient staff to be used throughout the planning process. He decided that the first two documents looked like common sense, and he felt that the process is really not all that different than the treatment planning that his staff has been doing for years. He sent the template to his staff by email and told them to use this person-centered planning form instead of the old one because it has been approved by the state. This transition is dangerously close to the 3 months that each mental health center is supposed to be using their new systems, but Donald feels confident that it will work.

MONTHS 3–6: BLACKHAWK COUNTY MENTAL HEALTH CENTER

Back at Blackhawk, the outpatient staff is receiving the training on working with consumers with severe and persistent mental illnesses at the same time that they are using the person-centered planning processes that they have been developing over the past few months. It seems clear that some of the staff are much more interested in working with consumers who have severe mental illness than others, but the training did stimulate interest in changing their person-centered planning template in two ways. Cathy suggested that some of the clients with disrupted cognition (hallucinations and delusions) needed an explicit reminder that the goals at the end of the planning session were connected to the consumer's dreams that they stated at the beginning of the planning time. A statement was added at the beginning of the goals section to this affect: "Goals and Objectives Developed for Psychotherapy based on Dreams, Desires, and Goals."

Dion was struck in the training with the importance of cultural differences that arose even with people with severe disorders and he suggested that "cultural considerations" be added to the person-centered planning template. Even though some of the therapists thought this was "overkill" for most consumers (after all Blackhawk county was not a particularly diverse area), no one saw any harm in adding it.

James checked in with the outpatient staff several times over the 3 months between developing the person-centered planning process and the visit by the state auditors. Although there were some lingering doubts about the process, for the most part, the staff was growing increasingly more comfortable with the process and didn't suggest any additional changes. James knew that each of the therapists used the process slightly different in ways that were consistent with their training, but as far as he could tell, they all seemed to maintain the spirit of person-centered planning. Best of all, they all seemed to take ownership of the process. Including them in the process seemed to lessen the initial stress and dread of this newest requirement. Moreover, they were now working together despite their differences and developing a team based on their strengths.

MONTH 6: STATE AUDITOR'S REVIEW AT BLACKHAWK COUNTY MENTAL HEALTH CENTER

The state auditor team that came to Blackhawk County Mental Health Center in June was comprised of two individuals: Gregory Levine, an MSW who had been an outpatient psychotherapist and an outpatient supervisor in a parallel mental health system for many years before joining the administrative team in Lansing, and Min Lu Huang, who had a long career in day programs for those with developmental disabilities and now worked at the state organizational level. They reviewed completed person-centered plans and then interviewed both the psychotherapist and the consumer who had completed the plan. The auditors generally confirmed James's impression about how person-centered plans were conducted.

Most of the interviews of both staff and consumers revealed that consumers had been encouraged to lead with their own needs and preferences in developing a plan for treatment, which is the essence of self-determination and person-centered planning. The values of self-determination seemed to be very strong in this outpatient department.

While reviewing the person-centered planning documents, the auditors were particularly impressed that all of the outpatient therapists had completed the section entitled "Dreams, Desires, and Goals" with a direct quote from the consumer and then wrote a short narrative right before the goals and objectives that specifically connected the dreams, desires, and goals with the specific measurable goals in that section. They also loved the section entitled "Cultural Considerations" and found some interesting things there including how the individual's culture affects the way he/she approaches problems in his/her life. In one document, the therapist had written a note that clearly helped to form the process of therapy: "Charles comes from an Odawa Native American background and realizes that he learns the best when material is given to him in the form of a story."

Some of the interviews did reveal some hesitations about person-centered planning. Several therapists suggested that the process was a cumbersome addition to an already limited course of psychotherapy. Most therapists thought it was a good idea to ask consumers about their global dreams for their lives but found that the goals often went back to the presenting problem that the consumer came in with. For instance Lorraine Van Buren said, "People come in with a presenting problem that they want to solve like feeling afraid of the people around them; then we have to widen the work to the global dream. Don't get me wrong I think that it is good to put this into the context of the consumer's life, but then we end up narrowing it back to the presenting problem to solve that problem. I feel sometimes that we lose valuable time in the process. You know we aren't given much time to do our work. When the push to have briefer versions of psychotherapy became important, forms of brief therapy were developed, but all of them really focus on very clear defined presenting problems. These global dreams can pull the therapist and the consumer away from that."

Min Lu had a difficult time understanding what Lorraine was talking about. After all, aren't mental health services about a person's life and future? Gregory, however, explained to Min Lu that the role of outpatient psychotherapists in state mental health systems, because those systems treat only the most severe mental health problems, has changed drastically over the last few years, and because they are very limited to how often they can see a consumer, they cannot be in the business of focusing on a person's future.

Min Lu understood better when they interviewed Natalie Brown. Natalie was referred for outpatient services after a series of suicide attempts and hospitalizations. Natalie told Lorraine in their first meeting that she needed to figure out how to stop trying to hurt herself when she had deep feelings of depression and desperation brought on by rejection by others. She said that Lorraine had immediately set up a safety plan with her to contact the hotline when she had these impulses and taught her some distraction techniques. She felt some sense of success. Lorraine then started asking her about what her goals were for her life. This was pretty hard for her because she had a hard time looking past the immediate problem. Eventually she said it was to "have a good job and get married to a great guy." That seemed pretty far away for her and she started to feel a little desperate. Lorraine did help her keep some of the distraction skills going but she felt like she was losing ground. When the planning meeting came along, Lorraine put the long-term goals down but then helped her get back to that goal of preventing her impulsive suicide attempts. Lorraine explained the process, but Natalie felt like what had been working was interrupted.

The problem of including the diagnosis on person-centered plans was also a constant theme in the interviews. Most of the psychotherapists felt that the diagnosis pulled them away from the strength-based nature of psychotherapy. Some of them, like Dion, stated that they just didn't like using diagnoses at all, but others felt that the diagnoses could be used to educate people but often the complexity of a diagnosis was a distraction to the task at hand.

Cathleen showed the team one of her cases, Luigi Comensoli, a man with paranoid schizophrenia. He had been referred by his case manager because he wanted to learn how to cope with residual hallucinations. He was more than willing to talk about how his voices "bugged" him but was very cautious around Cathleen, which indicated to her that he may have some paranoid feelings. He was able to plan about wanting to open a lawn business and needed to find a way to manage the voices, but when Cathleen got to the end of the person-centered planning form in preparation for the diagnosis, she started to explain that the hallucinations were part of a syndrome called schizophrenia. Luigi got up and left yelling that she was just like everybody else because she thought he was paranoid. Cathleen ended with, "Even though using a diagnosis to educate someone can be very effective, very often in psychotherapy it is very far away from the work that you are doing with a person, and it takes way too long to do this education well."

Min Lu nodded, even in work focused on developmental disabilities where people have known their diagnoses (like autism or Asperger's syndrome) all their lives using the diagnosis as a positive tool could backfire on a clinician.

The final theme that Gregory and Min Lu found in several of their interviews was the challenge of developing concrete, realistic, and measurable goals and objectives. It wasn't just that the goals were more specific than the global "dreams" they collected earlier from consumers, it was an honestly difficult task for consumers to understand.

"This is a very difficult skill," said Dion, "It took me awhile to learn how to do this well, but now I have to help people with major problems that interfere with their thinking establish clear goals and objectives. Look at the record of Sam Hill. He has such severe anxiety that it interferes with almost every aspect of his life. When we started to talk about what it is that he wanted to get out of therapy he just said, 'I want to get rid this,' and Sam pointed to his head and his 'fake' shaking body. 'I just have to get better.' When I tried to push him on what 'this' is and what 'better' would look like he just got more and more frustrated. Trying to explain to him that we wanted to be able to measure his progress, he said, 'What if I don't make progress?' Finally, I just showed him some ideas. I really tried to not put words into his mouth, but he seemed like he really wanted me to do this part for him. It is just hard."

Sure enough, when Min Lu and Gregory interviewed Sam they saw what Dion was referring to. "When we got to this point I just didn't know what Dion wanted from me. He kept saying 'put it in your own words' but I just kept thinking 'I am doing something wrong—why doesn't he do this—he knows what to do.' Then he showed me some choices that helped a little bit but how am I supposed to decide! I just didn't like this. It kept feeling like I was failing a test that he knew the answer to. And I have to tell you, he knows his stuff. I am not jingly in the nerves like I used to be!"

Gregory and Min Lu left Blackhawk County Mental Health feeling good about the person-centered planning work that was being done there. They both also went away with a better appreciation for the challenges of person-centered planning in the present day environment of an outpatient psychotherapy clinic. They gave the staff compliments for working hard on the task of incorporating person-centered planning and promised to take some of their input back to the advisory group at the state office.

MONTH 6: STATE AUDITOR'S REVIEW AT PHILLIPS COUNTY MENTAL HEALTH CENTER

The team's next stop was Phillips County Mental Health Center. They sat down with Donald Simpson who showed them the person-centered planning (PCP) template that was used in the outpatient psychotherapy department. They both recognized that this was the same (or a very similar) document as the one they saw at Blackhawk. They were confident that they would have similar results here as they did at Blackhawk.

Once they started to look at completed PCP forms, however, they found very different documents than those at Blackhawk. The first thing that caught their attention was that the section entitled "My Dreams, Desires, and Goals" never included a quote and the words often sounded more like a psychotherapist than a consumer. In fact one of the PCP plans read—"To overcome pathological dysphoria." The documents that did include what looked like global dreams did not connect those dreams to the goals and objectives that concluded the plan. They also noticed that the goals and objectives section often contained wording that looked like it came from a textbook. Finally, they noticed that the sections that were to demonstrate consumer choices in who, what, where and how the planning was conducted as well as the section about working toward community connections and natural supports was sparsely filled in with little variation.

When Min Lu asked Samantha Billings about how she goes about the "My Dreams, Desires, and Goals" section with a consumer she said that she doesn't really ask them those words.

"I tell consumers that we are writing down some of the things that we have already talked about that are important to you and what you want to change," said Samantha. "By the time I do this treatment plan, we have already talked about what they want out of psychotherapy, we are really just putting it down on paper."

One of Samantha's consumers confirmed this process. "Yeah, I remember this paper, it was something that she said we had to do to formalize how she was trying to help me. She filled it out in front of me and asked me a few questions while she was doing it, but I am not sure that I really understood. She really helped me with my depression though so that is all that I cared about."

"Do you remember her asking you about this section here about 'Dreams, Desires, and Goals'?" asked Min Lu.

"Not really, I know she told me that she was going to write down my goal about not being depressed."

"Do you know what this means?" asked Min Lu, pointing to the phrase "To overcome pathological dysphoria."

"Umm, no, not really; is that kind of like being a pathological liar? It can't really be that. It isn't one of my problems. I guess I didn't read this whole paper before I signed it."

Min Lu continued, "What about this part here? Did Ms. Billings ask you if there was anyone you wanted to come to the planning session? Or anyone that you wanted to come in with you to help you out with your problems?"

"Well," George said, "She asked me the first time I came in if I wanted to bring someone back with me, but I didn't quite get it, why would I want someone to come with me?"

"Sometimes, it helps for people who are close to you to come in and find some solutions to your problems together like a wife or a girlfriend?"

"That makes some sense," said George, "I never really thought about it that way, but my wife is always saying that she doesn't know what to do when I get in my funk"

Finally, Min Lu asked George, "How did you come up with these goals and objectives here?"

George took a look, "Oh, I do remember that. Sam told me that we had to put down some goals that we could measure. She pulled out a book and showed me which ones she was thinking about using and said it was basically what we were already doing. She wanted to know if it was okay with me. It seemed like what we were doing was working pretty good so I just said sure.

When Gregory asked Virginia Allen about how she approached the section on "My Dreams, Desires, and Goals," Virginia said, "Well, I would put it to them like this. 'What is it that you want to accomplish while you are here or what do you want to change in your life?' Yeah, because, otherwise it's like 'Your Dreams, Desires, and Goals' (said in a sing song voice) is kind of too ethereal for people. You know 'I want to be Queen' (said in a formal pretend voice)."

Gregory thought for a minute about how this approach was much more focused than the idea of global dreams. "How is this different than these goals that you do at the end?"

"I don't think it is really different," said Virginia, "you are really just adding the measurable part down here. You know we see a lot of people with severe mental illnesses and we really need to help them through this process. I rely a lot on some of the goals I have developed for other people. You know, why reinvent the wheel? But I always tell them what I am doing as I work through the form."

Gregory pointed to the section on the PCP about consumer choices of who will attend the meeting, what will be talked about, where the meeting would be held and who will be involved in treatment. "How do you use this section?" he asked.

"Actually, I don't really use this section at all. I thought it was for the day program because that is where family members are usually involved. It doesn't really apply to outpatient therapy."

Gregory decided to ask a larger question. "How do you think that person-centered planning is different than other treatment planning?"

Virginia said, "It is not radically different in outpatient. It's in a different form, but I am basically asking the same questions and doing the same things. It is only different words."

Min Lu and Gregory went on to interview Morningstar Frank.

"My dreams, desires, and goals," Morningstar said, "That question is very difficult for a client—'what?'—so you have to kind of rephrase that for them: 'Well, what are your plans for the future?' 'What is it that you would like to see happen in your life?' And so, you break that down and maybe you want to be a doctor, but, well, let's get through high school. You know they are having some difficulty with this, so to get realistic goals you have to help them, and sometimes its way out there, but it's their dreams, desires and goals, so you just put it down, because that's what they are saying that they want. 'I want to be a millionaire,' you know, that kind of stuff."

Min Lu and Gregory saw that Morningstar was much closer to the intent of person-centered planning—beginning the process of planning with the consumer's global dreams—even though she did adjust the global nature to a certain extent with her rephrasing of the question.

They then directed her attention to the goals and objectives at the bottom of the page. As they were going through some of Morningstar's files, they found some files on which she made notes right above the goals and objectives that seemed to be about the consumer's culture. On one they found a note about a Native American woman's tribe and clan requesting that she not be assigned to a provider from a different clan. On another plan there was a statement that a man attended the local synagogue.

"On some of your plans you have notes in this section," said Gregory, "What are these notes for?"

"Oh, those," Morningstar said, "As a Native American I am acutely aware of cultural issues in offering services. I don't know why we never put anything about this on our paperwork, but sometimes I just think it is important to record it.

You know, most nonnatives don't have any idea that certain clans within a tribe are very different—they just think they are being 'culturally sensitive' by assigning someone from the Odawa tribe to a case manager who is also Odawa. As far as people who are Jewish, this is a very small minority here and there is a lot of discrimination and bad Jewish jokes. I thought that I would at least put that up front. But frankly I didn't know where else to put it and I wasn't sure what these lines here were for, so I put it here."

Min Lu thought of the "cultural considerations" section of the PCP at Blackhawk and realized that there was not a parallel section in the forms at Phillips Mental Health Center. She asked Morningstar about how she develops goals and objectives.

Morningstar said, "I might get as far as 'what goals are we going to work on?' So we can get some ideas we will look back at the preliminary goals and look at the dreams and desires. A lot of times they don't really know how they want it. Based on the person, I might suggest, 'Well, what do you think of this? What do you think of that?'"

Finally, Min Lu pointed to the section on the consumer's choices as to who, what, and where in the planning process. "How do you use this section?"

"I love this part," said Morningstar, "I feel like I have finally been given permission to reach out to consumers and put them in charge of the process. It reminds me of when I worked inpatient. You know so many of the people who have persistent mental illnesses live pretty isolated lives—but when there is a crisis we were usually able to find family members or other support people to help. We all need people, and I really try to get consumers to figure out who might be good people to help them on their journey. And if they don't know of anyone then I work with them on how they are going to make friends and get involved in the community."

Morningstar went on, "I also love this part here," she pointed to the section defining where the planning would be held. "I work a lot with people who are hospitalized, and this has given me the flexibility to have meetings over at the hospital before someone is discharged. I had a new referral not too long ago from the hospital. The guy had a severe case of bipolar disorder that was treated well with medications, but he kept going off his meds. I was able to start making plans with him when he was still in the hospital and motivated to take his meds. I think that 'hook' into outpatient treatment will make him more likely to succeed at this goal."

"Just one more question," said Min Lu, "I notice that everyone here interprets the questions in this template in a different way. Have you talked about how to use it at all, or had any training in person-centered planning?"

"Well," said Morningstar, "Donald brought some information back from that meeting that he went to about person-centered planning. We all have copies of that information. I read mine but I can't say that I know if anyone else did. We are all really different in our training and how we do our work, so we really don't talk about it much. When Donald sent out the new forms we were supposed to use I looked at how it compared to the information he sent out early on and just took it from there."

Min Lu and Gregory returned to Lansing and put together a report that was sent to Donald Simpson. They placed the outpatient department on probation for not consistently using person-centered planning. A state representative would work with the outpatient staff to move toward compliance with the law over the next 3 months. This was based on the following findings:

1. Most of the psychotherapists did not seem to grasp the difference between effective listening, which is a traditional part of psychotherapy, and person-centered planning that places consumers' preferences and dreams at the center of the process. (Morningstar was mentioned as an exception to this rule.)
2. There is little evidence that the clients have participated in the planning process.
3. Psychotherapists are leaving some sections of the person-centered planning template blank as they plan with their clients.
4. Many of the things that psychotherapists write in the section regarding "Dreams, Desires, and Goals" and the goals and objectives of the plan seem to be straight from a treatment planning book rather than from the life desires of the clients.
5. One therapist told the auditors that the idea that clients should be involved in planning is simply not good practice in psychotherapy.

When Donald Simpson received the report from the state, he was disappointed and baffled by the response and was quickly reprimanded by his superior for losing money. In turn, he told his staff, "I am afraid that you have all done a poor job at pleasing the state on this latest demand. Here is what the state has to say. I must say that I am a little disappointed in some of their comments. Remember, that I gave you the materials to read. What stopped you from doing this? It looks like many of you didn't take it seriously. I honestly don't know what else we can do. We are using the identical paperwork as Blackhawk Mental Health Center, and they still don't like it. Well, it is clear that we need to let them know that we take this seriously or we will be losing more money and our jobs will be in jeopardy. The team will return for training in 2 weeks. Everyone clear your schedule for that afternoon. We must follow what they tell us to do completely."

CASE STUDY DISCUSSION QUESTIONS

1. In this case study, change is imposed on county mental health centers by statewide legislation. This is a powerful driver of change. Can you identify other important drivers of this change?

2. What barriers do you see for incorporating the needed changes into these two outpatient systems? Are there different barriers in the two systems or are they similar? Do the supervisors address these barriers in their actions?

Nurses from Other Lands

By Richard J. Tarpey

INTRODUCTION

A report released by the Health Resources and Services Administration (HRSA) in April of 2006 indicated that the U.S. nursing shortage will grow to more than 1 million nurses in the year 2020 (HRSA, 2006). All indicators concerning the nursing profession point to future shortages based on decreasing enrollment in nursing programs, increasing numbers of nurses approaching the retirement age, and increasing need for nurses due to an aging population. Additionally, according to the American Hospital Association survey, 44% of hospital CEO's report that it was more difficult to recruit and hire nurses in 2006 than in 2005. These trends are concerning for hospital administrators as they attempt to acquire an adequate labor force in order to meet the increasing demand of patients.

As just one of the several possible short-term solutions to the nursing shortage issue, the recruitment of foreign-trained nurses to work in the United States has received attention recently. In 2004, foreign-trained nurses accounted for approximately 4% of the nursing workforce, with the numbers of these nurses taking the U.S. nurse licensing examination increasing (Shaw, 2004). The recruitment of foreign-trained nurses does not come without controversy however. There are strong opinions in the industry as well as within individual hospitals concerning the practice, ranging from the ethical dilemma concerning the depletion of other countries' nursing supplies such as the Philippines where more than half of the foreign trained nurses immigrating to the United States have come from (Brush, 2004) to individual coworker and patient opinions concerning interactions with foreign-trained nurses. Culture and language barriers are common causes for conflict between foreign-trained nurses and U.S. trained nurses, physicians, staff, and patients.

THE PROBLEM

Bill Samuelsson, CEO of Mercy Hospital in St. Louis, Missouri, is faced with a difficult challenge. Mercy Hospital is a 200-bed nonunion facility offering multiple specialty services requiring approximately 500 nurses to adequately staff all departments and areas of the hospital. The hospital has a strong reputation within the community for its Labor & Delivery and Heart programs. He has witnessed the facility nurse vacancy rate (percentage of vacant, unfilled positions) rise steadily over the last 3 years from 15% to over 18%, representing over 90 nursing positions waiting to be recruited and hired. In order to provide patient care and coverage, the facility has been forced to work existing nurses on mandatory overtime, use incentive pay (extra pay per hour) to encourage nurses to pick up extra shifts, and use more expensive contract or agency nurses to fill the gaps. This steady rise in labor cost coupled with recent rising trends in uncollected debt has served to put tremendous pressure on the facility's bottom line. Adding to the hospital's troubles, nursing union organization activity in the neighboring state of Kansas has increased over the last 3 months. The union attempted to organize nurses at Mercy last year but failed in a vote that was a lot closer than the hospital's leadership expected. The board of directors of the facility has formally asked Bill to find a way to cut labor costs to more manageable levels. The challenge is difficult enough without the prospect of nurse dissatisfaction leading to union organization adding additional pressure.

Bill has spent the last 30 days analyzing various aspects of the facility's labor cost to identify areas of opportunity. He has considered multiple options including wage freezes, benefit reductions, and department or program closures. One morning as he was reviewing his straw list of unattractive options, a colleague (Joe Kamarand) from a sister hospital within the same health system in St. Louis called with a proposition. "Bill," Joe said, "we are having a terrible time recruiting new nurses to our facility given the nursing supply shortage in St. Louis. Have you ever given any thought to developing a foreign nurse recruitment program?" Bill had to admit that he had not considered this option to find new nurses to reduce the high vacancy rate. Last year he had attempted to partner with a local university's nursing program, but the annual supply of nurses graduating was simply too small to fulfill the demand of 18 facilities within the metro St. Louis area. Other nearby markets within the same region were in the same position, so hopes of recruiting nurses from those markets were limited given Mercy's constraints on labor costs that would preclude offering more favorable compensation packages. Bill has considered reaching out to other areas of the county but has hesitated for the same reasons. As Joe continued with his idea, Bill's interest continued to grow as this seemed like a viable answer to his problem. Perhaps the recruitment of foreign nurses would allow him to bring in more nurses at competitive or even lower rates than what would be required to attract nurses from other areas within the United States. Bill thanked Joe for the idea and indicated his interest in pursuing the idea for both facilities. He hung up and busily prepared his proposal for the rest of the hospital's leadership team.

THE AWAKENING

Bill worked for several days researching the details of a foreign nurse recruiting program and crunching the numbers on costs to see if the idea would be feasible. He was excited to see that the program's costs shared by the two facilities would easily be offset by the labor cost savings through a reduction in the use of overtime, premium incentive pay, and more expensive contract nurses. Additionally, Bill believed staff job satisfaction would rise given a more balanced workload from having an appropriate number of nurses on staff, resulting in less overworked nurses. Working excessive hours was the most common complaint he heard from the nursing staff and leadership. He could not immediately find a downside to the proposal, so he went to the Monday morning Leadership Meeting with confidence that he had a viable solution to the problem that he could present to the board of directors the following week. There was no conceivable way the hospital Leadership Team would not go for this idea. "This should be a quick formality," he thought as he made his way to his place at the table for the Leadership Meeting.

Bill sat through the presentations from the chief financial officer (CFO) on monthly financials, the chief nursing officer (CNO) on monthly patient quality metrics, and the chief operating officer (COO) on other various hospital business items. As the meeting continued, Bill became more and more confident about presenting his solution to the problem that everyone was so concerned about. When the initial presentations were completed, Bill stood up and proceeded to outline his new nurse staffing and hiring plan, going over the financial aspects and details. As he summarized, he looked around the room with the expectation of acceptance from everyone around the table. He was surprised at the immediate silence in the room.

After a couple of seconds of no response, Bill asked the group, "What do you think?" At first, no one responded. Then the CNO, Sherri Smith, spoke up. "Well, Bill, to be honest with you, I am somewhat concerned about the prospect of bringing 20–50 foreign-trained nurses into our facility. How will our current staff react? Will this give the nurses a final incentive to organize with the union? You know how close the last vote was." "How can we possibly turn nurses loose in our units without extensive training on our processes and procedures?" asked Jan Mulky, the Critical Care service line director. Bill Morris head of the Human Resources/ Payroll group chimed in, "When our IT group outsourced support of our payroll system last year, we could not get any help for months due to the language barrier between us and the outsourcing company overseas. Won't our employees and even our patients have the same problem with foreign nurses?" The chief medical officer (CMO) stated his concern as well, "Bill, if our physicians perceive an internal rift with our nurses or experience issues with working with foreign-trained nurses, they will simply begin referring their patients down the road to Memorial Hospital. You know most of the physicians have admitting rights at Memorial as well as Mercy. This idea could really backfire! Outside of emergency room admissions, our physicians are our only source of patients. We also need to consider the patients' reaction to a foreign nurse. We can't afford to let patient satisfaction decline." The next 30-minute barrage of questions were all along the same line concerning the ability of foreign nurses to work effectively at Mercy Hospital and the potential affects on the current staff, patients, and even the hospital's community reputation. Bill was completely taken aback by the response and was unsure how to react. The group discussed the idea for another hour before adjourning with the decision to create a task force to fully investigate the proposal.

THE TASK FORCE

The following week, the Nurse Staffing task force was established with key participants from the various areas of the hospital including: Clinical/Nursing, Human Resources, Financial, and Medical/Physicians. Bill, as leader of the team, had his work cut out for him. Each of the individuals on the team brought to the table a different perspective from which they would perceive and address concerns. The Clinical/Nursing area's main concerns would be centered on the clinical employee and patient care quality. This area would most likely focus on the potential negative impacts of employee–employee and employee–patient communication issues and conflicts and how they would potentially affect the quality of care provided at the unit level. Additionally, they would be concerned with foreign nurse qualifications and ensuring these nurses were certified and licensed accordingly. The Human Resources area would be most concerned with foreign nurse certifications and licensing to ensure they met all federal and state regulatory requirements as well as about maintaining employee satisfaction to ensure existing nurses do not leave the organization contributing to the job vacancy problem or lending support to union organization efforts. The Financial area would be most concerned about the potential foreign nurse impact on existing productivity of staff members to ensure that the facility still provides quality care in a cost efficient manner. The Medical/Physicians area would be most concerned about the potential impact on existing physician relationships and the facility's ability to recruit and attract new physicians to the facility.

In order to attempt to get everyone's thoughts on the table, Bill decided that the first task for the team was to create a list of potential areas of concern. The team met for a couple of hours and listed every concern they could think of from an employee, physician, patient, and administrator perspective. Once duplicate concerns were consolidated and any concerns that the team agreed were unwarranted were eliminated, they were left with a straw list of items to consider.

The list of items is included in **Table 33-1**, in no particular order:

As the team reviewed the list, it was clear that most of the potential issues identified shared root causes involving the impact of adding a foreign nurse to a unit group. The resulting impact would be either on the unit group as a whole (how would the unit team act or perform differently) or would be at the individual employee level (how would each individual staff member act or perform differently). Bill from HR observed, "It seems that our main concern is, first, how each employee will react to suddenly working with a foreign nurse and then how those reactions will affect the ability of the unit team to effectively accomplish their tasks." Sherri agreed, "Absolutely, Bill! We need to foresee how the employees and teams could potentially be affected by the additional stress, potential for conflict, and communication issues. Nursing units are close-knit groups with highly skilled interactions. Any potential distraction can be critical."

The team decided to adjourn with the task for each member to brainstorm and determine how the addition of a foreign nurse to the unit group might increase stress, cause communication issues, and add conflict to the employees and teams. Bill adjourned the meeting with the expectation that at the next meeting, each team member would come prepared with their thoughts about how the team could proactively address the identified potential issues to prevent negative impacts on employee performance and team performance.

Table 33-1 List of Potential Foreign-Trained Nurse Issues (meeting notes)

Area of Concern:	Notes
Quality Patient Care	Will the foreign nurses be able to provide quality patient care? Will any potential conflicts or communication issues affect patient care?
Foreign nurse training and productivity	Will foreign nurses be able to work within Mercy's systems and processes effectively and efficiently with comparable productivity of our U.S. trained-nurses?
Language and cultural barriers (potential source of employee–employee or employee–patient conflict)	Will there be communication issues among employees, physicians, and patients? How will our existing employees react?
Unionization issues	Lower wage rates seen by staff as way to eventually lower their wage rates. Possible incentive for unionization on the part of nurses?
Existing hospital nurse productivity	Will our nurses lose productivity assisting the foreign-trained nurses
Employee job satisfaction	Will current staff nurses have issues or problems working with the new nurses?
Physician facility satisfaction	Will our physicians be able to work with foreign-trained nurses? Is there a possible loss of physicians using facility services if satisfaction declines?
Patient satisfaction	Will patients accept a foreign-trained nurse? Will there be the potential for patient–nurse communication issues or conflict?

CASE STUDY DISCUSSION QUESTIONS

As a member of the team, your task is to prepare for the next meeting by (1) identifying potential concerns that may be presented by the addition of a foreign nurse to a unit group, and (2) develop strategies to address potential issues caused by additional stress, conflict, and communication issues. Explore all three concepts across the following areas of concern:

- Quality patient care
- Foreign nurse training and productivity
- Language and cultural barriers (potential source of employee–employee or employee–patient conflict)
- Unionization issues
- Existing hospital nurse productivity
- Employee job satisfaction
- Physician facility satisfaction
- Patient satisfaction

Keep in mind the three perspectives of employees, physicians, and patients, and also consider how existing staff members can be used to help mitigate the issues. Are there additional benefits you can identify to utilizing foreign-trained nurses besides financial benefits?

REFERENCES

Shaw, G. (2004, September). Recruitment of foreign nurses helping ease nursing shortage. *The Washington Diplomat*. Retrieved February 16, 2010, from http://www.washdiplomat.com/04-09/a7_09_04.html

The New Manager's Challenge

By Robert Vazquez

Benny, the newly promoted manager of the hospital's imaging department, answered his phone, "Good morning, imaging, this is Benny, how can I help you?" The phone's caller ID indicated the person on the other end was Lucy, one of the veteran radiology technologists. "We have a situation here and an infant patient's parents want to see you immediately. Can you come down to radiology's procedure room #1?"

Benny hung up the phone and quickly made it down to the radiology department's procedure area. Upon arriving, Benny introduced himself to the parents of an infant patient who quickly related that they were not satisfied with the information provided by Lucy in reference to the sequence of events that had taken place with their child's care. Benny had little background information on the situation prior to arriving, and this put him at a slight disadvantage. He only knew that the issue began in the pediatric nursing unit when an invasive radiology procedure, called a cystogram,[1] was ordered for the infant.

---

[1] This particular procedure involves the insertion of a urinary catheter that is removed at a certain point during the exam and is typically ordered to diagnose a multitude of bladder diseases.

Upon arriving to the radiology department, quick introductions were exchanged and the infant's father began to explain why he was dissatisfied with the hospital's services, alluding to the fact that he wanted something done immediately, stating, "I am a lawyer and I am very upset! I want someone to explain what has occurred here." His comments referred to the information he just received from Lucy, which conflicted with what he had observed in the pediatric nursing unit while his son was under the care of nurse, Marcia. The infant's mother, while present, added her thoughts only periodically such as, "I felt something was not right. I don't remember seeing the nurse use any lubricant." The father's demands were specific, which included a request for an immediate reassignment of his infant's nurse due to a series of events that occurred outside of the radiology department. The events on the pediatric nursing unit led the father to believe the RN in this particular case was incompetent. Although the issues involved specifically related to the urinary catheter implemented by the RN, there appeared to be an overall competence concern on behalf of the parents, which was the catalyst for their present hostility.

The discussion with the father focused on three specific issues. The first concern was that initially the incorrect sized catheter was selected by Marcia. The second concern was that the incorrect tape was utilized, causing the skin to be irritated and swollen upon removal. The final concern was a result of both the incorrect catheter size and tape—the catheter "fell out." This series of events led to the reinsertion of the catheter, which only served to further upset the parents.

Once Benny allowed the parents to explain the issues at hand, the father requested that the issues be addressed with Marcia immediately. To Benny, the request seemed reasonable as Marcia seemed to be the source of the parent's anger and dissatisfaction. Therefore, Benny thought that his direct communication with Marcia would quickly solve the problem at hand and prevent any further negative interactions between the nursing department (specifically Marcia) and the parents.

Benny notified Marcia that the patient's parents were requesting a nursing change. Benny spoke to Marcia in a semiprivate area and in the presence of another RN. Benny thought this best versus a more formal environment because he wanted to communicate the parent's request before the infant patient arrived back on the pediatric nursing unit. Benny proceeded to explain to Marcia the multiple errors she committed in reference to the infant's invasive radiology procedure preparation. Because of Benny's desire to be efficient due to the impending arrival of the parents and in an attempt to avoid any confrontation, he disclosed the parents' concerns and medical errors on her behalf prior to taking her version of the events into account. Also, Benny did not consider how sensitive this issue was, as Marcia was already distressed by the initial interaction with the patient's overbearing parents while attempting to insert the urinary catheter the first time, in addition to agreeing to cover a shift in the pediatric nursing unit, with which she was not familiar.

Benny's "information" was not well received by Marcia who took the comments offensively and considered them an insult to her nursing abilities. Marcia initially responded to Benny's claims with an increased rate of speech, only to follow with silence and disconnect. Marcia folded her arms across her chest, took a step back from Benny, and did not provide him any further verbal responses. More specifically, Marcia began a foot-tapping motion and lowered her eyes to avoid face-to-face contact with Benny. Benny ordered the nursing change to be made immediately without involving Marcia's clinical manager. Benny informed the parents that the nursing change was underway and offered his assistance to the parents "for anything they might need" during the infant's inpatient stay. The parents appeared to be satisfied that action had been taken, so Benny returned to his department.

Later that day, Benny visited the parents again. He wanted to follow up with the infant's care, verify that the parents were content with the way the situation had been handled, and to be sure that no other concerns had arisen. Upon seeing Benny, the parents expressed their gratitude with the actions he had taken, noting that they were extremely pleased that management stepped in to intervene on what they assumed had no solution.

The following day, the chief nursing officer (CNO) and senior vice president of the hospital contacted Benny for a meeting. Benny thought the purpose of the meeting was to provide him high accolades for the successful handling of the nursing issue from the previous day. In fact, Benny was quite pleased with himself. From his perspective, he was able to achieve a turnaround of the parents' negative experience without the assistance of any other managers as well as an unexpected extra bonus; a statement from the family indicating that they would return to the hospital for care, if necessary.

Regrettably, instead of praising Benny for his efforts, the meeting was to inform him of the inappropriateness of the exchanges between Marcia and himself. Benny was made aware of "how things were to be done" and given clear instructions how to approach similar situations in the future. The CNO indicated that all issues about nursing care must be addressed directly with the RN's clinical manger and never directly with the staff involved unless they were Benny's direct report employees. According to the CNO and senior vice president, it was not Marcia's actions but Benny's decisions regarding the proper course of action that needed improving! Benny agreed that after reviewing his interactions with Marcia, he could have been more sensitive and less aggressive with his tone and approach. Although Benny still had much to learn as a new manager, it seemed odd to him that the nurse who was the source of the issues was not part of this discussion. Benny wondered how Marcia's actions were being addressed by senior management. Was Marcia being reprimanded, disciplined, or at the very least (and probably most importantly), in-serviced in reference for her nursing errors?

CASE STUDY DISCUSSION QUESTIONS

1. Discuss the different forms of feedback present in the case study as well as any feedback strategies that were lacking and may have improved the overall outcome.

2. How was the lack of empathy present on behalf of both Benny and Marcia?

3. What conflict-handling style would you recommend the chief nursing officer (CNO) and senior vice president use in this case?

4. Evaluate Benny and Marcia individually and identify the various factors that may cause stress.

Reorganization and the Centers for Early Childhood Intervention

By Melissa A. Walker

E very day for the past 2 years Ernest Gibbs has battled to make Centers for Early Childhood Intervention (Centers) a going concern. He is the CFO (chief financial officer) of the only agency in the community serving children who have developmental disabilities. Friday is payday and Gibbs is certain none of the Centers' 300 employees will receive a paycheck. This is the last straw. Gibbs hands Curtis Graves, the executive director, his resignation. Graves contacts Carmen Sanchez, the board president, to let her know. He says he's not too concerned. Sanchez isn't so sure. She calls a meeting of the executive committee for next week.

For most board members, Curtis Graves *is* the Centers for Early Childhood Intervention. He has been executive director for the past 15 years. Graves reassures the board officers that Centers is on solid financial ground. After some discussion it becomes clear no one is certain about the current financial position. So the executive committee directs Graves to hire an independent CPA (certified public accountant) to sort this out. At this point no one has any idea how dire the organization's financial condition really is.

Adele Bonds, CPA, pieces together the situation. She discovers Gibbs has not balanced the checkbook for the past 2 years. He stopped making bookkeeping entries at least a year ago. The last time a trial balance was prepared was the year before last. When Bonds asks Graves the last time he saw financial statements, Graves says he doesn't know. He says his top priority has been to raise money for the new child care center.

Graves directed Gibbs to make the money for the new facility work out and that is what Gibbs did. Gibbs did not pay IRS (Internal Revenue Service) withholding taxes or other creditors. While CFO, Gibbs told board members the auditor did not have time to review the Centers' financial reports. It turns out the auditor did have time but the Centers' financial records were far from ready for review. There has not been an independent audit for 2 years.

BACKGROUND

Centers for Early Childhood Intervention began in 1976. It is the largest agency in the area serving children who have developmental disabilities. Autism, Down syndrome, impaired hearing or vision, learning disability, and developmental delay are examples of developmental disabilities. Services for children with special needs can include speech and language therapy, vision and hearing assistance, adaptive technology, physical therapy, and occupational therapy.

Each year Centers for Early Childhood Intervention serves 1,300 children. The agency provides early intervention services in the homes of 1,000 preschool-aged children. Research shows better outcomes when services are provided early on. Centers' programs engage caregivers in providing support that enables children to meet their full potential. Centers also has three child care programs. There are 100 children at each child care center. The loss of any part or all of these services would be a serious blow to the community.

EXPENSE GROWS, REVENUE SHRINKS

Like many nonprofit organizations, demand for Centers' services far exceeds the organization's resources. The mismatch between revenue and expense has grown steadily worse. Gibbs' resignation brought this to light.

Eighty percent of Centers' annual revenue comes from government ($10 million); primarily the local school district, state department of education, and Medicaid fee-for-service reimbursement. The United Way contributes 10% of total revenue. Ten percent comes from private sources such as individuals, foundations, and corporations.

The childcare centers are the largest expense. The three centers make up 50% of total annual expense. The school district pays Centers a daily rate for each child. This reimbursement does not cover all of the actual costs per child. This is one reason the Centers' expense exceeds revenue by $3 million.

Two years ago federal, state, and local government funding began to shrink. Rather than cut expenses, Graves elected to continue the same level of service. A visible and highly regarded member of the community, Graves is leading a campaign to raise money for a new childcare center. So far the capital campaign has generated $1 million. These are major gifts made by individuals and local business owners. The new center will serve children with special needs as well as children developing normally.

Over the past 2 years, Adele Bonds reports expense has exceeded revenue by $3 million. She found Gibbs used capital gifts to cover the cost of daily operation. Donors, as yet, do not know their contributions were used in this way. To free up cash, Gibbs did not pay federal or state income tax withheld from employees' salaries. The IRS has begun to ask questions and says it will impose substantial penalty fees. Bonds discovers at least 100 creditors are due payment for goods and services already delivered. She tells Graves, Sanchez, and the board that, in her opinion, the organization should stop spending immediately.

IMAGE IS EVERYTHING

Curtis Graves has carefully crafted his image and the image of Centers for Early Childhood Intervention. The organization has a reputation for innovation. Graves is an idea person. He's a development director's dream; a superb spokesperson full of new ideas that hold lots of appeal for donors. Graves' latest project is a child care center that will bring together children developing normally and children who have special needs. He devotes most of his time to meeting with donors, public officials, and business owners.

Some staff and board members find it difficult to work with Graves. As executive director, he controls information. Board meetings are devoted entirely to his executive director's report. He takes personal credit for all of the organization's accomplishments. Graves rarely attends weekly staff meetings. He leaves day-to-day operation to staff. When something needs to get done, he tells staff members what it is and then they figure out how to make it happen. Gibbs's job, for example, was to make the money "all work out." Graves wouldn't hear it could not be done.

As newspaper accounts begin to suggest trouble, the organization's reputation flags. Graves stands to be discredited. He does not believe what Adele Bonds, the independent CPA, has found. Within a month of Gibbs's resignation as CFO, Graves also resigns. He hopes his resignation will save his reputation. Sanchez's term as board president ends. Now the board must find a new executive director and a new board president.

Ben Samuels, a businessman who has served on the board for the past several years but never in a leadership position, agrees to become president of the board of directors. Samuels is a quiet, thoughtful person; not someone accustomed to being in the spotlight. He has a child with special needs and is passionate about Centers. He has been a strong supporter of Curtis Graves. Other than Graves, Samuels does not know other Centers staff. One reason is staff members have not been invited to board meetings. The only point of contact has been Graves.

Samuels quickly gets to know Beth Woodward. She's been Graves's director of operations. Woodward knows the most about the programs and about the staff. The board appoints Woodward interim executive director. Woodward asks Bonds to stay on as CFO. Samuels announces these changes at an all staff and board meeting. "Together" he says, "we will restore trust in Centers for Early Childhood Intervention." Samuels introduces Woodward who says her first priority is to "break down the silos that separate us." She encourages staff and board members to share ideas. Staff members begin attending board meetings as well as board committee meetings.

Woodward faces challenges that threaten the organization's existence. She, along with staff and the board, will have to: 1) negotiate payment with the IRS of $2 million in unpaid withholding, 2) appease donors who contributed a total of $1 million the capital campaign, and 3) prepare a reorganization plan for approval by a judge in bankruptcy court.

DOING THE RIGHT THING

Woodward, Bonds, and Samuels are an effective team. As new information comes to light, they talk and meet frequently to discuss it. Together they learn details surrounding the financial calamity that weighed so heavily on the former CFO. For the past 2 years, Centers has not paid quarterly withholding taxes on employees' wages. The Internal Revenue Service (IRS) is owed $2 million.

Another $1 million contributed by individual donors to the capital campaign for the new child care center under construction has been diverted to cover operating expense. So Centers is at least $3 million in debt. In addition, there are more than 100 creditors waiting to be paid. Woodward, Samuels, the board, and the leadership team pledge to put this right. Centers will pay all of its creditors in full. This is bold promise for an organization unable to make payroll.

Woodward gathers the administrative team. She wants to engage staff in a process that will generate solutions. In order to do this, staff must believe it is safe to share new ideas. Woodward's first directive is "Anyone can say anything, anytime." At the same time, the board enacts a whistleblower policy designed to encourage employees to report concerns without fear of losing their job. The fact that everyone could lose their job complicates the process of idea generation.

The first order of business is to find a way to meet payroll and start paying bills. Centers needs cash. Samuels, Woodward, and Bonds, with board approval, approach the bank that holds the mortgage on the largest building Centers owns. The building will be used as collateral on a $1 million loan that will be repaid once the building is sold. The bank agrees. This is a short-term solution to keep Centers afloat. It is clear that in the long run the cost of operating three childcare centers and soon a fourth is too high. Expense must decrease and revenue must increase.

REORGANIZATION PLAN

After much deliberation, Woodward, Bonds, Samuels, and the board agree the best option is to file a petition declaring bankruptcy. This is a painful choice. There is great concern it will further damage the organization's reputation. Under Chapter 11 of the federal bankruptcy code, Centers can continue to operate as a debtor in possession. This allows the organization to pay bills, sell assets, and reduce staff. Once the court accepts the petition, Centers has 4 months to prepare a reorganization plan. The reorganization plan, which also must be approved by the bankruptcy court, explains how Centers will become financially stable over time. A judge approves the bankruptcy petition and now Centers has four months to prepare the reorganization plan.

Centers' board and staff agree honesty is the best policy. Woodward, Samuels, and Centers' administrative team craft a message. A press release goes out the same day the bankruptcy petition is approved. It explains Centers' plans to reorganize; that it does not plan to close. The press release expresses deep regret. It includes an apology to children and families as well as to staff and the community.

Samuels fields questions from reporters, donors, and creditors. He's not comfortable in the spotlight but he is well prepared. With a steady hand, Samuels conveys a confident, upbeat message. He assures the community "We understand the problem and we are working to fix it." He asks for continued support.

What to tell donors is another concern. Woodward, Samuels, and Centers' administrative team adopt a straightforward approach. They meet with major donors who contributed to the capital campaign and explain what happened. This is a "new day" they say. They ask capital donors to once again contribute. They assure donors their gift will go to the organization's charitable foundation and be used exclusively for the purpose of building a new facility.

Woodward and the leadership team have begun work on a reorganization plan. The board will approve the plan. Then the plan will be presented to the court for approval. So far, staff have constructed this "before and after" picture of Centers.

Woodward and Samuels estimate it will take 10 years to repay the $3 million. Once the reorganization is approved by the court, Centers will negotiate a payment schedule with each creditor (IRS and vendors). When the new building is complete, Centers will locate all programs and administration in one facility. The proceeds from the sale of the largest child care center will be used to pay off the emergency $1 million bank loan. The plan is to reduce the number of staff by half. Annual operating expense will be cut from $10 million to $7 million. The annual operating deficit will disappear. A timeline follows.

Table 35-1 Before and After

Current	Proposed
Mission includes normally developing children	Mission returns to children with special needs
Capital contributions used for operations	Donors forgive and make new capital gifts
3 childcare centers	1 childcare center in new facility
300 children in 3 centers	100 children in 1 center All services & offices move to 1 center
1,000 children receive in-home services	1,000 children receive in-home services
300 staff	150 staff
$10 million revenue per year	$7 million revenue per year
$13 million expense per year	$7 million expense per year
$3 million deficit	No deficit

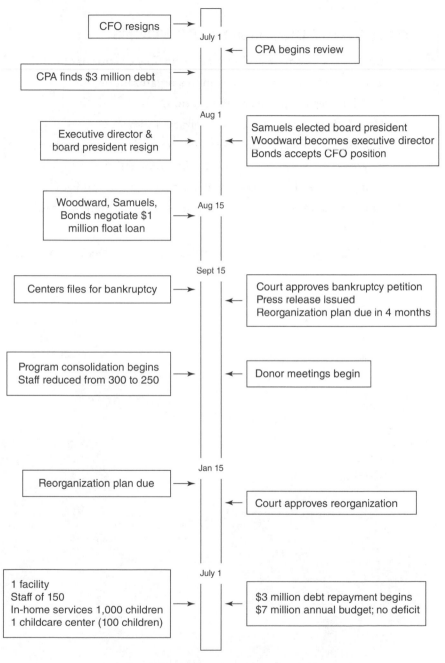

FIGURE 35-1 Reorganization Time Line

CASE STUDY DISCUSSION QUESTIONS

1. Leaders can promote and/or inhibit the flow of information.
   a. How does information flow in this organization?
   b. What steps improve communication?
2. How do leaders manage the organization's image?
   a. Describe how decision-makers use strategic communication.
   b. What is the message and how is it reinforced?
3. Compare how the two executive directors manage conflict.
4. What steps would you take to effectively manage communication and conflict in this situation?

Retail Pharmacies: Assessing Organizational Responses to AHRQ's Health Literacy Pharmacy Tools[1]

By Sarah J. Shoemaker and Melanie Wasserman

BACKGROUND

Only 12% of adults have proficient health literacy (National Center for Education Statistics, 2003), and persons with limited health literacy often have a poor understanding of basic medical vocabulary (Davis et al., 2006). Limited health literacy is associated with delayed diagnoses, increased medication errors and nonadherence, increased frequency and length of hospital stays, and a higher level of illness, resulting in an estimated excess cost for the U.S. healthcare system of

[1] DISCLOSURE: The information upon which this case study is based was performed under Contract HHSA290200600011 TO#5 entitled "Assessing Organizational Responses to AHRQ's Health Literacy Pharmacy Tools," funded by the Agency for Healthcare Research and Quality (AHRQ), Department of Health and Human Services. The content of this presentation does not necessarily reflect the views or policies of the Department of Health and Human Services, nor does the mention of trade names, commercial products, or organizations imply endorsement by the U.S. Government. The authors assume full responsibility for the accuracy and completeness of the ideas presented.

$50 to $73 billion per year (Kripalani, Gatti, & Jacobson, 2010; Keller, Wright, & Pace, 2008; Baker et al., 2002; Bennett et al., 1998; Friedland, 1998). Pharmacists can improve patients' understanding of medication instructions, yet relatively few pharmacies have implemented comprehensive practices to serve low-health-literacy patients (Praska et al., 2005). Although these findings indicate a need for quality improvement (QI) to address health literacy practices in pharmacies, QI leadership is relatively uncommon among pharmacists (American Society of Health-System Pharmacists, 2005). Obstacles include the often-hectic pace of pharmacies, high prescription volumes, low profit margins that limit pharmacy resources for QI, a workflow designed to dispense medications, and physical layouts that limit communication between pharmacists and patients.

Recognizing that pharmacists may need additional knowledge and assistance to improve their health literacy practices, the Agency for Healthcare Research and Quality (AHRQ) supported the development of health literacy QI tools for pharmacists. One of the tools, titled *Is Our Pharmacy Meeting Patients' Needs? A Pharmacy Health Literacy Assessment Tool User's Guide* (Assessment Tool), guides a pharmacist through an assessment of their health literacy practices—for example, the appropriateness of their physical layout and communication practices. AHRQ wanted to understand what happened when these tools were made available to pharmacies that varied in leadership, culture, organizational capacity, readiness, and innovativeness, and to understand how the pharmacies approached organizational change based on the assessment results. AHRQ funded Abt Associates, Inc. (Contract HHSA290200600011 TO#5) to conduct case studies to assess diverse retail pharmacies' organizational responses to the Assessment Tool, which was previously developed by academic researchers and tested in a safety-net hospital outpatient pharmacy. The following are from the case studies of Bella Pharmacy and Ocean Pharmacy.

BELLA PHARMACY

Bella Pharmacy was located in a federally qualified health center in an upper Midwestern metropolitan city. The patient population was largely low income (i.e., 69% were below 200% federal poverty limit), and 75% were people of color, many of whom were Hispanic. Given their patient population, they anticipated that their patients would have trouble understanding their prescriptions, and many would be considered to have low-health-literacy skills.

The pharmacy's prior experience with QI indicated a high level of readiness to change. For one QI effort, Bella Pharmacy queried pharmacy prescription records to identify asthma patients who regularly filled albuterol (for quick relief of shortness of breath) to determine whether they also regularly filled an inhaled corticosteroid (a maintenance medication that should improve asthma symptoms and limit the need for albuterol). The pharmacy was also very patient centered, providing direct-patient-care services such as medication therapy management (MTM)—a service through which pharmacists review patients' medication regimens and identify and resolve drug therapy problems. Finally, the pharmacy was trying to gain medical-home certification, an important motivator.

The manager at Bella Pharmacy agreed to complete the assessment as part of the AHRQ study and delegated it to the pharmacy resident. Although the pharmacy manager left shortly after the resident began the project, the succeeding manager was also supportive of the project. The resident recognized the importance of completing a baseline assessment of the pharmacy's health literacy practices given the high proportion of patients with low health literacy. She saw it as an opportunity to improve services for patients with low health literacy by better understanding areas to target for quality improvement. The resident was also doing the assessment to fulfill a requirement of her residency; as she put it, "The fact that it was my residency project meant that I needed to do it."

The resident initially found the Assessment Tool overwhelming, but because of its clear organization, she knew the steps she would need to take to complete the assessment, which reinforced her decision to use it in the first place. The resident recruited a pharmacy student to lead one component of the assessment (i.e., a patient focus group); the resident completed the remainder of the assessment herself. The resident did receive support from Abt Associates, the research organization, in the form of regular check-ins (to encourage timely progress) and guidance on how to conduct a focus group, which she found beneficial. As she stated, "Being able to talk to someone about each step of the assessment was helpful. It was helpful to touch base with somebody who knew what [the Assessment Tool] was about—it was helpful for moral support."

Although the resident's overall implementation experience was positive, she and the student who helped her with focus groups did encounter several challenges over the course of implementation.

Implementation of the Assessment Tool resulted in some concrete changes in pharmacy operations. For example, the pharmacy began using pictograms during patient counseling and began reminding patients of the number of refills remaining on their medications. They also improved their signage for the pharmacy. There was also a general increase in awareness of health literacy issues among pharmacy staff and leadership. However, the resident had trouble transforming the assessment results into discrete action steps that could be easily adopted by the pharmacy and felt that the change in the pharmacy's practices was not as significant as she would have liked.

The resident was motivated to complete the project so she could fulfill the requirements of her residency. Although she was required to write the report, she was not required to follow through on recommendations—nor did time permit because she finished her report in the last week of her residency. She left the pharmacy without having an opportunity to formally share her results with pharmacy staff beyond sharing a copy of her report with the pharmacy manager, the new resident, and another pharmacist. But as the pharmacy manager said, "I honestly didn't have time to read the report. We have to fill hundreds of prescriptions each day, and there's just no time to focus on this." Although the time-limited nature of her residency spurred her progress in conducting the assessment, it simultaneously limited follow-through on recommendations and the actual QI efforts to improve the pharmacy's health literacy practices.

OCEAN PHARMACY

Ocean Pharmacy was a large retail chain in a low-income neighborhood of a large Northeastern city. The pharmacy advertised their ability to serve patients in several different languages, in part because city law required that prescription information be provided in the 6 primary, non-English languages in the city; they had materials in 16 languages. At the time of this study, the pharmacy was planning to provide medication therapy management (MTM) to a Medicare plan's beneficiaries, but had not yet begun.

A clinical faculty member from a local college of pharmacy had a joint appointment with the pharmacy and the local college of pharmacy. The pharmacy served as a rotation site for pharmacy students, which she oversaw. The faculty member was interested in using the Assessment Tool because of her professional interest in health literacy and language access issues. The faculty member felt that completing the assessment would be a valuable experience for students on rotation. Her motivation was to improve the pharmacy and to help students develop as professionals by becoming aware of health literacy issues. The tool also aligned with her college's focus on disparities in health care and the pharmacy's focus on improving customer loyalty. The faculty member thought that the Assessment Tool seemed easy to use and was potentially valuable for her pharmacy. She expected that the tool would provide a "snapshot" of how well the pharmacy was serving low-literacy patients.

The faculty member did not need permission from upper pharmacy management to use the tool, and she knew staff in her pharmacy would support implementation. Motivated by her personal interest in health literacy, she said, "I'm working under the [college] umbrella when I do things like that, so I can make the time," implying that her affiliation with the college freed her to pursue initiatives like the assessment without having to obtain leadership buy-in at the pharmacy. Pharmacy students also contributed significantly to the feasibility of the assessment. As the faculty member explained, "We had the students, which was a tremendous help. Pharmacies who don't have the extra set of hands…I don't know if they would take the time out to do [the assessment]."

Students on rotation at the pharmacy helped to conduct the assessment. They completed the audit of the pharmacy's oral communications and written materials. Additionally, the students adapted the tool by converting the patient focus-group component to one-on-one interviews with patients in order to simplify recruiting and minimize resources, while facilitating completion of the assessment. The students completed the interviews with patients and reported these findings to the faculty member.

The freedom to pursue implementation and the availability of a student intern to conduct the assessment were essential to successful implementation for Ocean Pharmacy. Despite the faculty member's interest in health literacy and Abt Associates' periodic check-ins (which appeared to encourage some progress), the clinical faculty member was unable to complete the full assessment and did not implement any changes in the pharmacy as a result of the findings. This was in part because of competing priorities and the busy retail pharmacy environment. As she described, "As soon as you have down time, something happens."

CASE STUDY DISCUSSION QUESTIONS

1. According to Rogers' *Diffusion of Innovations* model, what apparent prior conditions existed for each pharmacy in their consideration to use the Assessment Tool (e.g., need, mission)?

2. What characteristics of each pharmacy might have affected the decision to adopt and implement the tool?

3. What perceived characteristics of the Assessment Tool affected each pharmacy's adoption of the tool?

(continues)

4. What factors appeared to positively and negatively affect implementation in each pharmacy?

5. Who were the change agents in each pharmacy?

6. What were the individual and organizational motivating factors for each pharmacy to implement the Assessment Tool?

7. What were some of the related problems in change management for the pharmacy?

8. What were some differences in the leadership support or buy-in to conduct the assessment?

9. What might have helped the pharmacies further implement identified changes or areas for improvement in each pharmacy?

RECOMMENDED READING

American Society of Health-System Pharmacists. (2005). Measuring the Quality of Medication Therapy Management Services. Retrieved from http://www.ashp.org/s_ashp/docs/files/MMA_MeasuringMTMQuality.pdf.

Baker, D. W., et al. (2002). Functional health literacy and the risk of hospital admission among Medicare managed care enrollees. *American Journal of Public Health*, *92*(8):1278–1283.

Bennett, C. L., et al. (1998). Relation between literacy, race, and stage of presentation among low-income patients with prostate cancer. *Journal of Clinical Oncology* *16*(9):3101–3104.

Davis, T. C., et al. (2006). Literacy and misunderstanding prescription drug labels. *Annals of Internal Medicine, 145*(12): 887–894.

Friedland, R. (1998). *Understanding health literacy: New estimates of the costs of inadequate health literacy.* Washington, DC: National Academy on an Aging Society.

Keller, D. L., Wright, J., & Pace, H. A. (2008). Impact of health literacy on health outcomes in ambulatory care patients: A systematic review. *Annals of Pharmacotherapy* *42*(9):1272–1281.

Kripalani, S., Gatti, M. E., & Jacobson, T. A. (2010). Association of age, health literacy, and medication management strategies with cardiovascular medication adherence. *Patient Education and Counseling, 81*(2):177–181.

National Center for Education Statistics. (2003). National Assessment of Adult Literacy. Retrieved from http://nces.ed.gov/naal/.

Praska, J. L., et al. (2005). Identifying and assisting low-literacy patients with medication use: A survey of community pharmacies. *Annals of Pharmacotherapy, 39*(9):1441–1445.

Index